Synagogue Life

Samuel C. Heilman

Synagogue Life

A Study in
Symbolic Interaction

The University of Chicago Press
Chicago and London

The University of Chicago Press, Chicago 60637
The University of Chicago Press, Ltd., London

Library of Congress Cataloging in Publication Data

Heilman, Samuel C
  Synagogue life.

  Bibliography: p.
  Includes index.
  1. Orthodox Judaism—United States. 2. Jewish
way of life—Case studies. 3. Jews in the United
States—Social life and customs. I. Title.
BM205.H44   296.6′5   75-36403

For the people
of Kehillat Kodesh
and for Ellin

Contents

Preface

> ... societies, like lives, contain
> their own interpretations. One has
> only to learn how to gain access to
> them.
>
> *Clifford Geertz*, "Deep Play: Notes
> on the Balinese Cockfight"

In this book I have attempted to describe from the perspective of
the participant observer, but with a minimum of sociological
jargon, the interaction generated within and by the members of a
small modern Orthodox Jewish synagogue located in a large
northeastern American city. It is perhaps easiest to describe the
purpose of this study by first describing what it is not. This is not a
book about the religion of Orthodox Jews, for it explains neither
their religion nor the essence of their Orthodoxy. Such matters of
the spirit do not fully reveal themselves in the context of interaction. One will not find the faithful Jew here—not because he does
not exist, but because the analytic perspective used here transforms

him into a person like all others, subject primarily to the imperatives of commingling. Thus observed, the interdictions and demands of Orthodox Judaism are qualitatively indistinct from the social constraints and claims made upon all people. If the book succeeds in its purpose, the reader will finally know little if anything about the meaning that the Orthodox synagogue has for the faithful; he will see only how Orthodox Jews, *as social beings*, act in their congregation. So while the manifest subject of this work remains the Orthodox synagogue—currently the primary (if not only) setting where interaction occurs within a totally Jewish environment—the study is more about behavior within a conveniently bordered and clearly defined setting, which just happens to be an Orthodox synagogue.

Such a synagogue is a place of daily worship, periodic study, and frequent assembly. An examination of it requires one to decipher all three activities as well as how they coexist within the same setting. Throughout, my emphasis is neither on the nostalgic nor the exotic but rather on the ordinary, daily, and familiar dimensions of the setting. Such an approach presumes that the ordinary, being the stuff of everyday life, must, even more than the unusually dramatic, be comprehended if one is ever to decipher a culture and a people.

While there are various ways to decipher a synagogue—historical documents, demographic surveys, questionnaires, and so forth—my approach was to enter into the setting as a participant observer and to learn by watching while doing. Such a strategy was made easier for me by the fact that I had all my life participated in the life of Orthodox Jewry and thus knew how to act like an insider. I knew where and when the action would occur even if I did not yet completely comprehend its social significance. A working knowledge of Hebrew, Yiddish, German, Polish, and all mutants thereof, all part of the language of the world I was investigating, was also helpful.

To find one synagogue embodying all the qualities of the species was not easy—some would say impossible. While my familiarity with Orthodox synagogues was helpful in recognizing obvious anomalies, the more subtle peculiarities of any one congregation would appear only after the research was under way. Moreover, familiarity, while on the one hand advantageous, on the other hand threatened to make me take for granted things which a complete outsider might consider puzzling or curious and hence worth examining.

I finally chose Kehillat Kodesh (all names are fictitious) less out of intellectual conviction than out of expediency. On the surface, it displayed many of the stereotypical qualities I had learned to expect in Orthodox synagogues. Moreover, when I decided to embark on my research, I was already a member and could thus expect few problems in gaining access to the group I would study and observe, as well as their permission and trust. Having originally joined the congregation with no ulterior motives of research, I had established a degree of intimacy with the insiders which is rare even among the most dedicated of participant observers. Finally, as an insider I could supply, both through introspection and a sense of the relevant questions to ask, information about dimensions of inner life not readily available to pure researchers.

Opposing the real advantages were the concomitant disadvantages. I have already suggested the epistemological liability of taking too much for granted. This danger was of course intensified by my being not only Orthodox but also a member of the congregation. There were personal drawbacks as well. Relationships which I had over time developed on emotional grounds would have to become instrumental; friends would be transformed into informants and I into primarily a collector of social facts. The depth of my friendship, and that of my wife, who was ineluctably implicated in my adventure, would be tested by my publicly announced research intentions.

Realizing that such a study was an opportunity both to examine my own traditions in ways I had never before considered and to present them to students of society in a novel way, I overcame my feelings of ambivalence about the project and acquired a passion to complete the task which sustained me through all the inevitable drudgeries of long research. I began to attend every prayer service, class, and meeting held in the synagogue as well as those congregationally sponsored functions which took place in other locations. Moreover, my visits with members in their homes and their return visits to mine also became part of the data of my research.

I engaged in this intensive participant observation for a period of a year. After each experience in the synagogue or with its people in other settings, I returned to my desk to write detailed notes on all I could recall, and for every fifteen minutes in the field I would find myself with an hour's worth of notes. It was not at all unusual to find myself in the early hours of the morning still writing up my notes on the previous evening's gathering, with only a few hours remaining before the start of morning prayers, which I would also attend.

Most settings did not allow for unobtrusive note-taking, especially on Sabbaths and holy days, the periods of most intense and involved activity, when writing is religiously prohibited. As a participant I accepted this prohibition and had to let such days pass without writing notes until the evening. After a time I had trained my memory so that on Saturday night, or after a holy day, I could sit down and remember, along with the help of my wife, who acted to check my recollections, all the salient events of the past day and even a few quotations.

When the events I observed in the setting ceased to reveal novelties to me, I took my six volumes of notes and began to look at what I had gathered. While certain themes had spelled themselves out in the course of the observations, others became apparent only after all the notes were analyzed.

Only a small part of the information I collected could be incorporated in this study. The themes that are treated must therefore not be presumed to describe everything there is to know about Kehillat Kodesh. Rather, they represent those aspects of the setting and action that are either most representative of American modern Orthodox Jewish synagogues, as I comprehend them, or vital for a comprehension of the particular social interaction at Kehillat Kodesh.

I have throughout combined the ethnographic approach, which in its description embodies explanation, with the sociological one, which tends toward analytic generalization. Such an effort to intertwine the ethnographic particular with sociological generalization dilutes the purity of both but makes the work of interest to a more varied audience. As a blend of my two loves—ethnography and sociology—the work runs the risk of scorn by the supporters of each. Ethnographers will complain about gratuitous sociologizing, while sociologists will murmur about overabundance of detail. I hope such responses will be few.

To those defenders of quantitative social science who will denounce my tendency toward a narrative style, I can only reply that, unlike the novelist, who seeks to make the facts conform to his art, I have throughout made my art conform to the facts.

In presenting my report, I have used a dramaturgical framework. I do so both because of the structural advantages it offers for ordering my narrative and because I wish to suggest the drama inherent in the ordinary. Opening with a brief discussion of the background and beginning of the congregation, as well as some definitions necessary for locating the world in which the synagogue exists, I go on to sociologically describe both setting and props, paying special attention to their inherent expressive and symbolic character. My study then successively details the three major constituent parts of the synagogue: the houses of prayer, study, and assembly. In each I begin with a sociological casting of the characters and then follow with an analysis and ethnography of the action. Finally, I complete my synagogue portrait with a brief word about the essence of the interaction taking place within it.

No effort such as this one is undertaken alone, and words of thanks are therefore in order. The people of Kehillat Kodesh, who by their existence made my efforts possible and by their hospitality made my life tolerable, must stand first. My teacher and dear friend, Renée C. Fox, was throughout the long months of research and the initial writing an invaluable source of ideas and encouragement. To Erving Goffman go thanks, not only for stimulating the project, but for his continued advice through all stages of the work. Otto Pollak helped me to be critical both of my own work and of my doubts about it. Philip Rieff, my intellectual conscience and guide, sensitized me to the implications of my perspective, enabling me to avoid becoming enslaved by it. For his helping me to recognize both what I had *and* had not done, I am sincerely grateful. To my colleague, Dean Savage, go my thanks for his helpful critical reading of parts of this manuscript during its last stages. Rabbi Philip Weinberger helped me to discover what I did not know and to verify what I did know about matters of Jewish law, observance, and language usage. The University of Pennsylvania Center for Urban Ethnography and its director, John Szwed, offered both the financial support and institutional affiliation which made possible a project which less imaginative institutions would undoubtedly never have encouraged. Finally, I thank my wife, Ellin, for her patience, suggestions, and willingness to allow her life to become enmeshed in a project which gave her little time with a husband who was forever "going to the synagogue."

Synagogue Life

1 Background, Beginnings, and Definitions

Although officially a part of the metropolitan area of Sprawl City, Dudley Meadows remains somewhat distinct ecologically. Lying on the western edge of this great metropolis, it is bounded on one side by a mammoth park, on another by the city line, on a third by a six-lane expressway connecting the western suburbs with the center city, on a fourth by railroad tracks, and on a fifth by an area of row houses which have become part of a black ghetto. Unlike the row houses in what has come to be called "Upper Dudley Meadows," the large and stately stone houses of Dudley Meadows are surrounded by large plots of land. A few high-rise, luxury apartment buildings and several garden-apartment complexes are fairly recent additions to the neighborhood.

To the uninformed observer, the Dudley Meadows area looks like a highly affluent neighborhood. Indeed, at one time it was, and it then served as one of the most exclusive areas in Sprawl City. Over the years, however, it went through many of the metamorphoses that have become common in American cities. Originally the meadows of Dr. Dudley, a respected physician of Colonial times, the area became the site of early country estates. In time it evolved into the neighborhood of the Sprawl City aristocracy. In the post–World War II period it started to become Jewish as the former citizens moved west and out of the city. These Jews made the area a middle-class one and in turn watched the construction of the row houses, which enabled their less affluent brethren to move in. Here people could live within easy commuting distance of the center city while experiencing few of the disadvantages of life in an urban environment.

In the late sixties the face of the neighborhood began to change again. Blacks began to move into the row houses, and, at the same time, Jewish whites began to flee, much as the earlier citizens of Dudley Meadows had fled when they, the Jews, had begun to move into the neighborhood. At the time of this study, from 1970 to 1973, the emigration was continuing, but at a somewhat slowed pace. The row houses had become almost completely filled by black middle-class families. The large stone houses were populated by both whites and blacks. The high rises remained white and primarily Jewish, while some garden-apartment complexes had become totally black and others remained totally white.

On Dudley Avenue, the main street of Dudley Meadows, there stands an old converted stone house that serves as a synagogue for approximately 130 men, women, and children. Its name is Kehillat Kodesh. These people are for the most part dispersed within the Dudley Meadows area, and only the *shul* (as the synagogue is commonly called in Yiddish)* allows them a space where their hegemony is absolute. An overwhelming majority of its members identify themselves generally as Orthodox Jews. As such they are

---

*The term "shul" comes originally from the Yiddish word for "school." In their incipient form, at the beginnings of the Diaspora, synagogues were nothing more than schools, or "shuls," where people got together to study Torah—Jewish law and lore (halacha and agada). In time, since the men were together during the times of prayer, they would begin and end each study period with prayer. Ultimately, prayer became as much a part of the shul as study. Today shuls are primarily for prayer, although they serve as locations for study as well.

committed not only to Judaism as a religious affiliation but also to accepting all the precepts, imperatives, and doctrines of Jewish law or *halacha* (translated literally, "the way"). The shul is one of the absolutely necessary institutions for Jews who wish to practice their religion in an Orthodox fashion.

In addition to the shul, Orthodox Jews need a Jewish day school for their children of primary-school age, to ensure that the young will be schooled in Jewish law, lore, and tradition; a nearby source of kosher meat, to supply the basic staple of food according to the Jewish dietary laws; and a *mikva*, or ritual bath, in which a married woman must immerse herself seven days after the end of her menstrual cycle to provide for ritual purity in procreative activity. Although other Jewish institutions are also necessary and useful, these four are mandatory for the establishment and maintenance of any Orthodox Jewish community. A large number of these institutions and others, as well, reflects a strong Orthodox community which can maintain them. Yet, of the mandatory four, none but the shul can count on the simultaneous involvement— albeit at different levels of participation—of men, women, and children. For this reason and others that will become clearer as the study proceeds, the shul is the central large institution in the life of the Jews of Kehillat Kodesh.

As part of their adherence to halacha, Orthodox Jews observe the law against any travel other than by foot on Sabbaths and holy days. Accordingly, in order to participate in the religious services of the shul on such important occasions, these Jews must live within walking distance of it. All Orthodox Jews, therefore, live in the neighborhood in which their shul is located. Hence, to say that one prays at Kehillat Kodesh is to say that one lives in Dudley Meadows. A look at the membership list of any particular Orthodox shul thus enables one to get an idea of how many Orthodox Jews live in the immediate geographic area.

In addition to praying together, these same people are very likely to join together in other activities as well. Unlike Conservative or Reform Jews, who, because they do not adhere to the ban on motorized travel on Sabbaths and holy days, may live in one area, worship in another, and have little in common with their fellow worshipers besides participation in the same religious services, the members of an Orthodox shul additionally experience one another as neighbors and friends. Inevitably they share a complex array of concerns, including maintenance of the shul itself as a building and a community; religious values, and the problems involved in adapting those values to the claims of a secular American society; and, finally, a general *Weltanschauung* which comes in part from these other mutual concerns.

Except for the shul, use of the other Orthodox Jewish institutions listed above is not limited to people who live near one another, for they may be used on weekdays, when travel other than by foot is permitted. Thus, other Orthodox Jews may use such institutions; however, they do not necessarily have much in common with one another, as is the case with members of the same shul. Of course in certain communities where there is a large concentration of Orthodox Jews, all institutions are nearby, and the same people who worship together also send their children to the same school, patronize the same butcher and the same mikva, and indeed make up the entire clientele of all the Orthodox institutions in the area. Or, if the Orthodox community is very small, with but one shul, one school, one butcher, and one mikva, the same situation may obtain. Neither situation obtains in Sprawl City. Only two day schools exist there, and two reliable kosher butchers and one mikva, but there are quite a few Orthodox shuls. Thus, while all the members of a shul use many of the same other Orthodox institutions, not all users of the other institutions are members of the same shul. For that reason, and for the others suggested earlier, people tend to identify themselves by the shul to which they belong, which they attend on the average of once a week all year long.

Although the members of Kehillat Kodesh are considered Orthodox Jews, especially by outsiders, not all Orthodox Jews are alike. While all such Jews agree that an ideological commitment to the entire halacha is mandatory, there are differences among Orthodox Jews as to the minimum observances necessary for sustaining that ideological stance. At one extreme are those who are almost constantly involved with other observant Jews and for whom Orthodox Jewishness is defined by strict adherence to halacha, from minutiae to broad legal principles, with emphasis on the equal importance of both; at the other extreme are those for whom the actual practice of Orthodoxy means minimally: (1) Sabbath and holy-day observance, with their correlated laws; (2) *kashrut*, the strict observance of Jewish dietary laws; (3) use of a mikva, that is, maintaining family purity; and (4) praying in a synagogue which has the formal characteristics of Orthodoxy. However, most Orthodox Jews fall somewhere between these two extremes of halachic fulfillment.

For the purposes of this study, Orthodox Jewry may be divided into two groups, both of which have in the past been referred to as "Orthodox" Jews: modern Orthodox Jews and traditional Orthodox Jews. The first group is defined by a desire to adhere faithfully to the beliefs, principles, and traditions of Jewish law and observance without being either remote from or untouched by life in the contemporary secular world. The second group is relatively more isolated from contemporary secular society. It is in America but not of it, concerning itself almost completely with Jewish life and seeing such aspects of reality as secular education, English language, or occupations outside the Jewish community as infringements upon their life. The most prominent, but by no means the only, representatives of this group are the Chassidim, the sect of zealots whose entire lives revolve around Jewish observance.

Kehillat Kodesh is populated primarily by modern Orthodox Jews. Its members are "oriented significantly to the world outside" the Jewish one, and they regard themselves "as an integral part of that [outside] world."[1] This cosmopolitanism may be seen, for instance, in the occupational profile of the adult males. Only about 5 percent have jobs, such as religious school teachers or kosher butchers, which allow full-time involvement and isolation within the Jewish community. Nearly 65 percent have careers in fields like medicine, law, university teaching, and the natural sciences, which require relatively long periods of training and initiation outside the Orthodox Jewish orbit; and, as Hughes suggests, "In general, we may say that the longer and more rigorous the period of initiation into an occupation, the more culture and technique are associated with it, and the more deeply impressed are its attitudes upon the person."[2]

These are people who, for the most part, use English as their everyday language and whose interests are not limited to matters of Jewish concern. Nor are their friends exclusively Orthodox Jews. Yet, at the same time that their occupations, interests, education, and friendships propel them toward cosmopolitanism, their commitment and strict adherence to the code of Jewish law draw them back. Such has always been the goal of halacha, whose imperatives cover almost every aspect of human existence, from the mundane to the ethereal, and frequently require the communal assistance of other observant Jews.

To the extent that Kehillat Kodesh Jews have ordered their lives according to halacha, they have remained "preoccupied with local [i.e., Jewish] problems. . ., strictly speaking, parochial."[3] The modern Orthodox Jew of Kehillat Kodesh is thus cosmopolitan in his desire for modernity and parochial in his commitment to Orthodoxy. When desires and commitments come into conflict, commitments must have primacy.

One member articulates the issue with reference to a conflict between his occupational demands and his Jewish constraints as follows:

> When I first found out about my job transfer, I was afraid.
> I thought that I'm going out of New York, and how will I find
> a place where I can observe my Jewishness. *Now* I would move
> anywhere, I don't care—of course, providing that my Jewish
> needs were taken care of. I mean I wouldn't have gone to
> Phoenix, Arizona.

Job transfers have to be accepted wherever possible, since careers are important. Nevertheless, Phoenix, an Orthodox Jew's no-man's-land, is out of the question. One gives up New York and its many Orthodox institutions for the career as long as the minimum of Jewish observance remains possible.

While the women in the shul are not generally involved in an occupational structure which pulls them out of the Orthodox community (about 63 percent have no paid jobs) and tend to be more strict in much of their halachic observance, they share the men's commitment to the modern world through their interests, friendships, and education. The children remain more encapsulated in a Jewish world. Of the school-age children, only one attends a public school (and this is a school for the brightest of Sprawl City youth), while the rest attend Jewish day schools or, if they are of high-school age, a *yeshiva* (academy of higher Jewish learning). One might say that the young are not trusted to choose Jewish commitment in the face of modernity. They are perhaps also the conscience and vital symbols of Orthodoxy in the community. As one member put it, "I send my kid to yeshiva because I want to have the proper atmosphere in the house."

The people of Kehillat Kodesh are primarily young. Although the age range of its members runs from infancy to past seventy, the median age of the male household heads (i.e., most of the men in shul) is about thirty-five, and the modal age is about thirty. The wives of course reflect this age structure, as do the children. This is, then, for the most part a young congregation.

Because Dudley Meadows is a neighborhood which is in the process of changeover from white Jewish to black, with a resultant decline in property values, many of the younger members of the shul (a minority of whom are Sprawl City natives) consider themselves sojourners and temporary residents of the area. Among homeowners, those who plan to stay, or who have already been in the community for an extended period of time, one finds few people under the age of forty. Among the younger group, most of those who plan to stay in Sprawl City eventually buy homes outside the Dudley Meadows area, though their choice of location is somewhat limited, since they wish to be near an Orthodox shul. Accordingly, much of the formal authority structure which has been built up over time at Kehillat Kodesh is in the hands of *balabatim* (a Yiddish term for community leaders and literally translated as "homeowners") above the age of forty. Most of those in shul government and a majority of the board members are all over forty; and this is true also of the three-member presidium of the ladies' auxiliary. However, if the people most responsible for running the shul are older than the average member, authority is still shared with the young, who make up the lifeblood of the congregation.

Beginnings

The situation in Kehillat Kodesh was not always thus. In its beginnings, about twelve years ago, the shul was an offshoot of another Orthodox synagogue, situated just across the city line in the more affluent community of Happiton. The membership was then for the most part older and far less ready to share authority. Every member learns the story of these beginnings and can repeat its salient facts; indeed, the very knowledge of these facts seems often to be the best evidence of one's membership in the group. The newer members repeat the story with the same assurance as the older ones. The freshness of detail makes a listener surprised to learn that most of the events under discussion happened between nine and twelve years earlier, before many of those telling the story were even members of the shul.

The story of the shul's early history can be divided into two parts. The first deals with the original break from Happiton and the three early years, which were not easy ones in the life of the institution. They were marked by a poor turnout of participants, even on such important occasions as Sabbaths and holy days. One member recounts:

> I remember how on the first *shabbos* [Sabbath] we could not get a *minyan* [according to halacha, the ten-male minimum

necessary for community prayer] together, and how once on *Shevuos* [the Feast of Weeks holy day] we had to wait and wait until we finally got together a minyan. Yah, those early days were not so easy.

In addition to the difficulties of assembly, the first years were scarred by dissension. Another member describes the scene:

> The atmosphere in the shul was like an inquisition. A lot of people had a holier-than-thou attitude. Those who had a position felt that they had to publicly express that position. They had to have special seats. So there were the "haves" and the "have-nots." There was always quarreling—I mean much worse than it would ever get now.

People judged one another's religious observance, relating power and authority in the institution to a proper exhibition of such observance. Yet only some people were doing the evaluating. These evaluations became translated into giving or holding back *kibbudim*, honors accompanying publicly assigned ritual performances during the synagogue service. Every *kibbud* (honor) required an investigation of whether the recipient measured up to the demands. In fact, many of these specifications were written into the first shul constitution, which proposed strict halachic adherence before anyone would be allowed to hold communal authority or receive any kibbud. The ones who met the demands were the "haves"; the others were the "have-nots."

Any version of this first part of the story inevitably mentions these facts: the smallness of the group, its tenuous existence, and its atmosphere of altercation. With mention of the latter comes the second part of the story.

Ultimately, the dissension became too much for the group to bear. The new congregation remained precariously small, as potential members were put off by the atmosphere of contention. Consequently, after three years, a second schism occurred. Now the original rebels themselves became victims of an insurrection. Some versions of the story recount an "expulsion," while others describe the "haves" being "voted out of office." Whatever the method, the clear result was a change in authority. Some founders left the shul by moving out of the neighborhood. Others began walking great distances to join other shuls, where they reportedly engaged in further quarrels. Finally, some began to stay at home, returning to shul on rare occasions and then only as passive participants without authority and subject to murmurs of gossip about their fate and identity.

In the new order, members were far more reluctant to hold shul office. By the time of this study, elections prompted widespread efforts to avoid authority, so much so that one vice-president could be tricked into office only by being elected while he was out of town. Instead of being denied authority, newcomers were now eagerly offered it, much in the way that Frankenberg discovered people in a Welsh border community giving office to neophytes "in order to avoid thrusting the responsibility for open schism upon themselves."[4]

Along with this change came a strong, albeit unstated, taboo against open quarreling in shul and a great emphasis on conciliation. A new constitution was written, which, although it included many of the halachic demands of the original, was far less strictly enforced. No one ever read it and, when asked, claimed, "It's probably illegal anyway." Kibbudim, and the ritual performances associated with them, became accessible to all, while halachic demands became subtly moderated. Except in rare cases, private religious observance was no longer to be publicly evaluted via either open quarrels or the withholding of kibbudim. The collective inclination became, in the words of the shul president (who had witnessed the last insurrection), "Let's *first* be one big happy family."

One cannot help seeing parallels between this institutional history and the character of small training groups. Like the congregation, these groups are distinguished by face-to-face relations and allow "for examination of elementary societal phenomena in microcosmic form." Both groups "generate some degree of emotional involvement in the participants."[5]

In describing T-groups, Slater explains that the leader is always attacked and ultimately expelled. The expulsion, or symbolic murder, is then linked to the development of group solidarity. "[T]he actual or threatened loss of members acts as a strongly inhibiting force with regard to revolt." Eventually, "the group members can either try to make the leader one of them or get rid of him altogether."[6]

The newfound solidarity following the second Kehillat Kodesh insurrection (which might be considered the true culmination of the shul's birth) can be understood along these lines. When the original leaders refused to share authority, they could be treated in one of two ways: (1) they could be forced to share power and hence become like all others in the group or (2) they could be removed altogether. After three years of struggle, only the latter alternative seemed feasible. A second act of rebellion was, however, potentially a very explosive model for members to legitimate. Accordingly, in the repeated telling of the story, emphasis was always on: (1) how much life had improved since the end of the quarrels and (2) how dire the consequences had been for the quarrelers. One narrative even ends by recounting that not only are the expelled no longer in the shul but the expellers are gone too.

As Slater suggests, "groups have a pronounced tendency to represent or even act out particular emotional constellations in which all members actually share."[7] The events of the insurrection and the traumata of the dissidents have clearly been shared by the entire congregation. As each newcomer learns the story, he too comes to share in that history, and his behavior in the collectivity is accordingly affected. No one fights in shul.

Relations with Other Jewish Sects

Although the shul members have begun to display a greater tolerance within their own ranks, they have not done so vis-à-vis other Jewish sects. Such groups are censured as either "too modern" or "too *frum.*" *Frum*, or *frumkeit* (the state of being frum), is a Yiddish expression referring both to the actual practice of halachic Judaism and to the religious outlook associated with it. Operationally, frumkeit is quite difficult to define, since its requirements vary in accordance with whom one asks for a definition. In effect, one must conclude that, for shul members, frumkeit is synonymous with conformity to Jewish observance as publicly practiced at Kehillat Kodesh. Any other form is deviant.

There is no lack of local embodiments of both extremes. The "too modern" Jews of Temple Or Chodosh, directly across the street, whose doctrine denies, practically as well as ideologically, the legitimacy of halacha and seeks instead to "reform" it, symbolize the excesses of modernity and are often targets of derision. For example, when Or Chodosh closes its doors for the summer while its membership is on vacation, the shul members jokingly ask if Heaven has closed its doors for vacation as well.

Shul members who make some complaint about Kehillat Kodesh prayers are derisively told to "go across the street," with the implication that nothing in Kehillat Kodesh could be as disturbing as what is found among Reform Jews. No one dares step into the Or Chodosh building, to say nothing of worshiping there, for to do so would be to step outside, in symbol and in fact, the border defining the Orthodox community. The members of each synagogue are faceless and nameless to one another, each representing a totally alien and unacceptable viewpoint rather than a real person. As such, it is possible for the shul Jews to call the members of Or Chodosh *goyim* (Gentiles)—persons totally outside the Jewish cosmos. Undoubtedly, it also makes it possible for Or Chodosh people to think of their neighbors as "fanatics"—persons completely outside the pale of contemporary normalcy.

While the members of Moriah, the Conservative synagogue two blocks away, are subject to criticism for excessive modernity, the attitude toward them is less extreme. Unlike the Reform Jews, these people have "conserved" some of the legitimacy of halacha even as they affirm the imperatives of modernity. They may, therefore, have much in common with their modern Orthodox brethren.

In fact, the congregations maintain contact in various ways. Friendships are shared. Moreover, some shul members were originally Moriah congregants. Others teach in its Hebrew school, while some occasionally attend public events held within its doors.

When an Orthodox minyan or quorum is unavailable during the week, shul members may occasionally even worship at Moriah. The halachic transgressions which distinguish it from Kehillat Kodesh are, for all intents and purposes, removed on weekdays. Primary among these is the mixed-sex seating which Moriah permits during public prayer. Since women do not customarily come to pray on days other than Sabbath and holy days, and since, liturgically, the conservative prayers are fundamentally indistinct from those of Orthodoxy, weekday communal prayer at Moriah is conceivable, if not encouraged, for shul members.

Although differences in Jewish practice divide Moriah from Kehillat Kodesh, the criticisms of Moriah's excessive modernity are associated more with ideology than with practice. While the modern Orthodox Jews in the shul, along with the Conservative Moriah people, recognize the mutual demands of Judaism and modernity, the latter, unlike the former, consider both equally important. Where the shul Jews have allowed their support of modernity to remain essentially *de facto*, the Moriah members have rationalized and ideologically legitimated halachic change *de jure*. One might see here an analogue between the criminal and the revolutionary as Merton describes them.[8] Both engage in the same act; yet for the former the act does not challenge the legitimacy of the law, while for the latter the transgression is revolutionary, challenging the rightfulness of the law. In terms of this formula, shul Jews can accept themselves as "criminals" while they criticize the members of Moriah as "revolutionaries."

Hence, whenever a shul member joins in Moriah activities, he accompanies his actions with lengthy explanations of his motives, lest his participation be interpreted as a wavering in his doctrinal commitment to halacha. The ambivalence suggested here is most clearly expressed in the comments of two members, both of whom have attended Moriah events. One derisively explains that Moriah is peopled by a preponderance of *trefniaks* (a Yiddishism describing those whose observance of Judaism is literally not kosher; it is within the Jewish cosmos but not properly so); the other remarks:

> I don't go for this whole idea of the breakdown between Orthodox and Conservative. I mean, 'cause there are people that I know that go to Moriah, which is Conservative, that are just as much practicing Jews as people that come to an Orthodox shul.

All members, however, agree that excessive modernity is wrong, and even this relatively tolerant member went on to say:

> On the other hand, I don't think you would find someone going to a Reform temple who in his own private life would be as observant as someone who would go to an Orthodox shul.

At its worst, excessive modernity arouses deep feelings of antipathy, as exemplified in one member's analysis of the consequences of becoming "too modern." He explains:

> Anyone who lets things go like that gives his children a sort of antireligion. You can't get so modern like Conservative or Reform Jews—I mean, you need some guidelines.

This statement, and the vehemence with which it was spoken, expresses antipathy; yet antipathy, as Toennies explains,

> can easily, as a result of close acquaintance or other motives, be transformed into real sympathy . . . ; the same or similar interests are sufficient to arouse sympathy to the extent that such similarities are in the consciousness of those involved, and by the same token contrary interests will evoke antipathy.[9]

A closer look reveals that the shul members feel certain sympathies for even the most modern of Jews.

To the extent that the modern Orthodox Jew of Kehillat Kodesh is conscious that his interest in modernity is not essentially different from that of other kinds of Jews, he will sympathize with their goal if not with their means. But when he sees that the means these other Jews have chosen lead to an undermining of halachic observance, toward "a sort of antireligion," which is intrinsically different from his own, antipathy overwhelms any feeings of sympathy.

Yet even the deepest feelings of antipathy toward the "too modern" are mitigated by one very important factor. Toennies suggests this additional ground for sympathy when he writes:

> We shall usually have a certain degree of sympathy, even though this may be small, for those who side with us, whether we have known them before or come to know them only as fellow fighters, comrades, countrymen, or even home folks, or as colleagues, or as persons of the same faith.[10]

At the very least, the threatening non-Jewish world makes the shul members realize that they share a common faith and ultimate destiny with members of Or Chodosh and Moriah. Thus, for example, when one weekday morning someone discovered a sticker which overnight had been placed on the door of Or Chodosh and which proclaimed, "Free Rudolf Hess," several shul members took the sign down, pointing out that, "We've got to do it, even for them and even though they probably don't know that they're Jews like us." Mingled with the general antipathy aroused by issues of frumkeit comes the inevitable sympathy for "persons of the same faith."

While those who are "too modern" are criticized for insufficient frumkeit, the "too frum" are faulted for the opposite excesses. In the Dudley Meadows area, one outstanding source of such Jews is the Sprawl City Yeshiva (often called simply "the Yeshiva"). Although primarily an academy for the advanced study of Talmud—rabbinic law and lore—it also has a chapel, which serves as a shul for students, teachers, and others who wish to pray with them. While there are Kehillat Kodesh members who occasionally worship there and who consider themselves as frum as the Sprawl City Yeshiva people, the Yeshiva is fundamentally a traditional Orthodox institution. Known outside Sprawl City and America as a bona fide place of Orthodox Jewish learning, the Sprawl City Yeshiva is the first stop for the traditional Orthodox Jews who come to Sprawl City and Dudley Meadows. Hence the attitude expressed toward the Yeshiva may be seen, at least in part, as a reflection of the general attitude toward the "more frum."

Perhaps the first step to take in considering the Kehillat Kodesh feelings about traditional Orthodox Jews is to define "more frum." These traditional Orthodox Jews have been described as relatively isolated from contemporary secular America and concerned almost completely with Jewish life and observance. Of course traditional Orthodox and modern Orthodox Jews must be considered as ideal types which reality approximates but with which it never fully complies. Nevertheless, the more frum the person, the more willing he is to concern himself with the demands of halachic observance and the Jewish world which it defines, and the less energy and effort will he expend on other demands. Thus, for example, for the more frum, occupation becomes completely subservient to Jewish observance. Unlike the modern Orthodox Jew, who makes certain compromises in the pursuit of both an occupational career and a halachically ordered life, the more frum will pursue only those careers which negligibly disturb halachic observance. They become yeshiva teachers, ritual slaughterers, kosher butchers, Hebrew book dealers, scribes and, in general, holders of occupations directly involved in Jewish institutions. They thereby force themselves into a community which can support such institutions, one necessarily filled with other traditional Orthodox Jews.

While the modern Orthodox Jew also looks for an area which enables him to practice Judaism, he is satisfied with a minimum of institutions: day school, mikva, kosher butcher, and shul. His more-frum counterpart demands more. He looks for a Sabbath-observant bakery whose baked goods are not only above suspicion in terms of kashrut but whose bakers make the proper ritual benedictions over the breads when baking them. He looks not only for the mandatory mikva for women, but also for a separate mikva for men, whose immersion is voluntary, and one for dishes, which are to be immersed before initial use. He looks not only for a school for his children but also for a group of learned adult Jews with whom he can engage in Jewish scholarship on a regular basis. Observing halacha means learning all about it, a full-time occupation, for which the occupations of the modern Orthodox Jew scarcely leave enough time. The more-frum Jew needs a nearby source of Jewish books for purchase and perusal. In short, the more frum need more Jewish institutions than the modern Orthodox Jews. Indeed, in Dudley Meadows, the Sprawl City Yeshiva students and faculty have in large measure been responsible for bringing many such institutions into existence.

The more frum also practice more of the halacha than their counterparts at Kehillat Kodesh. To accept the notion of a necessary minimum level of observance, as the modern Orthodox Jews do, is anathema to the more frum. Thus, for example, the members of Kehillat Kodesh may miss a prayer now and then when they are busy at work, but the more frum pray three times daily, stopping any secular activity they may be engaged in when it inhibits prayer. Or, the more frum regularly engage in the study of Torah, the entire corpus of Jewish law and lore, while the modern Orthodox Jews at Kehillat Kodesh do so much less regularly, putting secular pursuits first.

When queried about halachic observance, however, the shul Jews will more often than not express many of the same doctrinal beliefs as the more frum. In fact, through interviews one might gain the impression that no differentiation at all exists between traditional and modern Orthodox Jews, for both would express essentially the same thoughts about the importance and imperative of halacha. The distinctions between them become clear only in a comparison of how halacha is implemented, acted out, and indeed lived by each group.

The comparison might best be understood by using Fichter's distinctions between complete ideology, practical ideology, and actual behavior.[11] The first of these constitutes the "unattainable positive ideal of spiritual perfection towards which all parishioners should be striving." The second is "the value system which guides them in everyday life," which "seems to be a mental working compromise" between ideal spirituality and the demands of the real world. Finally, "The actual behavior of parishioners is usually assumed to be in accord with the second ideology, although it is 'expected' to follow the first." For the more frum, practical ideology must remain relatively indistinguishable from complete Jewish ideology, with actual behavior being an effort to live up to the latter. While the shul members subscribe to the complete ideology, their actual behavior suggests a practical ideology which differentiates them from their more-frum brethren. *De jure* all Orthodox Jews, traditional and modern, are in agreement; *de facto* they remain at odds.

One may, incidentally, use the same schema to explain the relationship between the shul Jews and their "too-modern" kin. While modern Orthodox and Conservative Jews appear to coincide in much of their actual behavior, they differ in that the Conservatives, by replacing complete ideology with its practical counterpart, have given a greater legitimacy to their actual behavior. As for Reform Jews, shul members (qua Jews) share with them neither complete nor practical ideology nor any actual behavior.

To return to the attitude toward the more frum: if actual behavior and its associated practical ideology distinguish modern from traditional Orthodox Jews, criticism of the latter must then focus on halachic practice. The following characterization of the more frum by a shul member suggests that such is the case:

> I think there's a difference between Orthodox and orthoprax. Some of these so-called Orthodox are nothing more than orthoprax. Orthopractice is just doing what everybody else [among the Orthodox] does, without understanding it or meaning it. People who are orthoprax may call themselves Orthodox, but they really are not so frum.

While admitting that there are some Jews who practice halacha more strictly than others, the speaker points out that such practice is subject to evaluation as to its genuineness and does not always indicate frumkeit. Being frum requires, additionally, comprehension and religious intent. Of course, religious intent, as well as understanding the point, purpose, and reasoning behind observance, is insufficient if one does not actually practice. The same member went on to say:

> People who are Conservative and who observe and understand everything they believe—they call themselves religious, but they're not really frum.

One must practice even if one does not comprehend or believe everything. Clearly, being a frum Jew, as one ought to be, is an ideal to be strived for but not easily reached.

Some Jews are unquestionably more frum. These are the halachic virtuosi who both understand and practice Jewish law and tradition. Usually these people are officially ordained rabbis (although they need not pursue a rabbinic occupation); but sometimes virtuosity is recognized when individuals take the role of teacher in various study groups or exhibit expertise in halachic questions of everyday life. Of such people it may be said, "He could have gotten *smicha* [rabbinic ordination] if he wanted to; he just never bothered." Such people cannot be criticized on the grounds of orthopractice. Other ways are found. Thus one such Orthodox man, a recognized halachic virtuoso by virtue of his leadership in various study groups, is described as "crazy frum" (senseless and totally unsound in his Jewish observance) by members of Kehillat Kodesh because, among other of his practices, he recites psalms as he works or invites people whom he is with at prayer time to join him in worship. At the same time that this man is "crazy," he is respected for his scholarship; he is crazy not because he believes in the halachic doctrine that calls for such behavior—after all, he is a scholar and knows what the law actually calls for—but because he follows through in his actual behavior. Again, one must remember that, if pressed to explain the label "crazy frum," members of Kehillat Kodesh will ultimately explain that this man is probably right on his observance and that they were just kidding. Like a slip of the tongue, the label becomes denied upon closer scrutiny and when the labeler is asked to defend his "slip."

As stated before, the Sprawl City Yeshiva is the local embodi-ment of the traditional Orthodox milieu. In talking about strict ritual observance, one member says of Kehillat Kodesh, "We probably don't come up to specs. The Yeshiva probably comes closest to it." While shul members admit, when questioned, their collective deviance from the Orthodox standard, their behavior and unsolicited comments belie the sincerity of this admission. For example, although all Kehillat Kodesh boys of high-school age attend a yeshiva (girls, not ritually required to study Torah, go to day schools, which, although completely Orthodox, do not empha-size intense and advanced Jewish scholarship), most do not attend the local one. Members readily explain why they have sent their sons to more modern yeshivas out of town. One characterizes the local school as "pretty good in Jewish stuff, but it's not so hot in English [i.e., secular studies]." Another points out the one-sided-ness of the Sprawl City Yeshiva in the fact that students who want to study Jewish mystical texts or anything else not in the curriculum have had to sneak away to a midnight class at his home, given by a teacher imported from New York. A third member remarks in anger, "The kids there aren't even allowed to read the New York Times—too modern, especially the movie page." A fourth criticizes the preparation for life which the Sprawl City Yeshiva provides: "They make 'em study all day and never tell 'em they have to go out and get a job." Still another parent explains why he sent his son to a school in Baltimore:

> I went with my son, Amitai, you know, to check out the
> place, and I decided against sending him there. I didn't like the
> types there. [Why?] Well, they're more isolated and also they
> have the attitude of "I'm the best, and everything I do is right"—
> that there's only one way to be a Jew. I understand why they
> need such an attitude, as a defense; but still, I don't like it.

Here then, in action—through the avoidance of sending their sons to the local yeshiva—as well as words, members of Kehillat Kodesh make it clear that they are not one and the same as the Orthodox Jews which that local institution has come to represent and that they do not want their sons to become Orthodox Jews of that "type." Although shul members "understand" and perhaps even sympathize with the more Orthodox way of life, they still do not "like" it and wish, therefore, to distinguish themselves from it.

This mixture of sympathy and antipathy which the members of Kehillat Kodesh feel toward the traditional Orthodox Jews of Dudley Meadows suggests, in Merton and Barber's terms, "an ambivalence [that] comes to be built into the very structure of social relations." The two social structures—one, whose associated roles and behaviors define a people dually committed to the contemporary and Jewish worlds; the other, whose roles and behaviors stress a cosmos totally controlled and defined by Jewish law and observance—in mutual opposition *and* apposition "generate the circumstances in which ambivalence is embedded."[12]

While their attitudes toward both the more and the less frum help to delineate the identity of "the modern Orthodox Jews of Kehillat Kodesh," reactions to other groups who would define themselves equally as modern Orthodox Jews complete the identification of the subjects of this study. If a group may refer its behavior to, and define itself in terms of, those it is not, it must also be prepared to characterize itself in terms of those similar to itself. In other words, for Kehillat Kodesh Jews, not only the more and less but also the equally frum serve as a reference group.[13]

Since evaluation is implicit in any such comparisons, two groups likely to be defined as identical scrupulously scrutinize each other. Each realizes that on the basis of the *other* group's action, *it* may be judged. Indeed, two groups which are alike frequently threaten each other's identity the most; for, once adjudged identical, not only by others but by themselves, any discrepant activity on the part of one group calls the other's activity into question as well. When such activities are closely related to identity, discrepancy becomes an even more crucial problem. The two cannot be alike and yet also different. If they do not change together, one must be evaluated as deviant, the other as normative.[14]

Displaying concern with such issues, shul members frequently compare their institution with other modern Orthodox congregations, especially those nearby, to see if a genuine similarity exists. Liturgical form and style, frumkeit versus modernity, the extent of active participation in shul life and other matters of Jewish or institutional behavior, become the crucial criteria of comparison. While there may be other similarities, for example, political-party affiliations or economic status, these are not part of the group's concern with its Jewish or institutional self-identification.

For Kehillat Kodesh, three other shuls serve as possible comparisons: (1) the Happiton shul, from which Kehillat Kodesh sprang, (2) a recently formed shul in the nearby suburb of Drumlin, an area to which several Dudley Meadows émigrés have moved, and (3) a *shtibble* (a Yiddish term meaning "little house" and referring to a small shul, used primarily for prayer and commonly under the complete authority of one man) called Ram Shalom. Ultimately, each of these other institutions is distinguished from Kehillat Kodesh and criticized.

Thus, one member compares the size of the Happiton minyan with the Kehillat Kodesh quorum and finds the former wanting:

> I've gone to Happiton, but you can't always count on a minyan there. Every time you go, you're really taking a gamble. All right, here we have problems too, but there even on a Friday night [Sabbath] you're taking a gamble.

Another member criticizes Happiton for utilizing, as part of the weekday quorum, the beggars who daily solicit funds from the Dudley Meadows synagogues:

> Even if we're one man short, we're not gonna have to ask one of them [the beggars] to make the minyan [i.e., to be the tenth man] like they do at Happiton. They'll take anyone in off the street, because they can't count on their own people to come to the minyan.

A third explains his absence on a recent Sabbath morning by saying he attended Happiton services, but he laughingly adds that only fourteen were present at this most important service of the Jewish week; that is to say, symbolically there was no minyan even if halachically there was one.

Hence, while tacitly admitting that Happiton is a place where they may pray without calling their Orthodoxy into question (for people do so without heavier penalty than a joke or two at their expense), shul members stress that, although the two shuls might appear to be alike, the informed insider recognizes crucial differences between them.

Shul members do not limit themselves to informing insiders about such differences. Joint activities with other shuls are shunned because outsiders might then think that, if these institutions do things together, they might in some way be considered identical. This is especially the case where such activities pertain to Jewish-identity-linked behavior. Thus, for example, although both Happiton and Kehillat Kodesh have trouble gathering a daily minyan, they refuse to pool their participants and thereby assure a quorum. Such a union might blur the differences between them. Or, both shuls schedule Torah study groups during the week, but at identical times, thereby assuring that no one will be able to attend both classes; thus they are saved from being regarded as having a unified curriculum. Even the topics of these classes are similar, with one group studying the laws of marriage, the other those of divorce. Although members of each shul may not be conscious of this competition, the outsider cannot help but see it.

Similar efforts at differentiation occur with regard to the Drumlin shul. Here, however, the distinction is made, not with regard to the collective level of participation at the prayer services and the frumkeit which that suggests, but in terms of the actual degree of Jewish behavior and observance on the part of individual members of each shul. With scorn one member of Kehillat Kodesh remarks of the Drumlin shul, "I don't even know for sure if everyone there keeps *shabbos* [the ritual observances of the Sabbath]." Another member goes further and says, "That place is filled with *mechallelei shabbos* [desecrators of the Sabbath and its laws, who do not keep even the minimum halachic observances defining modern Orthodox Judaism]." Indeed, when the members of the Drumlin shul approached the Kehillat Kodesh congregation for financial help in building a mikva in the Drumlin area (suggesting by this that the effort be a joint one), the latter refused, saying, "They have enough money in Drumlin to put up a stained-glass window in the shul but not for a mikva. You know why? Because only about ten people there would use one." Another Kehillat Kodesh man adds, "They claim that they had a mikva in the plans, but that shows that they are only frum on paper." To admit that the Drumlin shul is any kind of modern Orthodox Jewish institution is to admit that the definition of modern Orthodox Judaism does not have to include Sabbath observance or mikva use. It is thus to call into question many Kehillat Kodesh members' activities. Accordingly, shul members reserve what is perhaps their greatest scorn and antipathy for this new modern Orthodox shul. In addition, since it is "new"— younger in institutional life (and also located in Drumlin, that area to which many Dudley Meadows people think of moving)—it is a greater threat than the other shuls, which are older, for it might be identified as illustrative of the modern Orthodox Jewry of the future. This would threaten not only present but future Kehillat Kodesh identity as well. Indeed, the president has on several occasions publicly announced that he has heard from several former members now living in Drumlin, and all admit to missing Kehillat Kodesh and wish they had never left.

Of the three other shuls, Ram Sholom is perhaps the one toward which the Kehillat Kodesh members feel the least antipathy; this is undoubtedly accounted for in part by the small size of the institution. Moreover, Ram Sholom is neither stable enough nor sufficiently known outside the Orthodox community of Sprawl City to act as a threat by possibly being identified with Kehillat Kodesh. Of the three, it comes closest to traditional Orthodoxy, and many of its weekday members disappear on the Sabbath, to attend prayer services at the Sprawl City Yeshiva instead of the shul. Perhaps the major difference, other than size, that the Kehillat Kodesh membership points to is the fact that Ram Sholom is under the nearly total control of one man. Even one of this man's sons, who attends Kehillat Kodesh, admits that this fact more than any other differentiates the two shuls. In other words, since member involvement is limited at Ram Sholom, it is not considered a shul so much as a shtibble. Identifying it by this latter label removes its threat as an "identical" institution. Once something is defined as different, one need no longer worry about its definition standing for one's own. Such is the case for Ram Sholom.

One can see, then, that the members of Kehillat Kodesh differentiate themselves not only from groups which are obviously different from them Jewishly—the less frum and the more frum, who have institutionalized these differences in terms of the sectarian identifications of Reform and Conservative or traditional Orthodox and Chassidic—but also from groups which at first glance seem quite like them. The integrity of the shul is maintained.

Of course they must, lest they succumb to feelings of isolation, identify themselves as part of a larger group which also sees itself in similar terms. While I have emphasized the distinctions and feelings of antipathy expressed vis-à-vis other Jews, I should also point out that much time is spent outlining similarities to other Jews and congregations. Part of this effort is accomplished by Kehillat Kodesh's membership in a national federation of Orthodox shuls, all made up of essentially similar Jews.

In addition to stressing its national affiliation with other modern Orthodox shuls, the members often compare themselves with the members of other Orthodox shuls. The vehicle for such comparisons is often conversations with guests and strangers who have come from another Orthodox shul. One hears, for example, how similar the liturgical style at Kehillat Kodesh is to that of the stranger's shul: "You have kids lead the end of the service here? We do too." One hears comparisons of members' occupations: "We have lots of professors in our shul too." One hears discussion of differences which are seen to be minor and not affecting institutional identity: "You sing this? We say it quietly and later on in the *davening* [praying]." Indeed, strangers and guests are made to feel that Kehillat Kodesh is but one stop like others on the modern Orthodox Jewish railroad, one part of a larger network. It is not alone but is linked inextricably to other like institutions.[15] Only where these institutions, like the local ones, might serve to undermine the identity of Kehillat Kodesh by presenting a successfully discrepant identity or set of actions is the similarity denied, and is antipathy expressed.

Until now the description of Kehillat Kodesh has concerned itself with outlining the general characteristics of the group which inhabits the setting under study. The people have been defined as modern Orthodox Jews. They have been distinguished from other kinds of Jews in terms of both objective and subjective criteria and from similar Jews in terms of their unique group history and its consequent effect on the character of the community. The next step after this general presentation of the dramatis personae is perhaps to describe, first, the stage set—the props which fill Kehillat Kodesh—and then the roles of the actors.

2 *The Setting*

The physical setting may be considered at several levels of analysis. First, its props (including both objects and space) may be described technically, in an instrumental sense. Such a description seeks to clarify what the props are, what they look like, how they operate, the functions they fulfill, and their relationship to one another in the context of the general setting. Second, one may discuss the relationship among the people, their activities, and these props in an institutional sense. That is, one investigates how in fact the participants in the setting, the utilizers of the props, understand and treat these objects. Inevitably, different people infuse the same instruments with different meanings, and also the same people and the same objects may have varying relationships depending on the institutional context of that relationship. Finally, an analytic discussion of the props requires an examination of their meaning in the context of Orthodoxy in general as well as at Kehillat Kodesh in particular. Thus, for example, all shuls have a table that serves as a pulpit. But what specialized meanings in addition to these regular ones does the pulpit have at Kehillat Kodesh?

Since the setting in question is, at least on some occasions, a religiously defined one, the props may be discussed in terms of the two classificatory types: sacred and profane. Objects may be either the former or the latter; but, as will be seen, not all objects are always sacred or always profane. Rather, some props are sacred at one point in time and not at another, just as the entire setting itself is at times a synagogue and at other times simply a place of assembly. Objects which are sacred include those considered "holy," or *kadosh*, to use the Hebrew term. This Hebrew word has the same etymology as the word for "separate"; and indeed, objects which are kadosh are separate—"supramundane," as Rudolf Otto calls them[1]—and isolated from other items in the setting, which, relative to them, are called "profane," or *chol* in Hebrew. The word chol also connotes "weekday," suggesting that time has something to do with the question of whether an item is profane or not.

The Hebrew language, often called *Loshon Kodesh*, "holy tongue," is the language of ritual in the Orthodox synagogue. Ritual objects—for example, holy books, scrolls, arks, and most of the items described immediately below—are called by their Hebrew names. Yiddish, on the other hand, is the language of everyday Orthodox reality. It is used to label everything which pertains to the Jewish world, with the exception of ritual objects. "Shul" hence is not only the sanctuary, which is ritually used space, but is the entire setting, with all its sacred *and* profane dimensions, inhabited by the congregants; "davening," the common Yiddish term for praying, includes the profane as well as the sacred aspects of prayer in its meaning; "frum" is a Jewish way of behaving; and so forth. In the course of the study, it should become clear that terms commonly labeled as Yiddish refer to the sociological realities, while Hebrew words refer to theological or religious realities. Not all Yiddish and Hebrew, however, can be so neatly characterized.

Instrumental Description

We begin with an instrumental description of the setting, aided by a floor-by-floor map of the shul, reproduced in figures 1 and 2.

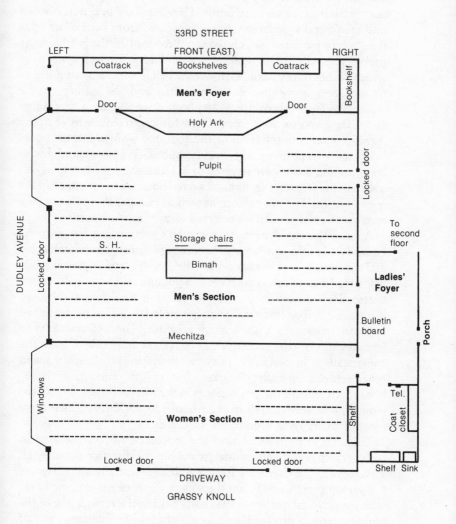

Figure 1. Floor Plan of Kehillat Kodesh (First Floor)

The first floor of the shul is divided into four enclosed areas. Two of these make up the sanctuary, or main prayer area, while the remaining two are anterooms. The sanctuary in turn is divided into men's and women's sections, separated from each other by a partition or *mechitza*, which rises to three-fourths the height of the room. This kind of separation is mandatory for any synagogue which wishes to call itself "Orthodox." While various shuls differ as to the form or height of the mechitza and the nature of the separation (some shuls, for example, put women on a mezzanine above the men's section), none allows for mixed seating by sex. The men's section is in the front of the shul, the women's in the back. With the exception of the prayer books (*siddurim*) and bibles (*chumashim*, as they are referred to in Hebrew by the members) on a shelf in the women's section, all sacred objects are contained in the men's section. For this reason, as well as because it is in front, the men's section is sometimes referred to as the "main section."

Among the ritual items in the men's section are the *aron ha kodesh* (holy ark), containing the scrolls of *Torah* (the Pentateuch), and the *bimah*, a pulpit on which the Torah scroll is placed while being read and which also serves as a podium and lectern at various times. This bimah may also be called a *shulchan* (table), to distinguish it from the smaller pulpit in front, which serves as the location from which the *chazan* (cantor), or *shiliach tzibbur* (congregational representative), as he is sometimes called, leads the congregation in weekday prayers. Siddurim, chumashim, and other *seforim* (literally, "books," but in shul connoting "holy" books) often lie on various surfaces in the men's section. Unlike the women, who seem to return their books to the shelves, men leave most of theirs lying around the sanctuary.

The seats in both sections of the sanctuary all face the aron in front, which is east and toward Jerusalem, the direction faced by all synagogues. The chairs are folding and all essentially alike. Hence, if a person prefers one to another, his preference has nothing to do with the physical quality of the chair. During the remodeling of the building from a private house into a chapel-like interior, most of the windows were removed or covered up, so that most of the people inside the sanctuary can see only what is going on inside.

The mechitza, which cuts the sanctuary horizontally, giving the men about two-thirds of the space, was once a topic of great community concern and discussion; some of the women pointed out that, if it were arranged vertically, they might be able to better follow the service. Horizontal placement was nevertheless decided upon, since manifestly it gave more space for seats. One should add that it continued to keep the men in the front and the women in back. Although the top quarter of the mechitza is a kind of cloth-like mesh, it is difficult for the men to see the women, and vice versa.

Outside the sanctuary proper are two foyers through which one may enter the shul. I have labeled the rear foyer the "ladies' foyer" and the front one the "men's foyer" because a sign on the front of the building requests men and women to enter through these separate entrances. In fact, however, while no women enter the sanctuary through the men's foyer, some men do enter the shul through the ladies' foyer.

Both foyers contain facilities for coats and outerwear as well as shelves for books. The scholarly books which make up the shul's library are kept in the men's foyer, while the ladies' foyer contains old, unused, and disintegrating volumes as well as some siddurim. Strictly speaking, one might say that the men's foyer, with its seforim and shelves piled with prayer cloaks, is filled with more ritual objects than the ladies' foyer, which, with its bulletin board and telephone, is more of a gathering place.

A staircase to the second floor begins in the ladies' foyer. Next to the staircase is a door which opens on a driveway outside. Members often take a break from services, especially the longer prayer sessions on Sabbath or holy-day mornings, and stand around in the driveway, chatting. In the winter, they use the ladies' foyer.

In the sanctuary are contained several props which are visible only at certain times. Among these is the *pushke* (Yiddish for "charity box"), a small metal container without sacred value which is often placed on the shulchan during the week and into which loose change is dropped in partial fulfillment of the ritual imperative of charity and for the benefit of beggars who frequent the shul. The deposit of change is not accomplished in a haphazard manner but rather in orderly and regularized fashion, which, although never formalized in manifest procedural codes, is predictable in its repetition.

At each weekday service, usually about three-fourths of the way through, someone will approach the bimah for the purpose of making a donation. The sound of the coins dropping into the box signals others to do likewise. Indeed, at times a donor will pick up the pushke and rattle it so as to make the noise clearly audible. In relatively rapid order, although with lackadaisical demeanor, each of those present drops in his share of coins.

When not in use on Sabbaths and holy days, money exchange

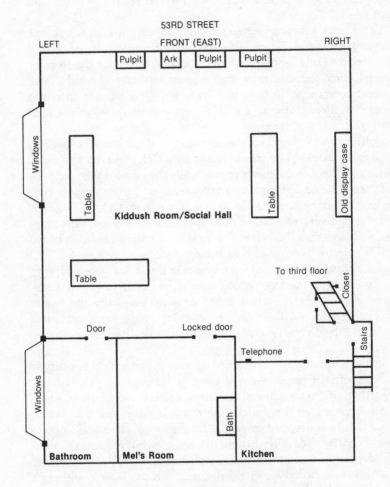

Figure 2. Floor Plan of Kehillat Kodesh (Second Floor)

being then prohibited by halacha, the pushke disappears, stored either under the shulchan or in the lower recesses of the aron, along with junk mail and other profane items.

Silver ornaments used to clothe the Torah scrolls are also stored in the depths of the aron, which is in a sense little more than a glorified closet. Inside it, as well, are some privately owned *talaisim* (prayer cloaks), which members leave in the shul for use there. Such props appear only during periods of utilization.

The second floor (see fig. 2), which is for all intents and purposes the only other floor of the building publicly used, is divided into four enclosed areas. By far the largest of these is an open space filled with three long tables and no chairs. These folding tables are for use at ritual meals or *kiddushim*. *Kiddush*, the singular form of the term, is the Hebrew word for "sanctification," but it also refers to the ceremony of blessing and drinking wine (or at times any other beverage, excluding plain water). Over time, kiddush has come to refer to the entire repast, in which the drink and its accompanying benediction are often of the least social consequence. Kiddushim are commonly made after Sabbath or holy-day morning prayers, and the food eaten during them constitutes the first food of the day.

At the far end of this kiddush room, which serves essentially as a social hall, are a small movable aron and three movable pulpits. These were at one time used for weekday prayers, which were held in this room. For almost two years they have remained unused and in a state of ritual inattention, not fully charged with sanctity yet not genuinely profane.

Off the large kiddush room are three other rooms: the kitchen, which serves as the site for kiddush preparation; the main bathroom for members' use; and separating these two rooms, a third, known as "Mel's room." This is a room rented out by the shul to a young man named Mel Stender. Although he is a college graduate, employed, and a paying member of the shul, many people seem to consider him the shul's caretaker. He is to lock the shul, put on the heat, take care of the lights, bring in the mail, and in general take care of the mundane necessities which come up in the everyday existence of the building. Although Mel denies that the responsibility is his, he continues to fulfill most expectations through his affirmative action.

The third floor, a garret, is little used. One room serves as a playroom for very small children, who are supervised by a different mother each week. Mothers can thus send their small children to shul with their husbands and be assured that the children will be cared for, the husband unperturbed, and they themselves free for the few hours of Sabbath morning shul.

Institutional Description

The same setting and props may be described in an institutional sense, with emphasis on understanding the physical realities as the participants do within the setting. Some items are seen as more important than others, meaningful in one context and perhaps meaningless in another. They become different things at different times for different people and may be described in terms of their relationship both with one another and with their utilizers. Inevitably, institutionally indigenous definitions of sacred and profane enter into an interpretive description of this kind.

The shul itself may be considered first, for it serves variously as a house of prayer, assembly, or study. Associated with each of these uses is a distinct set of behaviors, definitions of the situation, and props. Even these contexts may be broken down into subcategories. For example, different prayers, said on weekdays as opposed to Sabbaths or holy days, may differently define the setting. Not all assemblies are alike; some are purely for pleasure, others form a prelude to prayer, while still others are simply group meetings, and so on. Finally, not all study is the same; some is exclusively for men and requires intense involvement; other types are more like sermons; and still others take the form of question-and-answer periods. Since each of these categorizations of the shul has an effect on the way one might define and describe the setting institutionally, each inevitably requires contextual definition. Of course, some items remain essentially the same from one context to another, and those that change often do so only subtly.

To begin with, the shul is considered a house of prayer. As such, it must be further divided into a house of (1) weekday morning and evening prayers; (2) Sabbath and holy-day evening prayers; (3) Sabbath and holy-day morning prayers. While there is no legal variation in a Jew's obligation to pray on each of these occasions, at Kehillat Kodesh each respectively involves a larger proportion of the congregation. The first involves a small group of adult men, usually no more than sixteen or twenty; the second, most of the men in the congregation, along with some of the older children; the third, the entire congregation of men, women, and children. Although not everyone attends shul each Sabbath or holy-day morning, it is only at these times, when everyone is commonly expected to be present, that *anyone's* absence is likely to require explanation.

More than any other part of the setting, the sanctuary and the objects in it are affected and defined differently in these different situations. Although its physical makeup remains essentially the same throughout the week, the subjective quality of the space changes. On Sabbaths and holy days, for example, space in the sanctuary is highly structured in terms of areas where trespass is limited and those where it is permissible. During these times, only those especially appointed may approach and stand at the bimah or near the ark; the women's section is off limits for any and all men; for the most part, seats once selected are kept throughout the service; no chairs may be rearranged; and so on. All these restrictions are far less prevalent—and many are completely relaxed—during weekday services. On weekdays much more space is open, and some boundaries seem to disappear. On Sabbath and holy days people usually stay in one place during their prayers; on weekdays, changing seats during the service is not at all unusual. Finding men praying in the empty women's section is also common. And the bimah is an open space available to any and all men. In short, the sanctuary becomes on Sabbath and holy days an area allowing a minimum of movement, while on weekdays the space allotted each participant expands.

The setting changes in other ways, too. Consider, for example, the shulchan or bimah. When the Torah scroll is placed on the shulchan for reading, this location becomes off limits for all except those engaged in the ritual activity going on there. One may approach the shulchan only if the *gabbai*, the man communally designated to apportion ritual duties and honors (kibbudim), ceremoniously calls out one's Hebrew name (all names have a Hebrew equivalent) in a chanted recitation; and only after two more persons have been called up, or after the Torah reading has been completed and the scroll put away, may one leave the shulchan, and then by the most circuitous route. Similarly, during prayers, only the man designated by the gabbai as chazan may stand at the bimah, and he is permitted to leave it only at the completion of the portion he has been assigned to lead. Should one approach the shulchan at these times for any other reason—frequently because of ritual need, as when, for example, one wants a blessing for a sick kinsman (commonly executed during the Torah-reading preliminaries)—one must make clear, usually to and through the gabbai, the reasons for such an invasion and thereby have it legitimated.

The gabbai, of course, by virtue of his legitimating role, has freedom to go everywhere as long as he is on "official business"—an often ambiguous state of being which expands his freedom of movement.

During the week, with the exception of a brief period on Monday and Thursday mornings when the Torah scroll is being read, the shulchan is accessible to anyone. Indeed, it is the first location approached by incoming members. Although its primary and manifest function is a ritual one, connected with prayer and the reading of the holy scrolls, the shulchan reveals itself to be subject to other definitions during the week. Being in the center of the room and the largest flat surface available, it often serves as a repository for many smaller items, not all of which have sacred value. Indeed, most do not. Thus, much of the mail delivered to the shul finds its way to the top of the bimah, where it lies open and available for general perusal. In addition, the already described pushke sits there, easily accessible for those who wish to drop change into it. Holy books may also find temporary resting place here. On Sabbaths and holy days, all items are removed, the holy books usually being the last to go.

Perhaps most interesting of all, what is a ritually restricted table on Sabbaths and holy days, and even during portions of weekday prayers, becomes a gathering place for interaction and sociability during the week, especially before and after the prayers. Like a hitching post, drugstore counter, street corner, or any other "good place to meet and talk," the bimah becomes a focal point. Such places are characterized by a high degree of what Simmel has defined as sociability, by "associations . . . accompanied by a feeling for, by satisfaction in, the very fact that one is associated with others and that the solitariness of the individual is resolved into togetherness, a union with others."[2] They are defined as well by an institutionalized, "focused interaction," in which people assemble *regularly* to engage in the kind of interaction that occurs when persons gather close together and openly cooperate to sustain a single focus of attention, typically by taking turns at talking. Everyone located at such a place is involved in and incorporated into the ongoing interaction. These locations may be called *sociability spots*, and the bimah is one of them. Thus, although its manifest function is a sacred and ritual one, its latent one—which makes itself apparent on weekdays—seems to be as a sociability spot, social and profane rather than sacred.

In fact, the shul is filled with such sociability spots. When the bimah is not available, other focal points are found. The foyers often serve the purpose, and men repair here for talks, bull sessions, gossip gatherings, or any other form of sociability. The women and children also have their special sociability spots: the kitchen and the back row of the men's section, respectively (a meager provision compared to the men's). Finally, the second-floor kiddush room may become divided into dozens of small sociability spots when the congregation is assembled for eating.

Conversations which begin at the bimah may spread out into the space of the sanctuary, a spreading ripple in a sea of sociability. As the interaction starts to become multifocused, men move away from the bimah and create other such spots, in corners, around the smaller bimah, or in the foyers. When a spot becomes filled (i.e., when newcomers can no longer find sufficient interest or chance to participate in a given interaction), another is found.

While the bimah and its surrounding space remain on weekdays publicly accessible to any and all legitimate congregants assembled in the men's section of the shul, no one person may lay exclusive claim to it, nor may anyone constantly challenge a user's right to be there. Any insider may assert possession of all or part of the bimah and its surrounding area through his use of the space, signaled usually by placing on it such personal effects as a coat, hat, prayer book, prayer-shawl bag, or watch or by standing nearby. However, should another insider find a need for the space and challenge the first occupant's claim, the latter will usually vacate it without protest. Few such challenges take place among insiders, and at times the bimah area has the appearance of being one person's exclusive "stall," the "well bounded space to which individuals can lay temporary claim, possession being on an all-or-none basis."[3] However, the bimah area is a *collective* stall, open to the claim of everyone in the collectivity and to no one person exclusively.

The *appearance* of exclusive control is not really a result of the quality of the space but rather a reflection of the relationship among insiders which makes them solicitous of one another's needs, so that they avoid conflict and accede to challenges when these occur. That these actions are reflections of relationship rather than qualities of space becomes particularly clear in the handling of outsiders' challenges to spatial use. Beggars, for example, who walk in for quick cash without fully participating in the service are turned away from approach to the bimah by handouts at the door. To recapitulate: any insider using this table must be, and always is, willing to share the space with other insiders.

It is not unusual to see several men standing around the bimah during the prayers, some having stayed at what was once a sociability spot and has since become a prayer location. At the end of the prayers, this same location will once more become a sociability spot to which others return for a chat before leaving, if they have the time.

Another way that the sanctuary seems to change with the change from weekdays to Sabbaths and holy days is in the utilization of seats. Coming to shul regularly, members customarily choose the same seats in which to sit during communal prayers. Such seats are commonly called "shabbos seats" because they are consistently claimed and used on Sabbaths and on holy days. (The latter, as far as this setting is concerned, are equivalent to Sabbaths and will henceforward not be mentioned unless they differ in some respect from Sabbaths.) A look at shul seating patterns reveals much about the congregation.

To begin with, most people sit near friends, thereby exhibiting alliances. Moreover, those who sit together share other things besides friendship. They are often persons with similar occupations and levels of education, both secular and Jewish. And, as becomes clear after closer observation, seat neighbors tend, within the limits of modern Orthodoxy, to observe and deviate from halachic doctrine along the same lines.

While there are no formal boundaries dividing the sections and the cliques which fill them, such seating reflects a relationship which, in Weber's terms, is "closed against outsiders so far as, according to its subjective meaning and the binding rules of order, participation of certain persons is excluded, limited, or subjected to conditions."[4] Members all know precisely where one section ends and another begins, and no one ever makes the mistake of sitting in the wrong place, i.e., invades a section and clique where he is not accepted.

As Weber suggested, there can be exceptions, "subject to conditions." Any invasion, however limited, as well as any retreat, requires some sort of public explanation. Thus, when an outsider to the group decides to sit among the young professionals who make up one section, he explains, "I'm slumming it"; or when another sits in a section other than his usual one, he explains it by pointing out that there was no room left in his section by the time he arrived in shul.

When a regular participant arrives in the sanctuary on Sabbath, his seat neighbors, those usually seated adjacent or close to him, fully expect him to sit near them. They may signal this expectation by removing their personal effects from a nearby seat, giving it up as part of their possessional territory and making it available for the approaching member. The member makes clear his understanding of this expectation by making a beeline for his section in spite of the fact that many empty and ostensibly available seats may be closer to him. It is therefore not unusual to find one section of the shul sanctuary very crowded and another section completely empty.

Incidentally, I found that persons' reported perceptions of whether the shul is "empty" or "full"—that is, whether a large or small proportion of the membership is assembled on Sabbath—depends on whether or not one's seat neighbors are present. This is not the case on weekdays, when the whole notion of neighbors and sections is relatively nonexistent. On weekdays more objective criteria of "emptiness" or "fullness" are considered—for example, the actual number of people present.

The only people in shul without shabbos seats are strangers, newcomers, and guests. The stranger is a potential threat to the integrity of sections. Because of his ignorance, he may invade one without meaning to do so and jar its entire structure. Consider the following example:

> I am sitting in my regular seat, but all the usual neighbors in my row are changed tonight. [See figure 3 for a description of the dynamics of movement.] On my left is Jerry, and on my right Mel. On Jerry's left is Jake. These three men usually sit behind me; but tonight a stranger is sitting in Jake's seat, and so they have all moved forward to adjust to Jake's move. In fact, all the other seats in Jake's row are free, with the exception of his, so that the others could have, strictly speaking, kept their regular seats had they so desired. Nevertheless, they did not and chose instead to move with Jake. First Jake moved. Then, when Jerry came in, he sat next to him; Mel, in turn, sat down next to me, the closest spot to his other regular seat neighbors.
> Now, since the seats next to me were occupied by these inter-lopers, Harwood, who usually sits near me, had to move else-where, which he did, moving toward the front of the shul next to Irving, his friend. The others who usually sit near me are not present tonight. Indeed, the one stranger who sat in Jake's seat has caused a ripple of movement that could turn into a wave. And, the man does not even know what he's done!

When movement occurs from one section to another, seat neighbors move together, where possible, trying to recreate the social

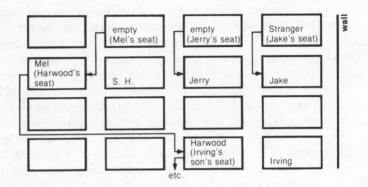

Figure 3. Front of Men's Section

dimensions of their regular section. However, one's seat neighbors are not one's only friends in shul (I have already pointed out that the shul is generally characterized by a high degree of solidarity), and so one may, on occasion, sit with others. Most members have a secondary section where they feel accepted and at ease if their primary seat section is unavailable.

The newcomer signals his newness by changing his seat from week to week. Eventually he finds his group and seats himself accordingly. Yet at times it becomes difficult to ascertain whether seats and seating patterns reflect or account for friendships. In truth, the relationship must be described as synergetic: people sit with friends and thereby confirm and intensify that relationship. Worshiping side by side, chatting, and generally touching one another, seat neighbors share a literal and symbolic vantage point. Indeed, a knowledge of seating patterns reveals much about the network of relations within the community.

While guests, like other outsiders, have no regular seats, they do have established ones, since they are commonly expected to sit near their member hosts. In an effort not to disturb a section, members frequently move with their guests to an open area, a section where no clique has established itself; they sit in their regular seats only if there is room for their guests as well. The open space is the place to find strangers, especially those familiar with the fixed character of seats in a shul.

Halacha also confirms the importance of seating patterns. When in mourning, one must, during that year, select a seat other than one's regular seat. Mourning, an event which has disturbed one's position in the Jewish community at large by transforming one from normal person into mourner, is acted out in seat change, among other ways. The law seems to reflect the realization that seating patterns are not simply physical arrangements but reflect social belongingness—something which cannot be unaffected by death and its accompanying social turbulence.

That people are quite conscious that their shabbos seats reflect their membership in various groups is exhibited by the fact that movement does not go unexplained. Moreover, seating, and the group membership which it implies, may also indicate status, power, and authority within the shul. For example, two men, joking about their relative seat positions, say that their seats reflect their merit in the community:

> Riken came back to joke with Jerry. They joked with each other about the relative merits of sitting in the back or the front of the shul. Riken joked that the *tzaddikim* [pious and righteous Jews] sat in the back. Jerry, reading the mocking tone of Riken's remark, responded by casting aspersions on those in front.

The fact that such seats are joked about must be understood in terms of the atmosphere of conciliation in Kehillat Kodesh. Recall that, in describing the shul situation before the expulsion, one member pointed out that people had "special seats" to reflect their authority and power as well as their implied piety. Now this topic is joked about, as are all sources of tension. Nevertheless, the potential for such socially disruptive interpretation still exists and exhibits itself.

In connection with authority and power, it should be recalled that the women's section has remained in the back.[5] Furthermore, the young boys, who make up one of the cliques of seat partners, sit in the last row of the men's section—as if they are lowest among men, yet still above women *in the sanctuary setting*. These last words must be stressed, since the women, while they have few prerogatives in the shul setting, are by no means the ones with least power and authority in the modern Jewish community in general. Nevertheless, in shul they have little power, and this is reflected in the material conditions of their existence (back seats, fewer sociability spots, few ritual objects in their section, etc.). Indeed, they have no vote (or dues obligation), although they have a voice.

On weekdays none of the seating sections exist. While men may sit in their shabbos seats, they do not always do so. For many their seat becomes simply a repository for personal effects while they pace around the open space of the relatively empty sanctuary. One may speculate about the reasons for such movement. Its absence on Sabbaths is only partly explained by the need to accommodate, in the same space, a larger group than on weekdays, since even on Sabbaths members sit in their regular places when, early in the service, only a few are present. One might suggest, somewhat instrumentally, that since on Sabbaths those who are present are sure of a large turnout, they lay claim to their space early by occupying it soon after their entry into the sanctuary. However, a more sociopsychological explanation is possible. Proud of its existence and integrity, the community stresses its large turnouts at services, which serve as representations of its collective might. On weekdays that impression is jeopardized, and members may want to camouflage, albeit unconsciously, the smallness of the assembly by moving about to fill up the space, a practice unnecessary on Sabbath—though it occurs even then on those very rare occasions when the attendance is poor. (Indeed, one finds generally that, the smaller a congregation is, in proportion to its sanctuary, the more its members pace about.)

A sociological explanation is possible too. Since weekdays bring few members to shul, those who do come seldom expect to meet their seat neighbors. With the extinction of the seat neighborhood, the need to remain in place disappears as well. Sociability spots decrease in number, leaving those present two options: convergence or dispersion. They may establish new neighbors or go it alone, as if at home. They do both, and this reflects the intermediary character of the weekday house of prayer. Just before the beginning of the services the men gather and socialize around the bimah and perhaps also in a corner of the room if the group is relatively large. Suddenly, with the beginning of prayers, they become like strangers and spread to all corners of the room in an eerie symmetry of which none save the observer seems aware. (When I once pointed out the pattern to a member, he ceased his movements; so I ceased my interventions.) If more than one man remains at the bimah, it is usually because he thus maintains the symmetry.

Our attention turns next to the two foyers. Here the major difference between weekdays and Sabbaths is the degree to which this location becomes a sociability spot. Examination reveals that during the weekdays when prayers are held, the foyers are used primarily as entryways, becoming sociability spots only when a subgroup of those present wishes to engage in a private and exclusive interaction of one sort or another or when members are simply waiting for a congregation to assemble. On Sabbath (i.e., Friday nights and Saturday afternoons), both foyers are used more extensively.

During the week's prayers the men's foyer—which on Sabbaths is used for coats and other outer garments, as well as for social purposes—is little more than an enlarged entryway. Coats and other outer garments are brought into the sanctuary and deposited on nearby seats or other suitable places. In other words, possessional territory grows inside the sanctuary, and there is no need for storage places elsewhere. The door between the men's foyer and the sanctuary stays open, since no counteractivity occurs there which might in some way disturb or compete with what is happening in the sanctuary. The small number of people attending a weekday prayer service demands the focused involvement of all those present; there is thus no allowance for retreat to, and subordinate involvements in, the foyer or elsewhere. On Sabbaths and holy days, however, when a large multifocused group is to be found inside the sanctuary, the men's foyer (as well as other locations) may become the locus for other interactions. At such times the doors are closed so that the two or more interactions may continue to occur simultaneously without affecting one another. The epitome of such separation occurs on Simchas Torah, the holy day when, among other things, everyone in shul must be called to the Torah scroll reading. At such times separate prayer services are set up in various locations, among them the men's foyer. Such services ensure that everyone will be called in the shortest possible time. During these readings the shul seems in effect to be made up of separate congregations, divided by closed doors, and each operating with its own rules of behavior, its own gabbai, chazan, Torah scroll reader, and even status hierarchy, reflected in the dispensation of kibbudim.

In the end, of course, all the separate shuls come together again at one large minyan in the sanctuary for the final reading, thus latently reaffirming the solidarity of the entire Kehillat Kodesh community, while manifestly coming together for the reading of the final chapters of the Pentateuch.

During Sabbath evening prayers the men's foyer gains in social importance. On Friday nights, before the beginning of prayers, it becomes a loitering place where prolonged greetings are exchanged. After the services it becomes again a sociability spot where the men linger and chat while ostensibly dressing and getting ready to go home. Frequently men stand here for quite a few minutes, all dressed for the outdoors; or they may linger by the bookshelves, engrossed in talk, and not put on their outer garments for a long time. Indeed, in the summer months, when for the most part no outer garments are worn, with the exception of hats, men seem to spend just as long a time in the foyer after services as during the winter months, when time there might be needed for putting on coats, hats, galoshes, and so forth. Clearly, at such times the foyer is more than a place to dress.

On Sabbath mornings the men's foyer is again used, in much the same way as the night before. In addition to being a combination cloakroom and sociability spot, however, it may become several other things as well. Because of the seforim (holy books) stored there, this space may become a kind of mini *Bais Medrash* (house of study). Men may take a book from the shelves and lean there while they peruse or study it. Occasionally the book may be taken elsewhere for more protracted study; more often it is not.

In addition to its function as a Bais Medrash, the foyer may become a playroom for young boys who have for one reason or another been freed from their obligation to stay in the sanctuary. Now the men's foyer may become the locus of a game of tag, a conversation, or some other profane activity. These boys are sufficiently socialized to know that this activity belongs outside the sanctuary. In a way, these youngsters are mimicking their fathers, who also step into this foyer during the Sabbath service for some profane activity. The difference between the two groups is in the nature of the profane activity, and it is interesting to note that the older boys tend to spend more time talking here, like their fathers (albeit about vastly different topics), while the younger ones treat the space more like a gym.

The men's foyer remains essentially closed to women, although they may occasionally pass through in the company of their husbands or kinsmen. The only exceptions are little girls, who, in addition to the men's foyer, have the run of many areas of the shul that are otherwise prohibited, either expressly or implicitly, to women. Goffman offers the following explanation for such a phenomenon: "Insofar as children are defined as 'nonpersons' they have some license to commit gauche acts without requiring the audience to take the expressive implications of these acts too seriously."[6] Hence, when little girls invade the men's foyer, they do so as children, not as women.

When members loiter in the foyers after Sabbath services, men will do so in both the men's and ladies' foyers, but women will do so only in their own foyer or outside the building.

It becomes increasingly clear as one investigates the shul setting that men have far more access than women to the space and objects in it. Even those areas open to women are never exclusively within their control, for men may on occasion legitimately invade that space. Thus men may, for example, use the women's section of the shul when the women are absent, but women very rarely use areas like the men's foyer, even when the men are absent. Indeed, during one women's meeting, the group moved to the front only after it became clear that the women's section could not accommodate the whole crowd. As one examines the ladies' foyer, then, one realizes that the designation "ladies'" refers more to the fact that the foyer is located near the section where the ladies sit than it does to the notion of female control over the space. Indeed, by the end of the book, the reader should realize that while women and children make use of the shul, it is essentially a world of men, in which the others are visitors and guests with limited rights.

Like its counterpart, the ladies' foyer tends to be used less during the week than on Sabbaths. On weekdays, however, men are more likely to mill about here than elsewhere. There are several reasons. For one, it is in this foyer that one of the shul telephones is located. Because of the frequent difficulty in getting the required ten men for the religiously mandated communal prayer quorum (minyan), telephone calls are often made to various members, requesting them to come so that communal prayer can occur. Inevitably the same people are called, usually either friends of the callers or regular attendants who for some reason have skipped this particular service. There seems to be a tacit understanding that the membership at large will not be called. If a newcomer to the daily minyan suggests that someone out of the ordinary be called, his suggestion is usually overlooked or rationalized away with comments about either the unavailability of the person in question or the fact that others have agreed to be "on call." These calls are often a stimulus not only for drawing men out of the sanctuary and away from the shulchan but for conversations which, more often than not, evaluate and gossip about those being called. While some who have gone out to make the call remain in the foyer, most come back to the sanctuary to report on their efforts—to say whether or not a minyan can be expected and who is coming.

The telephone is not the only instrument that draws members

into the ladies' foyer during the week. The bulletin board may act in the same way. When only one or two people are present, and especially if the only relationship between them is that both are members of Kehillat Kodesh (they are never seat neighbors, who always have something to chat about), they may linger at the board, reading its dated notices. Here one is likely to find strangers, especially before the beginning of services.

All such lingering is severely limited on weekday mornings, when getting to work on time is considered more important than waiting for a minyan and socializing. Hence, people pray individually even as they wait for the quorum to gather.

As an entrance, the ladies' foyer exhibits the male dominion in the setting. For women, this foyer is the only legitimate entry (although during the summer some women may sneak in through a door to the driveway, which has been opened for ventilation). For the men, this access is one of two. Here women *must* put their coats, while men may put theirs elsewhere as well. The women who enter through the ladies' foyer enter to the eyes of all others of their kind and are subject to inspection and gazes, but the men who come in at this entrance are slipping in at the rear of their section, facing the backs of those already present and thus remaining unnoticed.

For latecomers, this male advantage is significant. Coming late (though differently defined for men and women, since the latter are expected to come later) is negatively sanctioned (by gossip and deprecatory joking); it is thus to be avoided or at least camouflaged. Men are able to hide their latecoming via the entry through the ladies' foyer, but women must "face" the consequences.

During Sabbath morning prayers, the most extended prayers of the week, the ladies' foyer becomes a place in which to take breaks from the activity in the sanctuary. Such breaks are taken primarily during the reading of the *haftora*, the scriptural portion chanted by one man after the Torah scroll reading. At such times men will go out into the ladies' foyer and chat. This appropriated sociability spot seems then to become off limits for women. As the latter enter—for they are still coming to shul at this hour—they sheepishly greet the men standing there and immediately enter the sanctuary. During the services the ladies' foyer does not seem to act as a sociability spot for the women; if one or two small groups of women occasionally form there, it is usually by having something to say to the men. It is the latter, having hegemony, who legitimate the women's presence there.

The case is different at the end of Sabbath services on Saturday mornings. Then the ladies' foyer becomes a gathering place for both men and women. This is one of the few times and places that men and women interact in shul. Often the men will go first to the men's foyer to put on coats, put away prayer garb in the storage areas provided (women have no such storage facilities), or simply to accompany friends there. They then go to the ladies' foyer to meet their wives, who may be waiting for them there or outside. The men's hegemony over shul space seems to be almost complete. They can walk anywhere, but the women must wait to be picked up. On occasion an impatient woman will send a message by a male friend of her husband's, to let him know that she is waiting. Only as a last resort does she herself trespass.

Finally, the ladies' foyer has one more institutional definition or description. During Sabbath evening services on Saturday after-noons, in the period between the last prayer of Sabbath and the first prayer of *chol* (the profane portion of the week, which ends the Sabbath), one of the older men leads a Talmud class in the sanctuary. For both social and intellectual reasons, these classes, which provide homily and demand the attention of the partici-pants, do not attract all those present in shul. Some of those who skip the class but choose not to leave for home may spend the time in the ladies' foyer, which now becomes a place to wait for the class to end. To some extent it may at such times be described as a sociability spot, although it does not strictly fulfill the requirements of the definition, since not everyone present may be "associated with others." For example, men often stand alone, reading the bulletin board or occupying themselves in some other isolated way, hence not necessarily resolving the "solitariness of the individual" into togetherness. In short, only some of those present are experi-encing sociability. Others simply bide their time.

Institutional Sanctity

The setting may also be institutionally described in terms of the way some parts become sanctified and others not. Objects may appear to have ritual sanctity at one time and lose it at another, and vice versa. In describing the setting thus, one inevitably also re-veals, albeit indirectly, something about the people in it, those who consecrate, sanctify, and hence transform its reality. As the *Zohar*, the primary document of Jewish mysticism, puts it, "Only the holy may use holy things."[7]

Certain parts of the environment are always holy and are treated as such. For all intents and purposes these are all located inside the sanctuary. Paramount among these objects is the Torah scroll. Its reading, handling, housing, and in general all contact with it, are surrounded with ritual activity. For example, the penalty for dropping a Torah scroll to the ground is that the entire congregation must fast for forty days. That this has never occurred at Kehillat Kodesh is testimony to the fact that the scroll is handled with great care and attention. Thus, when one man was called up for the *hagba*, the ritual lifting of the scroll at the conclusion of its being read, he refused because the particular scroll was too heavy and he feared dropping it. Again and again he explained to those around him, "I'm not taking chances with the Torah [scroll]."

The Torah scroll is not only sacred in itself but is also able to sanctify anything with which it comes into contact. Hence the shulchan becomes a sacred object when the scroll is lying upon it during the reading. The ornaments which adorn the Torah scroll become holy because of contact with it. The ark which houses the scrolls is referred to as an *aron ha kodesh*, the *holy* ark. Even the people who hold or use the scroll become enveloped by a sort of sacred quality (being called into such contact is a kibbud), and this makes them shun most profane activity during the contact.

When the Torah scroll passes near one, it is kissed, either directly, with one's lips, or indirectly, by touching it with one's *tzitzis* (the fringes of the *talis* or prayer cloak) or one's siddur and then kissing the object which made contact with the scroll.[8] The tzitzis have no sanctity of their own but gain it from contact with the Torah scroll. The siddur, which has sanctity by virtue of the appearance of the divine name in it, is enhanced in its sanctity by contact with the Torah scroll. This sanctity in both cases is signaled by the bestowed kiss.

Not all contact with the sacred is, however signaled by kissing. Indeed, the sacred object is often defined by a restriction of contact. The actual parchment of the Torah scrolls may never be touched directly, and a whole set of proscriptions maintains this sanctity. Sacred objects seem both to attract and to repel contact. As Otto states,

> The daemonic-divine [i.e., holy] object may appear to the mind an object of horror and dread, but at the same time it is no less something that allures with a potent charm, and the creature, who trembles before it, utterly cowed and cast down, has always at the same time the impulse to turn to it, nay even to make it somehow his own.[9]

The indirect kiss seems a symbolic way of expressing this ambivalent attitude of restriction from contact with the Torah scroll and fascination with it. Its institutionalization captures that feeling.

The aron ha kodesh is an object whose sanctity, unlike that of the Torah scroll, is very much tied up with contextual considerations. Essentially, it is a closet or storage area whose qualification as a ritual object stems directly from the fact that the Torah scrolls are housed in it. Yet the ark, as mentioned earlier, serves also as a depository for profane objects. Nevertheless, when the doors of the ark are opened for the ritual viewing or removal of the Torah scroll, the congregation rises in a show of respect—not for the ark but for its contents. Accordingly, when on Simchas Torah the ark is emptied of its Torah scrolls, the doors remain open but the people sit. Indeed, children may even start to rummage through its insides without being called away by their parents, as they might be at other times of the year. The ark is then no longer holy.

Because the ark also houses objects other than the Torah scrolls, it may at times be opened for their removal. At such times no standing is required on the part of the congregants. Usually the removal of such objects is accomplished without a full opening of the ark. Thus, a man who wishes to remove the pushke or a talis or some other similar object sticks his hand past the curtain covering the front of the ark and slides open one of the doors behind it. He thus opens the ark only partially and removes what he wants. This is especially useful for latecomers who have stored their talis in the ark and wish to come in unnoticed. If everyone stood when these men removed their talis from the ark, no latecoming could ever go unnoticed.

The effect of context upon sanctity and ritual is perhaps best noticed when a Torah scroll is either removed from or put into the ark at times other than the ritually prescribed ones. This may occur when, early during a service or after the completion of one, a scroll is removed in order to prepare it for the next reading (i.e., it is wound toward the right place in the text). At such times the scroll is removed and the ark is opened without any response from the congregation. Again, the doors are not completely opened. Furthermore, none of the ritual activities of prayer, singing, or kissing occurs at such times. The removal is a functional rather than a sanctified activity. While the object, the Torah scroll, remains as sacred as at any other time, and all its accompanying restrictions are in force, the relationship to it *within the particular context* changes. The scroll is in the setting but is not a focused concern of all those present. Gone are the respectful standings, the institution-alized hymn-singing, and the kissing which characterize "official" removals or viewings. Instead, those assembled engage in a kind of *ritual inattention* toward the sacred object. That is, they know it is present, but that presence is of no ritual concern to them. Such ritual inattention may be analogized with Goffman's concept of "civil inattention," which he describes as, "a kind of dimming of the lights."[10] His concern, however, is in the mechanisms used when two persons passing each other in a public place wish to demon-strate their awareness of each other's presence and at the same time signal that neither has made the other a "target of special curiosity and design." In ritual inattention, however, since there is no other ego which must be defended from invasion, the emphasis is on the dimming of attention rather than on signaling (which, in any case, is directed, not toward the object, but toward others present, so that they may guide their behavior accordingly).

Such ritual inattention is expected by the persons who are mak-ing unofficial use of the ritual objects, for it enables them to make use of an object without including the entire congregation in some gratuitous ceremony for which no one is prepared. Should a Torah scroll be discovered to have some imperfection in it, it will be wrapped up rapidly and returned to the ark with a high degree of ritual inattention on the part of the members present. Although some people may stand on such occasions, for the most part the insertion of the imperfect scroll and the removal of a new one goes on with a degree of ritual inattention which allows the service to continue as if nothing untoward had really occurred. Such be-havior makes functional adjustments with ritual objects possible without creating and sustaining simultaneous ceremonial demands; thus the impression of ritual order and well-being is maintained in spite of functional chaos.

Other items in the shul may or may not be considered sacred, depending upon the particular context in which they are used. Among these items are the candles and wine of the *havdala* (separa-tion ceremony), which is recited between the *kodesh* (holiness) of Sabbath and holy days and the chol (profanity) of weekdays. Although such objects do not retain sanctity in and of themselves, regardless of context, as does the Torah scroll, they do gain a measure of sanctity in particular circumjacencies. Hence, a man who at the conclusion of Sabbath needed a light for his cigarette would not make use of the havdala candle but would rather make the long trip upstairs to the kitchen for a match. At another time, however, the candle might be used. The sacramental wine is another case in point. The same liquid which at one time may be simply an alcoholic beverage drunk at dinner becomes at another time a sanctified fluid which only a select few may drink, and then only after the required benedictions and actions. The objects themselves, then, do not change, of course; it is the context in which they are used that makes people relate differently to them.

Another category of objects in the shul consists of those items with which contact is at one time allowed or even encouraged and at another tabooed. This distinction cuts across both the nominally sacred and the nominally profane. A good example is the *tefillin* (phylacteries) which all adult men wear during the morning weekday prayers. These objects are always considered to be invested with a sacred quality, perhaps best seen in the fact that dropping them (to the "profane" ground) requires a penitence of a full day's fast by the offender; yet these same tefillin, which many men leave lying around the shul in various cubbyholes and storage areas, are taboo on Sabbaths and holy days, and one is not even permitted to touch them. They do not lose holiness yet are transformed by time. Such objects are called *muktza* (the Hebrew word which comes from the same root as "to cut off") and are literally cut off from contact. Such deliberate restriction is more than the simple ritual ignoring that characterizes ritual inattention. Rather it is *ritualized* inattention, constituted by formal and mandated avoidance behavior.

Besides such holy objects as tefillin, the shul as a house of prayer contains many profane items that become muktza on Sabbath and holy days. The telephone, the light switches, and in general any objects whose use is prohibited according to Sabbath laws become not only prohibited from use but also muktza-prohibited from contact. The avoidance which muktza demands becomes a way of life for the Orthodox Jew and causes a minimum disruption of his movement. However, Sabbath preparation requires, among other things, the removal of muktza items from the sanctuary proper, as far as the members of Kehillat Kodesh are concerned. Certain members take on this responsibility, often coming early on Friday afternoons to "clean up the shul." Such cleaning involves not only the functional tidying-up of the room but also its ritual preparation, which requires the removal or cleaning-away of muktza.

Seforim, siddurim, and *chumashim* (holy books, prayer books, and Pentateuchs, respectively) are staple sacred items in the shul. *Their* sanctity is not context-specific but rather constant. Dropping

them, however, requires at most their being kissed by the one who
has dropped them, their sanctity being of a minor order compared
to the Torah scroll or tefillin.[11] Many are gifts in memory of a
departed kinsman or in honor of a birth or some other happy
occasion and as such serve to associate the event with formal and
institutionalized sanctity. Without these items no shul can exist; yet
they alone do not make a shul.

Each person has his own favorite type of siddur or chumash, the
selection of which may express something about his status. Those
who choose a siddur which is all in Hebrew or a chumash which
contains many esoteric commentaries exhibit the fact that they
possess the scholarship which allows them to value such books.
Frequently a holder of such a chumash will quote a commentary to
his seat neighbors, thereby emphasizing his scholarship, a traditional basis of high status among Orthodox Jews. Interestingly,
women, for the most part, use only books with English translations. Jewish scholarly expertise is not a way for them to express
status.

The Setting as House of Assembly

The shul, as mentioned above, is, in addition to being a place of
prayer, a house of assembly, and it often serves both functions
simultaneously. People inevitably spend some time in assembly
before, after, and even during the prayers, chatting or otherwise
engaging in the sociability which characterizes shul assembly. Accordingly, the descriptions of the house of prayer and the house of
assembly to some extent overlap, as the discussion of sociability
spots, for example, suggests.

Sometimes, however, when the manifest reason for the people's
gathering is sociability or social action, the shul becomes primarily
a house of assembly. Such gatherings include shul-government
meetings, congregational dinners and banquets, celebrations, public speeches, and even group meetings to clean up the building. At
such times the focus of use shifts away from the sanctuary to other
parts of the building, particularly to the upstairs rooms. Most
official assemblies occur there; and even when a small group has
come together for a board meeting, for example, it will repair to the
upstairs rather than make use of the sanctuary.

When the group is too large for the upstairs, as is often the case
during public speeches, the sanctuary is used; but it then loses
many of its house-of-prayer qualities. If the speech is not on mat-

ters of religion or Jewish scholarship (these contexts being, as will be seen, more like prayer than assembly), the men may allow the women to sit in the main section. Some of the seats may not face the front of the sanctuary; indeed, on one occasion a podium and table were set up in such a way that those using them had their backs to the ark—something which seldom if ever happens during prayer. Seat neighbors do not necessarily remain together during official assemblies. In short, as a house of assembly, the sanctuary comes in many ways to be treated simply as a large auditorium. Of course, that is not to say that the sacred spaces and objects in it lose their sanctity. Rather, they are ritually unattended; they are *in* the space but not really *a part of* what is going on in the space.

Whereas sanctity and consecration often control access and movement in the shul as a house of prayer, sociability rather than halacha structures the shul as a house of assembly. Of course the shul is never *purely* a house of assembly, learning, or prayer. Instead, emphases move along a continuum between these various points. Nevertheless, as a house of assembly, space becomes subordinated to the desire to resolve the solitariness of the individual into togetherness, a union with others. The shul becomes primarily a mélange of sociability spots.

Some assemblies accomplish these ends more than others and thus make for more radical reshaping of the shul. As Simmel points out, "sociability in its pure form has no ulterior end, no content, no result outside itself."[12] Often assemblies do have ulterior motives and particular ends in mind which in some ways affect the use of the space. Thus during dinners women may be the last ones to find seats at tables and often end up standing, all the while serving food from the kitchen. Or, if the assembly is for the purpose of making some administrative decisions about shul government, the space and placement in it may reflect functional necessities, with the secretary, for example, sitting closest to the president. But other gatherings, such as the kiddush after services, are characterized by a minimum of such ulterior ends. Their primary function seems to be to give people a chance to converse; and, as Simmel states, "in sociability talking is an end in itself; in purely sociable conversation the content is merely the indispensable carrier of the stimulation, which the lively exchange of talk as such unfolds."[13] At kiddush, where the conversation of sociability occurs, the space becomes transformed into an array of sociability spots; tables, corners, stairwells, niches, and nooks become demarcated by the sociable assembly taking place in them. In short, as house of assembly, the shul approaches its most flexible territorial condition. The less specific the ends for which the people assemble, the more flexible and fluid the space and the more structured by sociability it becomes.

The Setting as House of Study

As house of study, the shul space may generally be divided into two parts: one for the teacher and one for students. No matter what space is used, some part of it, whether at the head of a table or at a podium in front of a large group, is reserved for the teacher. Indeed, the only notable spatial constant in the house of study appears to be this separation of teacher from students.

During women's classes this separation does not always obtain. Their classes, however, are usually held outside of shul, in the women's domain—the home. Moreover, women's classes are not always taught by a specially appointed teacher but may be led on a rotational basis by the class participants themselves. On the rare occasions when women do hold a class in shul, they too have a formal teacher (usually a male, who latently serves to legitimate their use of the shul), and the usual teacher-student spatial distinctions prevail.

The definition of the shul as house of study is no more absolute than the definition of it as house of prayer, for assembly and prayer may take place prior to, during, or even after a class. Nevertheless, since the manifest reason for the congregation is study, that definition is the "primary framework" and fundamental characterization of the setting and its props.[14] Thus, if a class occurs in the sanctuary, for example, the bimah becomes primarily a podium for the teacher rather than a sociability spot or sacred table. Or, if the class is on the second floor, the kiddush tables are transformed into long study desks, and chairs are brought up from downstairs.

From the institutional descriptions thus far offered, one ought to see that the setting changes with the activity in it. In the context of prayer it is used one way, in assembly another, and in study a third. Moreover, the relationship between activity and setting is synergetic. As space is transformed to fit the activity going on within it, so in turn activity is forced to confirm and conform to the setting. Thus, for example, when the shul is being prayed in, the setting becomes transformed, and this transformation in turn ensures that new entrants into the setting will pray rather than do something else.

Sheaths and Grooming

One part of the setting remains to be described. Having sketched the physical setting of the shul, both instrumentally and institutionally—the shell within which activities occur—one ought to describe the shell—or what Goffman calls the "sheath"[15]—within which Kehillat Kodesh individuals themselves exist. Basically, such a description is concerned with their appearance. To some extent it encompasses grooming and physical characteristics, but the primary focus is on clothing and costume.

For the shul Jews there are two large categories of garments: (1) the profane clothing of ordinary life and (2) the ritual, or prayer, garb which must be worn for religious reasons. These two categories may be further subdivided. The first contains both the clothing worn to shul on weekdays or chol and that worn on Sabbaths or kodesh. The second may be divided into items that are part of the mandatory religious "uniform" and items that are worn by some persons but not by others.[16]

Among their other qualities, clothes are expressive. As Schwartz puts it, "Dress is a communication medium. Clothing can function as a communication in various ways for different groups of people."[17] Like others, shul members communicate in this way. Moreover, since two types of clothing are worn—everyday apparel and clothing manifestly associated with religious ritual—two parallel messages may be given off. In general, one is tempted to suggest that the former type of clothing expresses something about the secular life of the people—functioning, perhaps, as what Veblen called "an indication of our pecuniary standing to all observers at first glance"[18]—while the latter type expresses adherence to halacha and religious doctrine—those who wear particular kinds of ritual garb indicate by it that they are frum. Both statements contain some measure of truth and are borne out by empirical evidence, but more needs to be said on the matter. One finds, for instance, that the communications given off by the two types of clothing are not always distinct or discrete. Indeed, certain items from the first category may communicate something to the informed insider about frumkeit (as when, for example, a more-frum man wears a hat instead of a *yarmulke* [skullcap]), and articles of ritual garb may serve to indicate pecuniary standing more than religious fervor or adherence (as when, for example, one man's talis is adorned with silver and another's simply with felt).

A closer look at clothing is thus in order. One might begin with headwear. For Orthodox Jewish males it is mandatory to wear a head-covering at all times. The halachic reasons for this are complex and for our present purposes are not of great importance. In fact, perhaps more than any other single identifying device, the head-covering has come to symbolize a male's adherence to the Law and to Orthodox Jewish philosophy. (One ought to add that the man's head-covering also makes a statement about his wife's level of observance, for no man who keeps his head always covered will be wed to a woman whose halachic adherence is not also high.) The head-covering takes various forms, which in turn may serve as indicators of identification with traditional or with modern Orthodoxy. The range of wear runs from a simple skullcap or yarmulke to the ornate fur cap or *shtreimel* of the Chassidim. In between are varieties of head-covering each of which may act as a subtle symbol of frumkeit (although no guarantee of such, since clothes are one of the easiest ways to project a false image—a disguise).

Consider various kinds of yarmulkes, for example. There are knitted yarmulkes, white linen ones, black ones, plaid ones, velvet ones, small ones, and large ones. Each may make a different statement. The smaller the yarmulke in relation to the head, the less likely is its wearer to be one of the traditional Orthodox Jews of Dudley Meadows. Knitted yarmulkes are more often worn by the young. Velvet yarmulkes, especially those whose sheen has worn away and whose surface has become crushed by the weight of an almost ever-present hat on top of them are usually the sign of the most frum, those for whom modern fashion and good looks are less important than proving that the head-covering is constantly worn. The smooth white yarmulke whose appearance indicates that it has more often than not been folded and stored rather than used is the first signal that its wearer is an infrequent sojourner in any shul. In short, the yarmulke can tell a great deal.

The requirement of covering the head is met by others by wearing a hat. Often the hats are worn in conjunction with yarmulkes, the latter sometimes showing from underneath. Here the kind of hat, the angle at which it is worn, and the occasions on which it is preferred to some other kind of head-covering may all serve as communications about the wearer's identity.

For example, young Kehillat Kodesh men do not for the most part wear hats in shul instead of yarmulkes. If they do so, there are two possible explanations. One is that the young man is married and is wearing the heavier hat—a traditional symbol of the weight of responsibility which marriage places upon the "head" of the family—as a sign of this status. (At Kehillat Kodesh this custom is observed by the more traditionally inclined young marrieds; their modern counterparts, influenced by the contemporary American premium on youth, continue to wear the yarmulke—the headgear that among traditional Jews is worn only by young boys—thus subtly, although not necessarily consciously, identifying themselves with the young.) The other explanation is that the young man who wears a hat in shul, especially during the longer prayer services, classes, or public assemblies, does so to indicate quite another thing, especially if the hat is black or dark brown and is worn at an angle, with its front far higher than its back and with a yarmulke showing beneath: such hat-wearing indicates the wearer's status as a student at the Sprawl City Yeshiva. (Some of the Kehillat Kodesh boys who go to this yeshiva do not wear hats to shul, as if to express—like some of the young married men—their greater identification with modern than with traditional Orthodoxy.)

A large black felt hat, or *biberhat*, is the headgear identifying the Chassid. This is the hat commonly worn by the *meshulach* (collector/messenger for yeshivas), who often makes his way into the Dudley Meadows area and Kehillat Kodesh to gather funds for a needy house of learning.

During the week the hats worn in shul are, like other garments, not always the same as those worn on Sabbaths and holy days. They may become caps or work hats—clearly not part of one's finery. It is the combination of time (Sabbath or holy day) and place (the shul) that creates the social expectations which bring out finery.

The observer also discovers that some hats, like many publicly displayed possessions, are, as Veblen suggests, signals of pecuniary standing. Indeed, the members of Kehillat Kodesh are acutely aware of all of one another's new articles of clothing. Each new coat I wore or that someone else put on was the subject of commentary. The comment *"Tischadesh"*—"May you be renewed" (in your new clothes)—ostensibly a blessing, is a common way for members to indicate their awareness of one another's new garments, and it is also a cue for the owner of the item to tell the story of its purchase and perhaps its source and price. On one occasion my comment of "tischadesh" about a new hat was answered with "It's a Borsalino," and a story of how the hat was acquired.

Women's headwear is also expressive. Those who are married must wear a hat to shul. Some women wear, in addition, a *sheital* (wig) as a further indication of the yoke of wedlock. These items, like men's biberhats or yarmulkes, are not, strictly speaking, either sacred or profane but are rather what Poll describes as "non-religious articles that tend to assume a semi-religious character."[19] More precisely, such garb, rather than being mandated along purely religious lines, is also ritualized, dictated *equally* by social and religious expectations.

A quick glance around the women's section should reveal, by simple examination of the heads, who is married. The accuracy of this indicator is somewhat jeopardized by the contemporary fashionableness and natural appearance of wigs, as well as by the fact that spinsters have taken to wearing hats. Nevertheless, such headwear serves generally to classify its users as wed or unwed, although one must look beyond the head to make certain.

Marital status is also expressed by ritual garb. This is particularly true for the men. The talis, used by men during morning prayers, is worn essentially only by married men. Single men called upon to perform some ritual act borrow someone else's talis for the occasion and then return it.[20] Hence, a look around the shul during morning prayers indicates who is and is not married. This bit of information is important to the members, for only the married members seem to be full-fledged members of the Kehillat Kodesh community.

I have said that ordinary clothing worn in the shul may be separated into that worn only on Sabbaths and that worn during the week. For men the difference is mostly in the appearance of suits, ties, and other finery.

Sabbath has always meant getting dressed in one's best. Whether or not this should be described as part of the Sabbath religious ritual is perhaps open to debate. Nevertheless, the following excerpt from Zborowski's and Herzog's description of Sabbath dress in the *shtetl* (the Jewish little town) of eastern Europe indicates that, if nothing else, dressing up for Sabbath became a ritualized activity, part of which, at least, included religiously oriented activity:

> . . . the men and boys seize their clean clothing [for Sabbath] and from all the streets they bear down on the bathhouse, their bundles under their arms. . . .
> Coming home from the bathhouse, dressed in their clean clothes, they put away the soiled garments and cover themselves with the carefully cherished sabbath caftan, tying in its fullness with a silken girdle. The sabbath caftan is usually of "silk." It may be sateen if the man is very poor, and the black fabric,

whatever it is, may be green with age, frayed and mended. But the sabbath caftan is made of "silk" and is a very special garment, stored away during the week with the rest of the sabbath and holiday clothes. There is a sabbath cap too, also of a precious fabric—satin or velvet perhaps for the opulent. The coat pockets must be emptied of all money, since none may be touched or carried on the sabbath. . . .

The boys, down to the very smallest, are dressed like their fathers in long black caftan and black cap or hat. . . .

For many women a sabbath without jewelry would be almost like a sabbath without chicken or fish. The ideal sabbath jewel is a necklace of pearls.[21]

The clothes themselves may have changed from the shtetl to Kehillat Kodesh, but the same care and sense of specialness still obtains as far as Sabbath dress is concerned. The well-scrubbed, clean Sabbath look is as unmistakable at Kehillat Kodesh as it was in the shtetl and, indeed, as it has been for generations of Jews.

During the week, the clothing worn to shul is associated with secular pursuits. It is work clothing; and, although some men wear jackets and ties to work, not all do. Accordingly, one difference between Sabbath and weekday clothing is that on the Sabbath everyone is in tie and jacket. During the week some men may come in casual clothes, without jacket or tie; some wear actual work uniforms; and still others wear the business suits required by their jobs. Sundays, on which casual clothes are the norm, represent a special case. Should anyone wear Sabbath finery then, explanations are requested, with members inquiring, "What are you all dressed up for?" In the opposite case, of failure to dress for the Sabbath, the joking question runs, "What's the matter—can't afford a tie?" (Failure to wear a tie was the only dress infraction I ever observed on Sabbaths.)

The wearing of casual clothes to shul is particularly characteristic of modern Orthodox Jews. This was neatly emphasized when, one weekday evening, a Chassidic visitor chastised a tieless member of Kehillat Kodesh. His criticism took the form of a contemporary folktale, in which he told the story of a man who had once, in desperation, taken his silk *gartel* (a ritual belt worn by Chassidim) to be used as a tie when he was told by the great Rabbi Aaron Gutman that the Talmud demands proper dress in the synagogue— which today means, among other things, a tie. Izzy, the member,

smiled, thinking that was the end of the visitor's story. Now the visitor said, loud enough for all in shul to hear, that he wanted to point out by his story that it was proper (for had not the great rabbi said so?) to wear a tie to shul. He added that, while he thought it was nice for people to come in off the street to pray, it would be more proper for them to wear ties in the future; it would be more frum. Izzy winked, and we smiled. We [the shul members] were too modern for that.

Indeed, at Kehillat Kodesh traditional Orthodox attire, such as a gartel, shtreimel, and so forth, is frequently worn for fun or masquerade, for example on Simchas Torah. This custom may express the already mentioned antipathy toward the "too frum." However, the willingness to wear such garb to shul as part of the joyful ceremony celebrating the end and renewal of the annual cycle of reading the Torah scroll indicates an element of sympathy as well. One ought, perhaps, to leave further interpretations to psychoanalysts.

Women, too, wear different clothing during the week from that worn on Sabbath. However, this difference is not often apparent in shul, since, as stated earlier, the women seldom come there during the week. On the few occasions that I have seen them I have noted: (1) The absence of a sheital and the presence instead of a *tichel* (a kerchief worn instead of a wig); (2) the absence of the ostentatious jewelry of Sabbaths; and (3) dresses which seemed in many cases more functional than stylish. Not being an insider and participant among the women makes it difficult, however, to accurately discuss them. One fact, however, is manifestly clear: women have no halachically prescribed prayer garb in shul.

An examination of the attire of shul children raises several issues regarding their socially perceived status. First of all, the presence of infants is, because of their incontinence, halachically prohibited and socially discouraged; thus, children in diapers do not appear in shul.[22] Children's shul clothing, ritualized in the regularity of its use, may be functionally differentiated into Sabbath and weekday wear. Children seldom attend shul on weekdays, and, when they do, they are dressed in the casual style of their American contemporaries. Their Sabbath clothing, however, will be of two extreme kinds: they will be dressed either like infants, with lace and frills, or like little adults, replicas of their parents, even down to the boys' miniature stetsons.

In his *Centuries of Childhood*, Ariès describes a similar set of extremes in children's dress during the thirteenth century, when the absence of a distinct social status of childhood resulted in children's being clothed either as babies or as adults, "like other men and women of [their] class," with no intermediary category.²³ Similarly, shul children have no "children's" clothes. Indeed, like women, they are halachically treated as nonpersons, a condition exhibited in part by the absence of any visible prayer garb mandated specifically for their use. The absence in shul of either ritual clothing for children or of clothing appropriate to their age affirms, as it did during the Middle Ages, that the child is not a legitimate role-player, not a person, in the setting. He is either a baby or an anticipatory adult.

The distinction becomes particularly apparent in the clothing of male children, who will one day take over the operation and religious responsibilities of the shul institution. Accordingly, after infancy their clothes immediately begin to reflect the fact that only as adult males (i.e., over the age of thirteen—*bar mitzva*) do they have halachic significance and, generally, count in shul. Only then can they be counted for a minyan, legitimately be given a kibbud, and begin to wear ritual garb. The females, on the other hand, since they will never gain such legal status or be able to wear ritual garb in the synagogue, tend to stay in the frills and lace of babyhood much longer than the boys.

For an Orthodox male, one of the exciting aspects of reaching ritual maturity is experienced in the donning of prayer garb, specifically tefillin, and the personhood it implies. Few males forget the experience of first putting on these items.²⁴

Little boys are given opportunities to don ritual or prayer garb before the age of thirteen and to perform certain ritual acts in shul, but all these are seen as prepatory for taking on the real and legitimate responsibilities. The little girls have none of this. Again, the shul is not for women.

On Sabbaths, little girls wear dresses with petticoats, ribbons, frills, and so on. Being summarily excluded from shul activity, they have no need to dress like their mothers. The little boys, for whom adulthood has promise, wear suits and ties, often as conservative-looking as their fathers'. As the males mature and pass the age of bar mitzva, they are released from the conservative restraints of an anticipatory social status, and their clothes tend to change a bit from those of their fathers, taking on more of the contemporary style of adolescent dress, with the flashy colors and progressive style common to young men's dress in urban America. (The local yeshiva boys are notable exceptions to this contemporary style, dressing more like Chassidim and less like secularized moderns.) Accordingly, as one looks around Kehillat Kodesh at the children, one sees the curious sight of little boys looking like old men, teenagers looking like either Chassidim or contemporary teenagers, and little girls in many cases looking much younger than their years.

Much more could be said, not only about children's clothing but about clothing in general. Suffice it to say that, like many other artifacts, the clothing at Kehillat Kodesh helps one to understand the people. It expresses two interdependent facts. First, garments may express one's membership in the group which populates the setting, the way a uniform does. They may exhibit the degree of that membership—whether it is partial (as is the case of women and young children) or full. Insiders know what to wear and when. They know how to be dressed on kodesh and how on chol. They know also that the wearing of certain clothes may be ritualized, even though in essence the garments remain profane.

Roles and status are also expressed through wardrobe, and especially through ritual or prayer garb. The little boy, as I stated, points up his entry into halachic responsibility at the age of thirteen by putting on tefillin. Yet these are but one part of the ritual wear available in the setting. When a man becomes married, he dons more and more ritual garb. Thus, only married men may wear a talis consistently at morning prayers, and only the married man may wear a *kittel* (white robe) on the high holy days and the Passover. As each rite of passage is achieved, more ritual and prayer garb is put on, exhibiting a rising status in the shul and a gradual role transformation from child to man and member.

In addition to indicating something about social, sex, and marital status, clothes may communicate one's frumkeit—and in a sense one's religious Weltanschauung. That is, within the definitions already established as a result of one's shul membership, clothes distinguish nuances of difference. Clothes may express one's partiality to Chassidim (as in the use of a gartel, kaftan, shtreimel, biberhat, yarmulke, etc.) or one's espousal of modernity (as in the wearing of fashionable contemporary attire). A trip from the shul to the Sprawl City Yeshiva often requires a change of dress—the wearing of a hat instead of a yarmulke, the wearing of a conservative-looking jacket rather than one with a loud pattern, etc. The key welded to a tie clasp or brooch and worn ornamentally on Sabbath represents another ritualized item of attire which may express one's frumkeit. Manifestly, such keys are so worn because carrying from one domain to another is prohibited on Sabbath; thus the only way to keep from being locked out of one's house is to circumvent the halachic prohibition by *wearing* (permissible) rather than *carrying* (prohibited) the key. Since such keys are worn even when there is no danger of being locked out (as when someone remains at home to open the door), one must assume that they are worn for expressive reasons as well, such as the fact that the key's presence indicates both the wearer's halachic virtuosity and his knowledge of how insiders dress.

Perhaps most interesting of all is the knowledge and self-consciousness of the actors in the setting. Like the mutinous soldier who puts on whatever uniform is considered correct for the occasion, knowing full well that he is not really convincing the informed audience of his dedication to the army and its principles, so too the members of Kehillat Kodesh who change their clothes to fit the setting know that at times they are simply putting on a front and engaging in staged behavior, especially when they change clothes to go to the local yeshiva. Ever conscious of standing out, especially in the secular world, where their religious Orthodoxy must be kept hidden so that they are not stigmatized by it, the modern Orthodox Jews of Kehillat Kodesh try to hide their religious deviance behind a veneer of ordinary clothing. This problem of passing in the secular world in spite of religious Orthodoxy and in the Jewish world in spite of secular fidelity is one that we shall return to; for, perhaps more than any other concern, it seems to be central to these Jews.

Now the stage is set. The objects in it, the costumes, the history prior to the observed action, have all been laid out so that in the next chapter we may concern ourselves with defining the setting in terms of the action in it. The discussion will again be divided into a consideration of the shul as a house of prayer, of study, and of assembly—functions not always distinct and discrete and whose interdependency is an important aspect of the setting. We begin in the house of prayer.

The House of Prayer: The Cast of Characters

The Jew's whole life becomes a
divine service with interruptions.

*Moritz Steinschneider, quoted in
A. E. Milgram,* Jewish Worship

The remaining chapters of this book will be devoted to defining and
analyzing the activities characteristic of the houses of prayer,
study, and assembly. Traditionally, these three have been the only
legitimate, and hence proper, activities in shul. Other activities
which may in fact take place on occasion are halachically defined
as incidental rather than legitimate shul activity.

From an interactional-analysis perspective, one discovers that
although the shul may at various times appear primarily as a house
of prayer or study or assembly, it is never any one of these to the
absolute exclusion of the others. In a sense, insiders experience the
setting as a combination of all these realities at once. Like a

chemical solution whose nature may be radically changed from one moment to the next by the addition, deletion, or intensification of any one ingredient, so also the shul is a mixture of activities which, performed in one combination, define a house of prayer and, in another, suggest a house of study or assembly.

The shul, unlike places of worship in other religions, was never the result of human implementation of a divine decree. Instead, it was always a construct inspired, organized, and designed by men. It may be further described as a "dialectic phenomenon in that it is a human product and nothing but a human product, that yet continuously acts back upon its producer."[1] Not only is it defined by activities in which its participants engage, but these activities have the paradoxical quality of being at once human creations *and* masters over the consequent behavior and consciousness of these same human beings. A person's activity "comes to confront him as a facticity outside himself . . . as *objectivated* human activity . . . a product of human activity that has attained a status of objective reality."[2]

Moreover, because the members of Kehillat Kodesh engage in many activities within the setting, its objective reality is a changing one. "Shul" is different things at different times. Accordingly, the members must continuously establish a relationship with it in its various situational definitions; this they accomplish by their ability to shift their activity among prayer, study, and sociability (later to be defined as the core action of assembly). A member may choose to act in conformity with a context defined by his prior actions and those of his fellow participants, or he may choose to deviate, change course, and hence transform[3] the setting along with his fellow deviators. People are thus constantly changing the definition of the situation, both by themselves and with others. To the nonparticipating observer who has analytically divided the life of the setting into formal categorizations of prayer, study, and assembly, such dynamics are often invisible, leaving him puzzled over what appears to be inconsistency between the manifest categorizations of the setting and the actual activity going on within it. What to the participant is the natural shifting from one context to another, from prayer to sociability to study and back to prayer, seems to the observer to be only chaos and contradiction. The observer seeing only objective reality, articulated in terms of prayer, study, and assembly, does not realize that these objective realities are dialectic phenomena—both the result of a particular flow of activity and also its cause.

Indeed, members engage in shifting involvements, which at times come close to being simultaneous and which enable them to shift from one context to another rapidly and comfortably. The context confirmed most often by most people *appears* to be the collective definition of the situation, with any other action seeming deviant. However, for the participant, no static objective reality exists: a prayer service is more than simply a time for praying; study sessions are more than merely occasions for learning; and assembly is far more than just getting together. To reiterate, the shul may be any one of these realities primarily but never exclusively. Bearing this point in mind, the reader must be prepared to sacrifice concise categories at times in order to have a truer picture of the setting. A close probe of the action may even temporarily leave him in doubt as to why people are in shul—to pray, study, or socialize—since they will be doing all three, and more.

Prayer

To begin, a few words about prayer in general and Jewish prayer in particular are in order. By nature, prayer is paradoxically both an intensely personal experience and one often performed in public with groups of others. In its personal nature it is difficult to define, for different personalities have infused it with different meanings; what is proper prayer for one is not necessarily so for the other. To categorically define only the public, most consistent, and recurrent behavior as prayer would be easy but inaccurate. While the language of social science cannot adequately define and delineate prayer, it may offer some operational descriptions to evoke a series of associations which may complete the picture.

Milgram, discussing Jewish worship, suggests several definitions of prayer. First he writes: "Prayer is essentially the product of man's yearning for the most intimate of all human communication, for the opportunity to open his heart and his mind in adoration and supplication to the divine presence." He then adds, "Prayer is also born of man's sense of wonder, from his awareness of God's marvelous creation and the miracles that daily bear witness."[4]

In other words, prayer, as a believer might say, is man's response to a world outside himself which, if ignored, might completely exclude him. At times, the other becomes personified as some sort of divine presence, a god, through which man may respond to that which is greater than himself. In any case, as people pray, they try to join with that power and existence beyond themselves and become partners with greatness, lest they instead become subservient to it. When such partnership requires subservience, it is submission by choice for some higher end rather than by default.

Prayer is but one way to accomplish such partnership. As Hubert and Mauss among others suggest, sacrifice accomplishes many of the same ends: "Sacrifice is a religious act which, through the consecration of a victim, *modifies the condition of the moral person who accomplishes it* or that of certain objects with which he is concerned."[5] That is, sacrifice is a way for man, by giving something away, to become partners with another. As such, the sacrificer is himself changed; his condition is modified.

For Jews, the antecedent of prayer was sacrifice. The three prayer services—*shacharis* (morning), *mincha* (afternoon), and *ma'ariv* (evening)—each of which is to be recited in its entirety only once daily, stand in place of the three regular sacrifices that were once daily tendered at the Holy Temple in Jerusalem before its final destruction in 70 C.E. Over time, and at the decree of the rabbinical leaders of the Diaspora, prayer became the surrogate for sacrifice, with the services themselves retaining the names of the sacrifices once offered at the temple. Implicit in this replacement was the understanding that as sacrifice could make for partnership with otherness and transform the individual, so too could prayer.

Yet such partnership with a power outside oneself may take various forms. At times men simply wish to display the partnership. Such demonstrations in prayer may become prayers of praise. Indeed, most Jewish prayer is of this form—so much so that the rabbis of the Talmud have suggested that, as much as men need God, he needs their praise. Like the actors whose acting may depend on their audience's approval, so the action of the divine depends upon the praise of men. Hence praise is a kind of partnership.

Prayers of petition exemplify another form of this partnership. In these a person seeks to exploit his ability to communicate with the divine presence. He demands mutual response and wants some control in the partnership. As the Sabbath liturgy states it: "May we see [our God] eye to eye when he returns to his abode." For the Jew, such petition is epitomized in the story of forefather Jacob's wrestling with the angel, in which partnership is stressed and absolutely exploited. As the divine presence struggles to break away, the response of man, in Jacob, is, "I will not let thee go, except thou bless me" (Gen. 22:28). That is, "Only if you respond to me and through a blessing reaffirm our union and communion, will I, man, allow you some independence." Much Jewish prayer takes this form, as well.

Finally, and especially for Jews, prayer may be a recitation of the history of the partnership. Here study, epitomized by the repeated review of Torah, the written and documented proof of a partnership between God and the Jewish people and, indeed, mankind, emerges as a form of worship. Whether the Torah deals with Jacob's wrestling with the angel or the building of a tabernacle for God, it ultimately reaffirms the partnership between man and the power outside him. For Jews, study is inseparably a part of prayer. Built into every service are not only the public readings of the Torah but also numerous prayers cataloguing such things as the story of the binding of Isaac, the proper material for Sabbath candles, or the order and list of objects required in the temple sacrifices of the past. Study then details both how men have related to their god and how the law would continue to structure that relationship.

Prayer for Jews is thus at least three things: praise, petition, and study. All three are forms of man's "yearning for the most intimate of all human communication," with the divine presence;[6] and the desire for response is born of man's sense of "wonder" at the world outside himself.

Yet wonder and intense yearning are fleeting experiences, which cannot be forever sustained by the individual. As Durkheim suggests, "A man cannot retain them any length of time by a purely personal effort." He stresses that "the only moral forces with which we can sustain and increase our own are those we get from others."[7] Accordingly, in prayer people have learned to bind themselves together with a liturgy and a law that allow them to reap the benefits of prayer even when they as individuals cannot initiate the effort. For Jews, this means, practically, that prayer is codified and objectivated in the liturgical format of the siddur and organized in the assembly of a minyan. Thus, what was once the result of individual thinking and feeling becomes instead the stimulus for it. Men made prayers out of emotional and intellectual inspirations, codified them, and now find that these prayers must recreate these same emotions again and again. That such prayers succeed at all is evidence of the power of their poetry; that they fail is not surprising. For in codification prayers may become the creations of everyone and the inspiration of no one.

The ironic dilemma of prayer should now be somewhat clear.

Indeed, the shul Jews cannot always pray as they, by their own definitions, ought. They cannot always pray with *kavannah*. This term has no exact English equivalent but refers to a combination of devotion, concentration, intensity, and intention. It is the emotion which stimulates the felt need for prayer and must remain in effect throughout its execution. To achieve a state of kavannah is obviously not easy, especially when one uses a siddur and prays in a minyan. That is, inspiration is diluted when one (1) uses others' words, as in liturgy, and (2) prays in public and so must simultaneously be concerned with prayer and the demands of relations and behavior in public. When Durkheim asserted the moral invigoration made possible by collective worship, he evidently ignored these devotional liabilities, which become apparent in the everyday practice of prayer. Indeed, many a shul member admits that kavannah is easier when praying alone at home; and students of prayer suggest that "It is natural for the mind to be distracted and to wander," especially in the stimulating context of public prayer.[8] Accordingly, Kehillat Kodesh Jews seldom if ever call their worship "prayer" or even (in the Hebrew) "tefilah," terms which, strictly speaking, connote a spiritual experience infused with kavannah. Instead they allude to their "davening," a Yiddish term which, while it denotes "prayer," also refers to the context, both spiritual *and* mundane, within which prayer occurs. Hence, while only the inspired may be able to pray, everyone can daven—even those who, like children, know nothing of the majestic spirituality of tefilah. A closer look at the actual practice of Kehillat Kodesh davening seems in order.

Communal prayer, *tefilah sheh be tzibbur*, occurs thrice daily, as already stated. On Sabbath and holy-day mornings an additional prayer, *musaf*, is added in commemoration of the additional sacrifice formerly presented at the now destroyed Holy Temple in Jerusalem. Individual prayer, *tefilah sheh be yochid*, follows the same pattern. Liturgically, the two types of prayer are simply differentiated. When praying alone, one cannot recite certain prayers, cannot respond "amen" (the affirmation of prayer and of the relationship which it asserts), and cannot hear or read the Torah scroll. Sociologically, the difference between individual and communal prayer is much more complex, for here the distinction is embedded in all the differences between the private and public spheres of life.

Although not all shul prayer halachically meets the requirements of tefilah sheh be tzibbur—these are met only when at least a minyan has gathered—all *observable* shul prayer must be sociologically considered public and communal. The solitary shul worshiper whose prayer might qualify (sociologically as well as halachically) as tefilah sheh be yochid is beyond the scope of the participant observer, whose presence assures at least a two-person sociation. Hence, for all intents and purposes, the prayer considered in this study will be communal.

The Cast of Characters

Like any action, prayer may serve to define a situation. Communal prayer, however, is not one unified action but rather a panoply of behaviors carried on in a variety of roles. Accordingly, an examination of such roles may offer a means of deciphering the house of prayer. Some of these roles are temporary, even fleeting, while others are more lasting. Some, like officially instituted roles, determine action, while others emerge extemporaneously from it and still others are combinations of the two. Finally, in all roles a distinction can be made between the "normative aspects of the role and a particular individual's role performance."[9]

Males and Females

Perhaps the most important role to consider in the setting is the sex role. As already stated, Kehillat Kodesh Jews, for all their modernity, segregate the sexes quite strictly among adults, especially within the sanctuary. In fact, this segregation is one of symbolic absolutes in a shul which defines itself as Orthodox. The scope and nature of this sex segregation, however, goes beyond moments of prayer.

In addition to the segregation manifestly enforced during prayer services, segregation occurs at other occasions during which a gathering may in some way be considered to be sponsored by Kehillat Kodesh. That is, whenever the members get together to affirm in some way their collective membership in the Jewish world, they segregate the sexes. This affirmation need not be the manifest purpose of the gathering. At such times, sex segregation of some sort is always observed, often in what seems an unconscious manner. (The same people might, however, get together at another time simply as friends, along with Gentiles or non-Orthodox Jews, and mingle sexes with the same regularity or irregularity as occurs in American society in general. Only, however, when their gathering is not in some way an affirmation of their Jewishness will even slight mingling occur.)

For example, although there are no formal restrictions on mixing during the kiddush after services, the men and women continue for the most part to remain segregated. They stand at different tables, with the women occupying the spaces closest to the kitchen and the men going into the interior of the room. When a woman breaks this barrier, she does so with obvious display of purpose; the same thing is true for men. Thus, a woman holds a garbage bag as she steps into the interior and thereby signals she is coming into the area to clean up; or she holds some food on plates, to indicate that she is going to serve. The man who is passing through the women's area stands in such a way that his forward motion is exaggerated: he is passing through, not staying.

Again, at parties which are sponsored by the shul or some other Jewish organization, any dancing that occurs is segregated by sex, with women dancing in one circle and men in another. Any mixing of sexes that does occur operates within the confines of special rules, to be outlined shortly.

When a woman stands about in the foyer after the end of prayer services, she does so with other women until her husband joins them. His appearance in this group of women is temporary and a signal for his wife to make her good-byes. The segregation is soon reestablished upon the couple's exit, either to the kiddush upstairs or, lacking a kiddush, outside to Dudley Avenue, where men and women stand or stroll in separate little groups.

Segregation of sexes also occurs during shul-government meetings. Not only do women then sit separately; they are also assigned tasks different from the men's. While men make policy decisions, women implement them. Rather than being only a delegation of "dirty work," such implementation in fact becomes a way of altering and overriding policy, as exhibited in the frequent and notable variations between the men's decisions and actual outcomes. In spite of such subversion of certain policy decisions, men continue to delegate implementation to the women, segregating spheres of authority. Thus, while women are not officially allowed by shul charter to vote, the board (composed of men) officially announced in an amendment to that document that it was prepared to "take into consideration" suggestions from the ladies' auxiliary.

The segregation of the sexes described above is not particularly unusual. We live in a world essentially separated by gender; hence, to find one more manifestation of this reality within Kehillat Kodesh tells us perhaps nothing more than that, in regard to gender, this group does not behave in a radically different way from others in American civilization—although that is useful information, too, especially when one is talking about a group that is notorious for its "differentness."

Nevertheless, the segregation practiced by the Jews of Kehillat Kodesh and by other Orthodox Jews is perhaps unlike the segregation common among men and women in our culture, in that it is intimately connected with frumkeit and evolves from a religious principle which demands that men and women approach divine otherness in separate and different ways.

While both males and females have religious responsibilities, women have fewer of these and are generally dependent upon men for the fulfillment of all public ritual requirements like those performed in shul. Thus it is the men rather than the women who must wear sanctified prayer garb. It is they who lead the prayers in the role of chazan and they who chant the Torah scrolls or make the benedictions at kiddush. In the segregated atmosphere of the kiddush room, for example, it is not unusual to find several women standing around a man who holds a drink in his hand over which he makes the kiddush benediction, which all, including women, must hear before eating but which only men may recite. For a moment the women, often led by the man's wife, approach the man, listen to his kiddush, and then move away again.

It is men who receive kibbudim, not only on their own behalf but also for the honor of their family—the women and small children. When a woman or minor experiences a sad or happy event of public concern, they religiously respond to it through a husband or father. He receives the kibbud for her and thereby gives the event religious and social as well as personal significance. Thus, for example, when one member's daughter became *bas mitzva*, twelve years old, and hence a halachically mature woman, the father received the call to the Torah scroll reading (unlike the parallel case of *bar mitzva*, the thirteen-year-old male's coming-of-age, when the celebrant himself is called for the kibbud). Men mark rites of passage in the community, no matter who has done the passing.

Even the space, as already described, asserts the public dependency of female upon male vis-à-vis religious responsibility. It is the men's section of the sanctuary where holy objects are primarily located.

Women may not even be counted for a minyan. The reasons given are manifold but focus essentially on the notion that women express their Jewishness through their actions in the home and family and that these concerns preclude time for public gathering and prayer. Prayers are said in the mornings and evenings—both busy times for the mother, the role for which all Jewish women are supposed to be destined. Not counting them in the minyan institutionalizes their freedom to pursue other obligations. Indeed, by law women are freed from the observance of all positive commandments which are dependent on a particular time for their observance. The law recognizes that the conditions of everyday existence cause men and women to come to terms with time differently; hence among Orthodox Jews a woman's life transcends institutionally arranged time, while, for a man, such time is what matters most. That is not to say, however, that a woman has no need for the human experience of prayer; she may, if she chooses, pray alone, without a minyan. Nevertheless, her father or husband *must* pray in a minyan and share with her the religious benefits of his communal prayer. Prayer, indeed, is but one of the many ways in which the conjugal pair is linked. Upon marriage, the woman's communal prayers are no longer said by her father as much as by her husband. It is the male who bestows blessings upon the woman. He goes to the Torah scroll and tells the gabbai the name of his wife, and this man in turn blesses her.

One ought not, however, jump to the conclusion that males alone are the guardians of the faith. On the contrary, it is and has always been in the Jewish home, where woman reigns supreme, that Jews are made and nurtured. Without such a home behind it, the shul remains an empty fortress. Perhaps in recognition of this reality the Talmud asserts: "A man's home is his wife," (Yoma 2b). The woman is no second-class citizen of the faith. As the Sabbath liturgy asserts, "Her worth is greater than rubies." Her domain is simply not the shul; her turf is her home.

The almost total sexual segregation of religious responsibility and domain is characteristic only of traditional Orthodox Jews. As one moves along the continuum through modern Orthodox, Conservative, and, ultimately, Reform Jewry, one finds an increasing effort on the part of women to share male custody of public religion. More often than not these female initiatives occur in the house of prayer; as one moves away from traditional Orthodoxy, one finds the proportion of women and men coming to shul becoming equalized. Women's participation has also increased to the point where some non-Orthodox congregations have taken to giving women kibbudim, counting them for a minyan, and, most recently, ordaining them as religious virtuosi—rabbis.[10] It is difficult to say whether this growing influence of women in the house of prayer is simply a reflection of present feminist trends in American society or whether it represents an effort to deepen involvement in religious life.

While the modern Orthodox Jews of Kehillat Kodesh are somewhat influenced by these trends in contemporary society, their modernity, in this case as in others, is restricted. Accordingly, while women come to shul, they do so only on Sabbath and holy-day mornings (and later and less often than men). Moreover, when they do come, they participate only peripherally in the activity of the house of prayer. Theirs is a prayer with a minimum of involvement shifts. They cannot easily change the prevailing definition of the situation—i.e., move from prayer to study to sociability and so on—as do the men, who as masters of the setting are far less restricted.

The men's authority to define and maintain situations is nicely reflected in the way they conduct conversations during communal prayer. They are constantly talking and shifting their involvement away from prayer, especially during the services at which the women are present. They walk out of the sanctuary to take a break from the activity of prayer. They make speeches. They plan the service and generally negotiate the dispensation of kibbudim. All this time, the women sit still and pray or follow the service. Their conversation is limited; they have no foyers in which to recess; they have no politicking to engage in *during the service* (although they do so at other times). When the women occasionally shush the men in order to better hear the service, they are usually ignored—the implication being that it is not important for them to hear, for they are not legitimate participants in the house-of-prayer activity. Indeed, when the women requested a seating change in order to better see and hear the service, they were overruled. However, if some noise should come from the women's section during the course of a service, the men will jokingly and sometimes vehemently ask for quiet, stop the progress of the service, and wait for silence to come, which it soon does. Plainly and simply, the shul is for men; and prayer as practiced in shul is for men, too. The women's place to pray is at home. (Indeed, among the most traditional Orthodox Jews, women appear in shul only on Yom Kippur, the Day of Atonement, when mankind has no home but hangs in the limbo of divine judgment.) If they do choose to come to shul, they must remain "in the back," with all the impotence that that location symbolizes.

On some occasions when men and women gather together,

women are able to overcome sex-role barriers. These occur when
(1) the setting is in the home, and the hostess ministers to those who
are gathered there; (2) the woman is in some way the stimulus for a
gathering; and (3) the interactants are married or engaged couples
rather than participation units composed strictly of individuals.
(Young adults courting each other constitute a fourth and very
limited case. They break the norms of sexual segregation only so
long as they are "playing the field"; once engaged, they segregate
like other adults.)

A closer analysis of the third case reveals that the sexual
integration that occurs here is more physical than interactional. In
spite of the apparent mixing, men continue to talk primarily with
men and women with women, and it is not at all unusual to see
such circles of couples break up into lines of men and women.
Nevertheless, only in a gathering consisting of such couples is it
commonly possible to talk for any extended period of time to a
member of the opposite sex. Indeed, only when my wife was
nearby did I ever have any long interviews with women.

The Gabbai

More specific to the Kehillat Kodesh house of prayer than sex roles
are the roles of the gabbai and president. Let us begin with the
gabbai. In premodern times, the gabbai served primarily as shul
treasurer and fund collector and as such had an authority second
only to that of the political lay leader, the *parnas* (today called
"president"). To increase the treasury, the gabbai was given the
right to dispense kibbudim in return for donations. This power
over privilege, which ultimately superseded his duties as treasurer,
endowed the gabbai with political power like the parnas. But the
gabbai's authority became religious as well, for he had to know
both the halachic requirements of each kibbud and what constituted privilege.

Since Jewish study has always been an essential and universal
religious responsibility, communities Orthodox in their observance
of ritual have always had high concentrations of knowledgeable
Jews and hence a ready supply of potential gabbais. Ironically,
selection as a gabbai, while assuring institutional authority, has not
always guaranteed the respect of one's peers, who often fancy
themselves as equals in Jewish scholarship.

The Jews of Kehillat Kodesh have tried to avoid such challenges
to their gabbais by appointing to the post persons whose Jewish
scholarship is generally respected. The office is normally held for

one year. The most secure occupants of the role have been those who, while not actively pursuing a rabbinic career, have rabbinic ordination (i.e. extracommunal credentials) in their educational background.

As dispenser of kibbudim, the gabbai becomes a most important shul functionary. To entirely comprehend his importance, however, one must first fully understand the significance of kibbud.

As already stated, a kibbud is the public honor associated with the ceremonial performance of a ritual act, usually within the house of prayer. While not all kibbudim are of equal prestige (the honor of chanting the haftora is, for example, considered a "bigger kibbud" than opening the ark), all easily qualify as *prestations*, defined by Mauss as "any thing or series of things given freely or obligatorily as a gift or in exchange, [including] services, entertainments, etc., as well as material things."[11]

The public presentation of kibbud is bestowed upon individuals by the collectivity, represented by the gabbai. If, as Mauss observed, "to give something is to give a part of oneself," the group—when, through its gabbai, it gives out kibbudim—gives of itself to itself, thereby linking individuals to the collectivity "by the mechanisms of obligation which are resident in the gifts themselves"[12] In some instances the kibbud may incur obligations of repayment, while at other times it serves as such repayment. More specifically, such acts as making a donation to the shul, sponsoring a kiddush, or volunteering one's time and energy for community benefit may either generate a kibbud or repay one.

As individuals rather than collective representatives, gabbais may occasionally use their power over privilege to either actuate or fulfill personal obligations. Such exploitation of their office for personal benefit is publicly discouraged and is often the source of criticism of particular incumbents of the role.

However, on special occasions, usually celebrations, such personal use of kibbudim is allowed and even institutionalized (as if to say that, in times of personal pleasure, one must remember one's social obligations). The father of a bar mitzva, for example, may either temporarily become gabbai or may hand a list of names and associated kibbudim to the gabbai, who dutifully follows it. Nowhere does the obligatory nature of kibbud become clearer. On one such occasion, when the celebrant began to select those to be honored, one of my seat neighbors announced, "Now we'll be able to tell who his friends are." Everyone now paid careful attention to each kibbud, and, with a logic exquisitely intricate in its comprehension of social networks and obligations, selections were reviewed, rationalized, judged, and often even predicted. What might have appeared at first glance to be simply an ad hoc and arbitrary dispensing of tasks and honors was to the insider a series of prestations clearly "actuated by mechanisms of obligation."[13] Favors were being returned, relationships confirmed, and credits generated by a dispenser obviously sensitive to the implications of kibbud. Moreover, the general attention given the matter by everyone in the congregation suggested that they too knew what was at issue.

Like any gift, the kibbud, in assuring reciprocal obligations, proclaims a relationship between donor and recipient, whether the exchanging parties are groups or individuals. At times kibbudim reflect changes in relations brought about by a change in status of one of the parties. Such changes, marked by rites of passage like bar mitzvas, weddings, funerals, and so forth, assure the receipt of a kibbud. The more dramatic the change in one's status (either socially or halachically), the "bigger" the kibbud. At other times, kibbudim affirm constancy as well. Hence, everyone may expect a certain number of them throughout the year even if nothing special happens to him. To fail to receive any is to have it publicly proclaimed through the gabbai that one lacks any links of obligation with the collectivity and so has failed to share in its symbolic wealth—its honor—and hence that one is implicitly rejected. Not a small number of Jews have left shuls precisely because they received either too meager a kibbud (too little of community "wealth") or none at all.

Although they are outsiders, guests and strangers customarily receive kibbudim. In bestowing such honors on outsiders, the congregation indicates both its magnanimity and its wealth—it has honors enough to give away. To fail to do so is to risk a reputation of collective niggardliness at best and impoverishment at worst. On the other hand, to give away too many honors to outsiders, who cannot be expected to repay such gifts, is to risk impoverishment. Not surprisingly, the distribution of kibbudim to outsiders is subject to much discussion. One hears members complain that outsiders receive more kibbudim than insiders. Yet one hears an equal number of complaints about omissions in honoring guests and strangers. Such ambivalence can only suggest the depth of collective concern about kibbud. Perhaps Durkheim can be helpful here. He suggests that "collective sentiments can become conscious of themselves only by fixing themselves upon external objects."[14]

For Kehillat Kodesh, kibbudim serve as these "external objects" through which the collectivity represents itself—both to itself and, in the case of guests and strangers, to others.

To be sure, the actual ceremonial performance does not in itself constitute the kibbud; there must be an accompanying public affirmation of honor. An act executed in the presence of only a few, or even among many but commanding little attention, is a lesser kibbud than the same act performed before a large and attentive public. To remove the Torah scroll from the ark for a weekday reading when only a handful are present in shul is, for example, not nearly as honorific as to do this on Sabbath morning before the attentive eyes of the entire community.

Public affirmations of honor are both liturgical and social. The former are represented by the gabbai's ceremonial summoning chants made in conjunction with the reading of the Torah scroll. As part of liturgy, these guarantee at least a modicum of attention. Social affirmations take the form of ritualized ratifying handshakes, accompanied by formulaic blessings, which commonly are offered to a kibbud recipient. Relatively difficult ceremonial tasks, such as leading the service or reading the Torah scroll, occasionally stimulate outright compliments. In general, the lesser the kibbud, the less extensive the public response to it, and vice versa. Accordingly, weekday kibbudim are perfunctorily accepted and perfunctorily responded to. Missing here are the extensive handshakes and compliments attached to the greater honors of Sabbath.

Such weekday kibbudim are, however, by no means altogether worthless. Indeed, the appearance of a guest at a weekday service often stimulates much of the controversy about kibbud dispensation. While of low value to insiders during the week, the kibbud still remains part of the collective wealth, not to be given away recklessly.

I have called the kibbud a medium of exchange. As such it has currency in the community outside the house of prayer as well—especially in gatherings which have a ritual character similar to prayer. Thus, for example, during a circumcision ceremony and the meal that followed at one member's home, much the same concern about kibbud was in evidence. Who would hold the infant, who would carry it in, who would hand it to the *mohel* (circumciser), who would lead grace, and so on were all questions of kibbud, whose answers, as always, revealed the nature of the tie between donor and recipient (though here the host rather than the collectivity is the donor).

In spite of its importance (or perhaps because of it), the kibbud may sometimes be mocked. Although the mock kibbud may be associated with an act identical to the one connected with a real kibbud, the underlying attitude varies, and therefore the social significance of the act varies as well. A mock kibbud is not charged with the same sense of prestation as its legitimate counterpart, and so it neither fulfills nor generates obligations. Such kibbudim appear most commonly during the playful atmosphere of Simchas Torah. On this holy day every male must, by tradition, receive the kibbud of a call to the Torah scroll reading. Yet, now, unlike the rest of the year, a prestigious *aliya* (call to the reading) may be given to a local n'er-do-well or teenager (a male low in the status hierarchy) amid much laughter and joking. This is a false exchange, for neither donors nor recipients may take the prestation seriously, as the obvious joking ensures. Yet, even as sham, the kibbud speaks, since it serves to mark the lowly for what they are. To be honored on a day when honor is dishonor is indeed no honor.

To recapitulate: in its representative qualities, the kibbud offers the collectivity a means of becoming conscious of its own worth. As a prestation, it provides expression for collective sentiments which functionally serve to link individual members to one another and to the group. Since the dispensation of kibbud is a public process, it also serves to display these sentiments and their associated relationships to all informed and interested observers. The gabbai, as keeper and dispenser of kibbudim, thus handles what is perhaps one of the group's most essential properties. As such, he shares in its power and importance.

When kibbudim become relatively unimportant, as on weekdays, the role of gabbai concomitantly declines in importance. Accordingly, it is no surprise to find that on weekdays when the permanent gabbai is absent, or is late in arriving, various others take over this role with relative ease. Of course, because even on a weekday the kibbud is potentially highly charged, these substitute gabbais are often those who command a certain respect—for example, older men, shul officers, or those with reputations as Jewish scholars. Yet on Simchas Torah, when playful kibbudim are given out, the person playing gabbai may also be a mock gabbai. Thus one is not surprised to find young boys, who during the rest of the year are systematically excluded not only from kibbud dispensation but from receipt of it, becoming gabbais for the morning. Mock kibbudim are distributed by sham gabbais.

Inextricably, the gabbai is associated with the kibbud. Just as it is among the central concerns of the congregation, so, too, is he: the members, ambivalent about the kibbud, wanting it and yet wanting to give it away, are ambivalent also about the role of gabbai, wanting the role and its power and yet almost universally refusing to fill the post. During the selection of one gabbai at, Kehillat Kodesh, everyone questioned refused the post; finally they appointed a man who was out of town during the selection process. Moreover, weekday substitute gabbais, at the same time that they expect to be offered the post, invariably at first refuse it. When they finally do accept the gabbai task, they do so in an offhand manner, thus indicating a degree of role distance.

The gabbai is potentially a schismatic influence on the congregation. A group measures itself by those whom it chooses to honor, and the gabbai, who exercises the group's choices, has the capacity to turn the group against itself and threaten or destroy it. Should he choose improperly, he is likely to set friend against friend, foment jealousy and insult, and ultimately destroy the unity of the group, tearing apart the very fabric of conciliation that Kehillat Kodesh so painfully established. If a gabbai seems to be headed in this direction, he must be renounced and abandoned. Men who will soon become outsiders are best for the job. Thus, one gabbai moved to Israel at the end of his year of duty, another moved out to Drumlin, and a third, because of his old age, became incapacitated and retired.

Yet, in spite of the social dangers, the gabbai's post is a desired one as well. People are forever trying to steal a bit of his power, wanting to dispense a kibbud, especially to personal guests—indicating by this, among other things, that they are true insiders who have communal favors at their diposal. The gabbai is deluged by suggestions from the membership—especially from the president, its lay leader—as to who should get what. The adroit gabbai deftly steers his way through such suggestions with a minimum of friction.

The task is not an easy one, and the Kehillat Kodesh institution has engaged in many efforts to mitigate the problem. They have divided the post into three parts—three gabbais. The first, traditionally the chief gabbai, chooses the kibbudim; the second, during the Torah scroll reading, calls out the names of kibbud recipients; and the third keeps records and finds out the names of those to be called. During the Torah scroll reading, all three gabbais work. During the rest of the time the first gabbai usually issues directives, to be carried out by one of the other two or at times by himself. As this is being written, all three gabbais have, for the first time, agreed to serve only on condition that none would be considered first gabbai—an effort aimed at avoiding the miseries of the post by avoiding ultimate responsibility while still maintaining the full power of the office.

In return for the pain of the post, the congregation allows the gabbai various prerogatives. Foremost, of course, is the power over kibbudim; but there are other advantages as well. For example, when no one else is allowed to talk during a prayer, the gabbai may speak, despite halachic prohibition, in order to assure the smooth dispensation of kibbud. When, on Sabbath mornings, everyone must sit in place, the gabbai, in fulfillment of his duties, freely roams the space. When most men must wait for ceremonial occasions to handle sacred objects, the gabbai, in preparing these objects for use, may handle them when and as he sees fit. As both representative and servant of the public, he retains access to everything the public holds and protects, and as such he acquires a power greater than any single member of that public.

Within the boundaries of the house of prayer, the gabbai dominates. While himself talking frequently, he dares chastise others for their unceasing conversations. While wholly concerning himself with the business of kibbud, he lectures on the importance of kavannah. In short, as manager of the house of prayer, his ultimate concern is not for his own prayer but rather to see to it that communal prayer is smoothly effected. He is one of those responsible for gathering a minyan when there is an insufficient number present for a particular service. His call to a member to come is not the plea of one man but rather a request from the entire congregation, just as a kibbud from him is really a kibbud from the whole group. It is the gabbai who programs the activity of the assembled prayer group and sorts out the ritual roles for those present.

The absence at Kehillat Kodesh of the competing authority of an official rabbinic leader has made possible the gabbai's dominance. In shuls who have rabbis, the gabbai's power is diluted. Yet even at Kehillat Kodesh his power is not absolute or completely distinct from that of a *parnas*, or president, for the latter may frequently assume many of his powers. As one member pointed out, "A president anoints a gabbai." That is to say, for all the power of the gabbai, the president is often the group representative who selects him (sometimes through the thinly disguised form of a nominating committee which follows his "suggestions") and who "anoints" him with a portion of power.

The President

If one considers the gabbai as a collective representation of the people, as one who serves as an instrument by which the group honors itself and thereby reaffirms its existence and unity, one may perhaps also see the president as a collective representation, since it is he who often selects and occasionally overrules the gabbai. An examination of the presidency seems to lead inexorably to this conclusion. Consequently, this role is the next one to be discussed—not only in order to discuss the relationship between the group and its president but also to help set the stage for an understanding of the experience of communal prayer at Kehillat Kodesh—the topic of ultimate interest in this section of the study.

At Kehillat Kodesh the presidency is far more than an elective office. Although nominally the term of the president is, like that of the gabbai, for one year, the presidency, unlike the post of gabbi, has in fact been held by one man for three consecutive terms and has become almost synonymous with its incumbent—Velvel Brillant.

Velvel, as he is called by old and young alike, is a man in his fifties, a first-generation Jewish immigrant from Europe who arrived after World War II. He, his wife, and several of his children came to Sprawl City at the behest of the Hebrew Immigrant Aid Society, which was then trying to channel the flow of immigrants from Europe out of New York. After a sojourn in other parts of the city, Velvel, an interior decorator by profession, ultimately settled in Dudley Meadows, where he bought a house and joined Kehillat Kodesh. He recalls the days before the final revolt at the old shul and knows all the characters who played key roles in it; thus, although he leads the "new" Kehillat Kodesh, he remembers the old times. This memory no doubt haunts him at times and may account for his never-ending efforts at congregational conciliation. This peacemaking is one of his most important qualities of leadership. As one member put it:

> Everyone talks to Velvel. I talk to him, too. Anyone who's dissatisfied talks to Velvel. You could talk to him about anything that concerned you. That's why Velvel is a good president—if anyone's unhappy, he'll try to satisfy him. He tries to keep everyone happy. Everyone uses him as a vehicle for his own purposes.

While the Kehillat Kodesh constitution clearly outlines the rights and duties of the congregational president, to list these and thereby suggest that they describe Velvel's role would be to obfuscate rather than clarify his true position. It is better to describe him as combining numerous roles, in which he may be either group servant, representative, or leader. He is variously a mediator of particular arguments, a conciliator and mitigator of states of general tension, a complaint recipient, a shul host to outsiders, a bearer of all group-related news and gossip, a charity-gatherer of last resort, a contingent minyan-assembler, a power-anointer, a lay authority, and, finally, everybody's friend. In short, the president's ultimate duty is to keep the group alive; and its destruction or disintegration is his own—as is the case for any leader whose authority dissolves with the disappearance of his followers.

These various role responsibilities may each be considered more closely. I begin with the mediator and conciliator roles. The mediator concerns himself with the details of a particular quarrel, while the conciliator aims for a general spirit of peace in the group. As mediator, Velvel often seems to enter arguments which appear not to concern him at all. Thus when two men argue about a procedure relating to a Torah scroll reading (something related to a religious or halachic decision, which for the most part lies beyond the scope of his lay power), Velvel nonetheless enters the argument and quietly asks them to sit down and discuss the problem after services—by which time it will no doubt be moot and forgotten.

As conciliator, Velvel talks to everyone, shares gossip with the men, makes a few jokes, defuses tensions, and plays down intramural discord by agreeing with both sides (but taking great care to hide his tactical duplicity by always agreeing "off the record").

It is Velvel who ends the fights that the quarrelers themselves fail to stop. On the increasingly rare occasions when such disputes get out of control and erupt in full view of the assembled congregation, it is Velvel who leads the efforts at ending the altercation. In the most simple yet often most effective efforts at mediation, Velvel shushes, cajoles, and sometimes caressingly touches the disputants, telling them, like a father, that they should not shout and argue. In conciliatory efforts afterwards, he may confer with each and then generally joke about the matter with anyone who still seems perturbed over the outbreak. Along with Velvel's efforts and words come those of the other members, who, acting like a chorus, reiterate, amplify, and confirm Velvel's demands for peace.

Velvel does not act as a mediator for the women. He need not, since women, unlike men, seldom if ever quarrel in shul. (One sees here incidentally, more evidence that the shul is a man's domain and that what men may do there women may not.) Indeed, the only public quarrel I ever witnessed involving a woman in shul occurred in the kitchen—the women's domain—between a woman and a man; they quarreled over what food should be put out for a kiddush, and the man had his way (which suggests, once again, that, even in the shul kitchen, ultimate power and control over the setting belong to men).

As complaint recipient, the president abets his role as conciliator. By accepting and responding to complaints, he defuses potential states of tension and conflict which might otherwise break out into open quarrel. Thus, when one member complains that the siddurim he has donated to the shul are starting to come apart at the seams, he adds, "I'm going to talk to Velvel about this." Velvel will admit guilt on behalf of the group he ultimately embodies and personifies. By complaining to Velvel one finds a focus for one's anger and avoids the feeling of alienation which resentment expressed toward the entire group might arouse.

But Velvel is more than a scapegoat for all that is wrong with the shul, for he represents its strengths as well as its faults. Thus, when outsiders visit the shul, Velvel is the one who greets them, either in a formal welcome from the pulpit during his announcements at the end of the service or during informal conversation. When other groups make use of shul facilities, they thank the president for his hospitality, knowing that they are thus thanking the entire group. When the president is in attendance at such meetings, he comes not as an individual but rather as the embodiment of Kehillat Kodesh; his presence is an official sanction of the outside group's use of the shul's facilities.

All guests and visiting relatives are introduced to Velvel by host members. In this way the visitor is made to feel that he has been formally presented in shul, while the host exhibits insider status through his access to the president. Often Velvel will make sure that the guest is offered a kibbud, thereby confirming the feelings of guest and host. If an unescorted stranger comes into the shul, Velvel more than anyone else takes the initiative, approaching the outsider and greeting him and, not incidentally, finding out information about him. This information in time is passed on to the other members, who trust Velvel to know all about the strange faces in shul.

This last point brings us to the next presidential function, that of bearing all group-related news and gossip. In addition to knowing all about strangers, Velvel knows all about the members. Approaching a member who has been absent for a time, he asks where the person has been and often jokes, "How could you leave without telling me where you were going?" Even more remarkable than Velvel's inquisitiveness is the readiness with which members answer his questions, a topic to be more fully considered in the discussion of shul gossip in chapter 5. While Velvel is by no means the only holder of news and gossip in the shul, he ultimately hears and bears all matters pertaining generally to the group. As a member, anyone may gain access to Velvel's knowledge. His is not a secret gossip, shared only within a personal clique. Rather, as one becomes more and more a congregational insider, one may share in progressively larger portions of this news and gossip, including the mildly slanderous and scandalous. Velvel, as embodiment of the group, simply acts as keeper of gossip, much as community leaders have at other places and times been guardians of folktales and myth, reciting these only to the initiated.

Perhaps the announcements which the president makes at the conclusion of the Sabbath morning services (when the entire community is present) serves best to underline his role as gatherer and bearer of news. Unlike other parts of the morning service, these announcements receive the congregation's undivided attention. As one member exuberantly exclaimed, "The announcements are the best part of shul!" Although mocked and amended in a chorus of shouted commentaries and laughs, announcements are never omitted. This institutionalized ritual of public gossiping does not, however, reveal anything new, since more often than not insiders already know most of the information, which the announcement simply formally confirms as fact. Thus when Velvel announces such things as an engagement, a wedding, a death, or a circumcision, everyone has already learned of it beforehand. The formal announcement provides the opportunity for members to display their informed-insider status either by telling one another that they already knew the information or by adding some extra information (fact or commentary) which Velvel has left unsaid. As any member can tell you, the outsiders and insiders are clearly distinguished during Velvel's announcements; the event thus has significance for everyone in shul.

Velvel is also the charity-gatherer of last resort. His pledge of funds is among the earliest called out during public appeals. His home is on every mendicant's list of stops in Dudley Meadows. Finally, it is Velvel who initiates charity appeals in the shul. When various individuals or agencies wish to make a public appeal to the membership for money, they must get Velvel's permission to do so. While others, like the treasurer or first gabbai, handle charity more directly, it is Velvel who presses the people to give when all else has failed. He stimulates and embraces the charity effort, always being the first to give so that others will follow suit.

Just as he stimulates charity-giving when no one else can, so, too, Velvel assembles a minyan when all others have failed. A trouble-shooter, he remains ever ready to call forth his members by cajolery, trickery, or simple insistence, at times bordering on eloquence. His concern for the minyan is great. Around Passover time, when many of the younger members leave town in a mass exodus to visit family, Velvel explains, "I was going to go away also, but I'm going to have to stay to take care of the shul and the minyan." When Velvel does go away or miss a minyan, he makes sure that everyone knows where he can be reached and the reasons for his absence. In this practice, Velvel does not differ qualitatively from other members, all of whom make sure to account for ab-sences. In the scope of his disclosures, however, Velvel is unique, for he tells everything to everyone rather than simply to a select group of friends, the way most do. This, coupled with his frequent willing-ness to forego vacations in order to come to shul, makes him stand out.

Velvel's desire for well-represented assemblies is not limited to those taking place in the house of prayer. While these are of special concern, since they reflect both collective vitality and frumkeit (strong and frum congregations are expected to have large min-yans), any gathering, whether in the houses of study or assembly or in other Orthodox Jewish settings in Sprawl City (for example, school banquets, rabbinic lectures, Israel Day parades) likewise concerns him. He is forever counting and accounting for shul representation at all sorts of assemblies, and at the very least he makes sure that he himself makes an "official" showing. The members know this, for he often calls them to come to some meeting "because we need some people from shul there." More-over, when members do assemble, they may remind themselves, as one put it during an Israeli Independence Day gathering, "You're not getting together for Velvel's sake but for [in this case] Israel's."

Whenever an assembly is required, either for religious purposes (as when, for example, a member needs a minyan in order to recite the memorial *kaddish* on behalf of a departed kinsman) or for social ones, Velvel is asked to help in collecting people. While he may sometimes succeed in delegating such responsibility to others, in the end he is always prepared to try once more where others fail. He may spend hours on the phone lining up commitments for appearance. His persuasions often consist of little more than a straightforward request, along with an explanation that, without this particular member's attendance, there may be no assembly at all. When he succeeds, as he does more often than not, it is perhaps due less to his persuasive powers than to the fact that he calls members together in the name of the collectivity. His success thus represents the success of the group, which, in being able to assemble itself, remains, as Durkheim suggests, viable, active, and alive.[15]

Finally, as power anointer and lay authority, Velvel makes use of and shares the power the group has invested in him. Unlike the gabbai, however, whose power is restricted to the ritual life of the shul, or the other officers, whose powers are associated with the life of the community as a political structure, the president shares in both worlds. He is at once invested with control over ritual life—as when he takes over the gabbai's role or chooses who will be the halachic virtuosi of the shul by inviting guest rabbis—and over the political life—as when he decides on social affairs, their rate and time of occurrence, and their substance.

In trying "to keep everyone happy," the president must know the limits of his power. He may not exploit his powers for personal benefit, and he must know when his directives have become too authoritarian. Paradoxically, if he succeeds in remaining popular, his power increases; yet, if he exercises that power to excess, he loses popularity. As a result, Velvel finds it almost impossible to make and implement decisions which will change prevailing realities. Hence, as even his strongest supporters agree, the president does not really change much; he just keeps the peace. The task is difficult, and Velvel walks a tightrope between scorn and love, often using jokes and gossip as a balancing pole, a sociability tool whose character will be more fully discussed in subsequent chapters.

In return for his efforts, the congregation gives the president freedoms and prerogatives in all houses of the shul. Some of these have already been mentioned: full access to news and gossip, introduction to all strangers and outsiders, power to anoint, and, finally, a universal affection. In addition, Velvel as president receives some of the most prestigious kibbudim of the year. (Since the president stands as a collective representation, the group, by offering prestations to him, in fact honors itself.) As president, Velvel may enter and leave all conversations with relative ease, since nothing which may openly be said in shul is "none of his business." Moreover, he may, within the house of prayer, pass easily and without explanation from one seat neighborhood to another. In short, in whatever he does, whether praying, studying, or socializing, the president's primary role responsibility remains keeping his congregation happy. As long as he maintains that pursuit, he fully complies with the situational demands of all shul settings.

The Chazan

The cantor, who has already been mentioned several times in passing, is next to be considered. Formally he is called the *sheliach tzibbur*, a Hebrew term denoting "congregational representative." As sheliach tzibbur he is halachically mandated to pray on behalf of the congregation. His role is thus a religious one.

In the informal parlance of the shul, however, the role incumbent is sometimes referred to in an Anglo-Yiddish amalgam as the "person davening," which means simply "the person praying." The Yiddish hints at a social as well as a religious dimension of the role. Moreover, since everyone is supposed to be "davening" in the house of prayer, this title does not definitively distinguish the cantor from the congregation. Indeed, at Kehillat Kodesh, which, unlike larger, more affluent congregations, has no professional cantor to lead prayer, all male members take turns in the role. Unlike the gabbai and the president, the cantor is a relatively temporary role.

The cantor is additionally called *chazan*, a neutral Hebrew and Yiddish term for cantor. In its linguistic bivalence (cf. p. 26, above) the word "chazan" neatly captures both the social and religious dimensions of the role, and it is the term most commonly used by the members to refer to the role.

Essentially the role of chazan requires that a male above the age of thirteen stand at one of the two pulpits and lead the congregation in prayer. He accomplishes this by beginning and ending the stanzas of prayer in a loud voice, at times in song and at other times in a sort of operatic recitative.[16] While he nominally has the power to cue the service through his cantillations (which serve as both benchmarks of progress and signals for proceeding), the chazan must, if he is to abide by situational proprieties, gauge his progress according to cues he receives from his fellow congregants. In short, individuals cue him so that he may cue the group. As he leads, he is also led; the interactional interdependence between congregation and chazan is thus perfectly synergetic.

The quasi-chazan

The mechanism by which the chazan learns when to end one prayer and lead into the next involves a form of aural communication between him and the congregation. No commonly accepted term seems to exist for this mechanism, perhaps because its existence has largely gone unnoticed, except perhaps by the ethnographer. Instrumentally, it consists of a prelusory singing by the members of the same lines and words the chazan is about to repeat. In a sense, the members become quasi-chazanim (plural), in that they anticipate not only the words but often the tune which the chazan traditionally uses at the ends of various prayers. The only community term that I have been able to find which describes at least a part of this quasi-chazanic activity is one suggested by one member who is prominent for both his chazanic and quasi-chazanic abilities. He called the process *oistzelozen*, a Yiddish term which means "to let oneself go." The Yiddishism again suggests that the term refers to a social more than a liturgical phenomenon.

Be that as it may, such quasi-chazanic activity, while manifestly offering a way to let oneself go in prayer, also acts to make the chazan aware that the congregation has reached the end of the prayer and is waiting for him to give the cue to continue. He in turn, guided by one or two prominent quasi-chazanim and his own general idea of how long a particular prayer ought to take, repeats the proper words as the congregation moves on to the next prayer. Experience teaches would-be quasi-chazanim that a cue that comes too early will not be picked up. Similarly, the chazan learns that failure to pick up on the proper quasi-chazanic cues subjects him either to outright requests to go on (an embarrassment at best) or to general criticism as a poor chazan (leading, at worst, to exclusion from the kibbud of the chazan role).

Quasi-chazanic activity should not be confused with communal singing, which involves a uniform tune and set of words which everyone engages in together. Such singing, which plays a very different role, will be discussed later. Unlike this singing, in which one can perhaps project himself only by singing more loudly than others or by harmonizing, all quasi-chazanic activity necessarily implies that one sings a kind of solo. Of course, not every person can have his quasi-chazanic activity be accepted as the ultimate cue. Nor does each quasi-chazan get to finish his singsong, especially if the chazan himself begins his repetition right in the middle of someone's quasi-chazanic activity. Indeed, every quasi-chazan, no matter how inspired, blends his voice into the general hum of the congregational prayer as soon as the chazan begins to sing.

Quasi-chazanic activity occurs for the most part on Sabbaths and holy days, when prayers proceed at a relatively leisurely pace. It may all but disappear on weekdays, when both chazan and congregation rush to finish the prayers quickly so that they may either get to work or get home to supper. One should add that when there is no quasi-chazanic activity, as is the case during some of the weekday services, the chazan provides the only cues— though others may provide indicators, such as lip movement, standing or sitting, and eye gestures, to name a few.

Besides its function in helping to pace the chazan, quasi-chazanic activity has certain other latent functions. A prominent display of it attests to its practitioner's liturgical knowledge as well as to his familiarity with the shul's prayer practices; both indicate that in this setting he is neither neophyte, sojourner, nor outsider. This latent function is particularly useful to strangers and guests, who, being in the shul for the first time, want to indicate their Orthodox Jewishness and reap the benefits of an insider's status. Often the loudest quasi-chazanim, these strangers call attention to themselves by managing to give off impressions which emphasize their situational belongingness. Such quasi-chazanic activity often cues the gabbai or president to offer the stranger the kibbud of acting as the chazan for the next section of the prayers, a sure way to be universally noticed, communally embraced. In the house of prayer, men can sing themselves into the action.

Another latent function lies in the fact that the quasi-chazan may by his action project, at least to those within hearing distance, the demeanor of someone intensely involved in prayer, someone who is frum. As such, he displays himself not as someone who is incidentally praying in an Orthodox shul but rather as one who is self-determinately present and spiritually at home there.

Because quasi-chazanic activity is a relatively simple way to exhibit frumkeit, its reliability may at times be doubted by those evaluating it as a signal. As is the case with many other performances, actors may try to misrepresent themselves.[17] Accordingly, the other congregants review and evaluate quasi-chazanic activity in light of other communications, both directly given and indirectly given off by the performer, which must confirm and substantiate the impression he is seeking to create. In the absence of such demonstrations, his quasi-chazanic activity is interpreted as a masquerade, and this calls all his consequent actions into question; he is then characterized as alien rather than autochthonous.

On certain holy days when the liturgy becomes amended or changed, quasi-chazanic activity serves two additional functions. By singing out the first few words of the additional or altered prayers, the quasi-chazan ostensibly reminds those within the sound of his voice (including, of course, the chazan) to make the necessary changes in their prayers; latently, however, he indicates his alertness in independently remembering to make the liturgical changes called for by the occasion—an alertness inevitably associated with the communally esteemed qualities of knowledgeability and presence of mind. Accordingly, it is not unusual to hear people racing through their prayers simply to be the first, among those around them, to sing out such liturgical changes.

It should also be pointed out that quasi-chazanic activity is exclusively a male prerogative (yet it is not exclusively for *adult* males, since children engage in it too; but, when they do so, they seldom succeed in pacing the chazan—another sign of their relative powerlessness to determine action in the setting). Women's solo voices are never heard during communal prayer. Indeed, women, here as in most shul matters, seem to have very little to say with regard to the cuing or pacing of the service. If it is too fast or too slow for their tastes, their only recourse is to complain to their husbands, who may act for them. Sometimes a woman will complain to her husband in the ladies' foyer, asking him to speed things up, slow them down, or perhaps see to it that they become loud enough for the women in back to hear. Only in this indirect way can their will at all affect tefilah sheh be tzibbur.

Another point deserves to be made with respect to this activity. At times it may take the place of conversation during the prayers. The same person or persons who were talking a moment before may, when such talking is halachically prohibited, engage instead in quasi-chazanic activity. The one activity seems to be transformed into the other, as if the person were compensating for his prior inattention to the prayers with a kind of spiritual catching-up and intensification of involvement—which quasi-chazanic activity suggests.

One must recognize that quasi-chazanic activity seems to arise out of the experience of tefilah sheh be tzibbur without being either a totally conscious or even formalized practice. Indeed, few who practice it are aware of either its function or its implications. As Durkheim has put it, "which of us knows all the words of the language he speaks and the entire signification of each?"[18]

While essentially an informal role open to all adult male claimants, the position of quasi-chazan is at two points in the service reserved exclusively for the rabbinic or religious leader of the shul—at Kehillat Kodesh a position in part filled by Rabbi Housmann, the retired ritual animal-slaughterer. Without a cue from such a religious authority, neither the *Shema*, the prayer affirming God's commitment to the people of Israel, nor the *Amida*, the silent meditational prayer around which every service is oriented, may be consummated by the chazan. At Kehillat Kodesh the chazan traditionally waits for Housmann to finish these prayers before going ahead with the other prayers. The wait is longer than during other prayers because *only* Housmann's quasi-chazanic cue frees the chazan to continue. The other congregants often complain about the duration of the silent wait for Housmann to finish. The latter, aware of this dissatisfaction, has struck a compromise with traditions. Perhaps in the spirit of conciliation, or perhaps out of a sense of reality—which suggests that, if he is not careful, he will overstep the threshold of the group's tolerance for his situational demand for respect and bring about an end to his *de facto* position as religious leader—or for whatever reason, Housmann does not ask the chazan to wait for him during the morning weekday prayers, when everyone is in a hurry to leave shul and get to work. Furthermore, the careful observer will notice that during weeknight prayers, when the congregation clearly has little patience for waiting, Housmann only simulates prayer (he leafs through the pages of the siddur in pace with the chazan but does not move his lips, as is required for prayer) and then mumbles aloud the final lines in order to cue the chazan. Indeed, in a moment of candor, Housmann once admitted to me that he usually prays at home after shul because the tefilah sheh be tzibbur goes too quickly for him. He attends the prayer services out of a sense of communal obligation, only to help make the minyan, and, one might add, perhaps to retain his prerogatives as rabbinic leader, for these are reaffirmed at each service that the people wait for him to finish the Shema and Amida.

Returning to the chazan, one may classify the role in terms of two distinct taxonomies: (1) variations in the personal style of role enactment and (2) variations in the social meanings attached to the role.

The first category includes a range of ideal types. At one end are those cantors best described as "hams." These are men who not only know the liturgy well but ostentatiously display this knowledge by turning a maximum number of prayer repetitions into bravura performances of arias. To Kehillat Kodesh this type of chazan is anathema; as he warbles his way through the prayers, his performance is often greeted with snickers, knowing glances, grimaces, grumbles, complaints, and a general response somewhere between ridicule and anger. If the ham is also a good singer, his ostentation may at times be overlooked and tolerated at Kehillat Kodesh; yet, more often than not, he will be passed over in favor of a speedier and less obtrusive performer.

At the other end of the range is the quick and efficient chazan who either sings or says the prayers with a minimum of exhibitionism. He leaps liturgically forward at the first cue of quasi-chazanic activity and therefore is commonly selected to lead both weekday prayers and prayers which end fasts, where the emphasis is on rapidity rather than kavannah. Such prayers, like a quick lunch, cannot be skipped; but also like a quick lunch, they cannot be lingered over.

This chazan need not have a pleasing voice, but he is expected to know the liturgy and its customary applications at Kehillat Kodesh and to know where he can rush and where he must retain a modicum of proprietary slowness (strangers, to whom no such expectations can be attached, seldom qualify for this kibbud). Although suited for the weekday tefilah sheh be tzibbur, this chazan leaves something to be desired for the more leisurely prayers of Sabbath and holy days, when a chazan must not only move the service ahead but also stir the religious sentiments of the congregation.

Somewhere between these two extremes lies the sweet-voiced chazan who is relatively efficient in the management of time while sounding neither rushed nor uninvolved. He can sing well in solo but chooses more often to lead the congregation in group singing. As the congregation joins him, not only does their prayer become intensified as the singing captures more and more of their attention and involvement, but their positive opinions of the chazan and his leadership qualities intensify also. A "good chazan" is one who "knows a lot of good tunes" and can use them to inspire the congregation in prayer with him. He is the one most likely to be selected to fill the role whenever kavannah is a mandatory appurtenance of prayer, as it is in services which are important both liturgically and religiously, i.e., on Sabbaths and holy days. On those most holy of days, Rosh Hashonah (New Year) and Yom

Kippur (the Day of Judgment), when involvement in prayer is greatest for the greatest number of people, this type of chazan is generally deemed an absolute institutional necessity.

The second category of chazanim includes those who receive this kibbud not because of their ability to play the role satisfactorily but because of the dictates of halacha, tradition, and social circumstance. Such role incumbents are those who have *chiyuvim*, religious or social obligations to lead the prayers (in practice the line between the religious and the social becomes blurred). Holders of such obligations are themselves called chiyuvim ("chiyuv" in the singular), their obligation consuming their identity; chief among them are persons who must recite the kaddish. As chazan one may recite this prayer more often and thus derive additional spiritual benefits. Group norms, as well as Jewish tradition and halacha, demand communal assistance in the performance of religious ritual and the acquisition of spiritual benefit. These norms stand behind the appointment of such cantors, and theoretically a shul explains its raison d'être in terms of its ability to fulfill these halachic requirements. Allowing someone with a chiyuv to be chazan is an expression of this traditional communal responsibility for individual ritual performance.

At Kehillat Kodesh the chiyuv is given priority in being the chazan, especially during weekday prayers. Not all chiyuvim, however, are alike. Someone who becomes bereaved is a mourner and has a chiyuv to say kaddish daily for the next eleven months. Another kind of chiyuv attaches to someone who has a *yartzeit*, the anniversary of a bereavement. Let us refer here to the former mourner as a "chiyuv" and the latter as a "yartzeit." The yartzeit receives precedence over the chiyuv and the chiyuv over the plain congregant in the prerogatives of chazan. The chiyuv retains his rights and privileges only during the weekday prayers; while he may be chazan on Sabbaths and holy days, his prerogative then is challengeable. The yartzeit retains unchallengeable privileges even on a Sabbath or holy day; this leads at times to the appointment of a ham chazan praying simply because he has a yartzeit. The chiyuv or yartzeit who becomes a chazan does not receive a full-fledged kibbud and its attendant status enhancement the way the individual does who is freely chosen. Of course, the fact that the gabbai knows that one has an obligation to say kaddish is an indication of one's association, and in a sense this status as an insider enhances one. Nevertheless, to repeat, a compulsory kibbud such as this one does not retain its full measure of honor and value.

Still another possible taxonomic distinction in the chazan role crosscuts the two categories already described. This distinction is between the weekday and the Sabbath, or holy-day, chazan. As in other weekday ritual performances, the role of weekday chazan is a semiprecious kibbud, a social fact reflected in the few and perfunctory audience responses following the end of one's tenure in the role. A Sabbath or holy-day tenure in the chazan role conversely brings with it attention, thanks, honor, and all the benefits of a full kibbud. Accordingly, an individual's aspirations to the role depend on whether he is to be a weekday chazan or a Sabbath and holy-day chazan. The same person who, often by elaborate quasi-chazanic "broadcasting," pursues the cantorial kibbud on Sabbaths and holy days may refuse selection on a weekday.

As leader of communal prayers, the chazan may easily serve as an external object upon which collective sentiments may be focused; as such, he may come, at times, to represent the group. Nowhere is this situation more clearly manifested than in the common selection of the most popular chazanim on occasions such as holy days or celebrations, when many guests are present in shul and the congregation wishes to present the best possible impression of itself.

As collective representation, the chazan may at times symbolize the group's existence. This possibility is neatly exhibited by the appointment of a weekday chazan even when no minyan exists and when, accordingly, there is no halachic obligation for such an appointment.[19] The group insists on playing such scenes as if there were indeed the minyan mandatory for tefilah sheh be tzibbur. The chazan, here more socially vital than ritually necessary, signals to those assembled that, in spite of their collective insufficiency, they ought still to consider themselves a group and thus require cantorial direction. By his presence he transforms tefilah sheh be yochid into tefilah sheh be tzibbur—if not halachically, then socially. He sustains the social fiction that a minyan exists, even long after the clock indicates that legitimate hope for a minyan must be abandoned.

Some discussion of the minyan and its meaning to the congregation is relevant here. At Kehillat Kodesh one of the most constantly expressed communal concerns is continued maintenance of a well-attended minyan. On Sabbaths and holy days, times almost exclusively consecrated to Jewish concern and involvement, gathering a minyan is not a problem, and one can then count on assembling far more than the minimum quorum of ten. These congregations become the standards by which the members gauge their shul's ability to assemble a community. The daily morning and evening minyan is quite another story. This is the tefilah sheh be tzibbur which takes place at a time when most men are enmeshed in their secular and occupational lives—the time when they stand with one foot outside the Jewish world. As I have already pointed out, these minyans suffer from rapid prayer, which often serves less as collective worship than as a simple reaffirmation that the group exists—even between Sabbaths.

Few attend the daily minyan, yet everyone seems to care about its existence. An announcement from Velvel that the daily minyan is floundering often brings forth expressions of concern from the membership. Members often use the criterion of the presence or absence of a daily minyan in other Orthodox shuls as a measure of the associated communities' strength or weakness. In criticizing the Happiton shul, for example, one member pointed out, "They never have a minyan during the week; and, if they do, it's 'cause they pay the beggars to come." Another says,

> I'll tell you why people who move here to Dudley Meadows come to Kehillat Kodesh—and I say this with a minimum of *gaivoh* [haughtiness]. Most of the people who move into this area—all right, so they're transients here for one or two years, I'm not talking about that. But most of the people move here because of this shul, because we got a good minyan—especially on Shabbos—that you can count on. I mean, we got the only real shul around.

The shul must have a minyan; without one, it is not a "real shul."

Furthermore, the minyan is testimony to the members' public commitment to being frum. In a sermonette about the importance of the minyan, for example, Housmann says:

> There are three sins which a Jew must die before doing: murder, adultery, and idolatry. The *gemara* [Talmud] says that if the entire Jewish community is being threatened with no minyan, then a person must die before letting that minyan die. The existence of a daily minyan is a way to practice *kiddush hashem* [sanctification of the (divine) name].

These words were met at first with an embarrassed silence and later with suggestions of how to improve the minyan attendance.

Again and again Velvel appeals for the minyan. The members have tried various approaches. They have tried appeals for each male to "donate" time for a service and pledge himself to come. There are telephone calls before each minyan. A yartzeit may draw upon his entire network of friendships for a minyan on the day of his yartzeit. This practice often results in expressions of bitterness on the part of the regulars, who resent such occasional attendance. As one said, in a mixture of joking and anger at the end of one yartzeit minyan, "See you again next year, boys."

Any effort to form a second and separate minyan—for example, one for latecomers or one for those who prefer a more quickly paced service—is met with much criticism. "That would kill the shul." "That would be the end of us." Indeed, one man who once began such a minyan was expelled from the shul and could not come back until he promised not to take on any shul office which would empower him to affect the minyan again. The minyan, like its organizing group, must remain one and indivisible.

In his discussion of the elementary forms of religion, Durkheim describes collective representations as phenomena which "are the work of the group" and "have within them a sort of force of moral ascendancy, in virtue of which they impose themselves upon individual minds." Moreover, their "stability" and ascendancy reflect or represent the strength of that group.[20]

The concern for the minyan, its power to represent the group, and the quality of "moral ascendancy," which suggests that one sins by not participating in it, all seem to point to a conclusion that the minyan is a collective representation of the shul. The strong minyan represents a strong collectivity, just as the frum minyan attests to a frum community. When there is a consistent and well-attended Orthodox minyan, the members take it as a sign of group strength and translate that feeling into personal triumph. This personal involvement is particularly marked for those members whose identity is closely intertwined with the shul—members like Velvel and Housmann, who themselves represent the collectivity. The success of the minyan indicates the existence of the religious community.

Yet not everyone comes to the minyan; and, when people come, their prayer does not always exhibit extravagant frumkeit. No simple answer exists for this paradox. The same man who will complain, "We've got to have a better minyan; I just don't understand it," explains his consistent absence with a series of excuses about work, time, and so on.

Perhaps the answer lies somewhere in the fact that the men, who alone can make the minyan, are, for reasons which cannot be deciphered within the boundaries of this book's analytic frame, involved in a secular world to which they are also highly committed.

During the week, secular and religious commitments compete and collide, with the result that people do not always come to shul yet continue to believe in the need for a strong minyan. Or, when men do come to the minyan, their prayer is diluted by their rush to reenter the secular world of work. The influence of each world grows weak in the face of the other. Only on Sabbath and holy days, when the Jewish world is transcendent, does the conflict to some degree subside.

In short, because the maintenance of the daily minyan represents one of the most crucial problems for a group which seeks to be both modern and Orthodox at once, concern about it crystallizes the problems generated by biworldly (i.e., Jewish and secular) demands. These contradictions of dual involvement will be seen in other aspects of shul life and will be returned to later.

To round out the discussion of the chazan role, which stimulated this discussion of the minyan, the child chazan ought to be mentioned. This chazan holds but a shadow of the power and status associated with the adult chazan. He is the young boy, usually between the ages of five and eleven, who takes over the lead in singing the last few prayers of the Sabbath and holy-day morning prayers. This boy in a sense plays *at* being chazan and is thereby socialized into one day playing the role in reality. This first chazanic duty, although not part of formal religious ritual, is an institutionalized *rite de passage* for the young Kehillat Kodesh boy. He has perhaps earlier passed his first few other *rites de passage* in the shul. These include, first, coming to shul and sitting with his father; second, having his first kibbud, which consists of opening the ark while another child acts as chazan; and, third, becoming the chazan himself. While halacha makes essentially no distinctions among boys younger than thirteen, the institution clearly and strictly does.

The child chazan has become a necessary part of the Sabbath and holy-day morning service, the prayers allotted to his leadership being systematically avoided by the regular adult chazan. Situationally, it is not really clear whether the child chazan is receiving a kibbud or is simply relieving the adult chazan, whose adult stature is thus accented. Perhaps it would be most accurate to say that the practice, which has become an institutional ritual, is a blend of status enhancement for both the child and the preceding adult, the former indicating his growing entrée into the adult population and its associated higher status, the latter exhibiting his position as full-fledged chazan, with the honor attached to that role.

In the discussion of the chazan and the minyan, two other house-of-prayer roles have been mentioned: the chiyuv and the rabbinic or religious authority. Both these roles deserve more characterization. Let us return first to the chiyuv.

The Chiyuv and the Yartzeit

It has already been pointed out that the chiyuv is given certain prerogatives by the congregation; for example, in recognition of his ritual needs he often has guaranteed access to the chazan kibbud. This easy access, however, devalues the enhancement qualities of the kibbud. Like other valuables, a kibbud has worth in part because it is relatively scarce and not easily or habitually received; but the chiyuv may take the role of chazan automatically, without even a formal appointment. Honor has for him become duty, the latter being far less desirable than the former. Indeed, one might say that the acquisition of kibbudim on weekdays is much easier for everyone and so loses some value for the entire congregation, but never as much as for the chiyuv.

In return for the unchallengeable right to certain kibbudim the congregation seems to make certain informal demands on the chiyuv. Among these is the expectation that he will be present at every minyan, a guarantor of the quorum. The members make this expectation manifest in various ways. They may obliquely remind the chiyuv that he is expected at the minyan; for example, Velvel said to one chiyuv who had failed to show up for the evening minyan for quite a few days, "You know we are getting together a minyan at 6:30 for mincha and ma'ariv every day now." Here Velvel was not only notifying the chiyuv of the time of the daily minyan but also pointing out that his absence had been noticed.

If such circumlocutory warnings fail to bring results, members may start to joke with the chiyuv about his absence and gossip about it as well. The delinquent chiyuv who does not settle his social accounts payable, who does not understand the warning underneath the jokes or receive and heed the gossiped message, will come to shul and find himself stripped of many of his prerogatives as a mourner. One such member, who had stayed away from the minyan despite all efforts to bring him back, found that when he did at times return to the daily minyan he was no longer accorded the right to be chazan. His kibbud was no longer taken for granted; it had to be shared with others. Although most persons with a chiyuv seem to stop short of this extreme, those who approach it do so late in their eleven months of mourning, when the memory of bereavement is not as strong as in the early months. Furthermore, the yartzeit never misses a minyan on the anniversary of bereavement. Evidently the immediate loss of kin or the renewed memory of a death is enough to maintain religious involvement and stimulate minyan attendance even in the face of everyday secular demands.

The chiyuv who seeks to maintain his rights and prerogatives in the face of less-than-total repayment for kibbud on his part (that is, in spite of his poor minyan attendance) finds that, in place of his presence, he must reciprocate for the continued prestation of kibbud by offering an explanation for his absence. Thus, a chiyuv may explain that he sometimes attends a minyan in town, near his place of work, or that he must leave for work too early to make the minyan, or that he has been out of town or ill. At times the explanations become almost confessional in nature, as in the case of one man, who volunteered, "I really wanted to come yesterday; I don't know what happened. I planned on it, but somehow I just couldn't get out of bed in the morning. You know, when it's dark and cold and. . . ."

Implicit in such explanations made to other members of the daily minyan is that these others can somehow forgive the absence. Indeed, those who attend the minyan daily—the so-called regulars—have a power beyond what might be expected of simple members holding no higher office. An examination of the social meaning attached to these regulars indicates that these men, by their constant attendance, do not simply fulfill their own religious needs and exhibit their own involvement with the Kehillat Kodesh group; by maintaining the minyan they also come to stand for it and, in turn, for the entire collectivity which it represents. In thus affirming group life, they become collective symbols, with a power greater than their own individual being.

In return, regulars seem to expect, though not consciously, some social repayment for this service. Such repayment comes in the form of (1) the power to negatively sanction the absent chiyuv (e.g., by gossip and joking), (2) the power to forgive (which Thomas has called "one of the functions of the community")[21] or to excuse others from attendance, including the chiyuv (often accomplished by lending a sympathetic ear to excuses), and (3) increased status by being known as a regular—a status recognized whenever an appeal is made to bolster minyan size ("We all should be like Mr. Eppess, who comes all the time; we'll miss him when he goes on vacation").[22]

Explanations or apologies for having missed prayer services must be strategically handled by the chiyuv who wishes to hold on to his kibbudim. He cannot appear to be paying simple lip service to an ideal that he does not really believe in; rather, he must convince his listeners of his sincerity. Here, however, as in so many other circumstances of life, action speaks more convincingly than words, and information given off is often more believable than information given directly. In short, no amount of explanation can compensate for habitual absence.

While in many synagogues the daily minyan is often a collection of chiyuvim and yartzeits, at Kehillat Kodesh such participants are in the minority. Were they in the majority, few would be able to receive daily kibbudim. As it is, when more than one chiyuv is present, the chiyuvim decide among themselves, often on the basis of age or some other status measure, who will be chazan or will receive other kibbudim. When the chiyuvim are relatively equal in social stature, they may simply alternate, one being leader at one service and another on other occasions.

The responsibility of the yartzeit deserves more attention. I have pointed out above that the yartzeit at Kehillat Kodesh never misses the morning, afternoon, and evening minyans on the anniversary of his bereavement. For the man involved in an occupational life which makes heavy demands on his time, such shul attendance is not always easy and may require sacrifices in the secular world. Nonetheless, the impetus to say the *kaddish* (memorial prayer), which may be recited only during tefilah sheh be tzibbur, seems to be quite strong. Indeed, in this respect the Orthodox Jews of Kehillat Kodesh are not too different from other Jews, for whom the kaddish is also a stimulus to visit shul. For some Jews, however, such a visit is one of the few made during the year; for the Kehillat Kodesh Jew, it is, on the contrary, but one more special event on a very busy Jewish calendar.

An examination of the yartzeit illuminates both the social networks and the substance of religious interdependence within the community. As stated earlier, the weekday minyan is often difficult to assemble. The person observing yartzeit is more often than not an insider and is thus aware that, to be assured of halachically acceptable tefilah sheh be tzibbur, he must himself assemble ten men on the day of his bereavement anniversary. This he does. He begins to solicit members for the minyan, by telephone and in person, saying something like, "Look, I have yartzeit next Tuesday. Do you think that you could make the minyan that day?"

Most of the people asked will agree to come. Unsure of how many regulars he can count on—in part because he is not one himself—the yartzeit will try to line up a full quorum of ten and then find that the minyan on his day turns out to be a relatively large group of seventeen or eighteen.

What makes this process sociologically interesting is the particular people who appear for a particular yartzeit. These persons tend to be seat neighbors and/or friends. Indeed, the yartzeit occasion is often a good time to discover various communal webs of affiliation as well as friendship networks. For the regulars it is a simple thing to figure out who has come as a favor to the yartzeit and who has come for other reasons. In fact, many regulars, in gossip among themselves, can account for each new face; and, knowing of a particular upcoming yartzeit, they can accurately predict who will turn up to fill out the minyan.

In return for their attendance, one's friends may make a reciprocal demand for a minyan on the day of their yartzeit. Thus:

> Zinger: I want to thank you for making it to the minyan today.
> Lonsky: Sure. You know I have yartzeit next month on the fifteenth. Can you make it?
> Zinger: I'll be there; I owe it to you—just remind me the Shabbos before.

Although short of being a written contract, this agreement is no less binding; on Lonsky's yartzeit, Zinger appeared, as promised.

Regulars, of course, are always assured of a minyan on their yartzeit, since they have, over time, built up credits by their consistent minyan attendance. This "insurance" is one of the benefits of their status.

The aid one receives in performing the religious rites of yartzeit must be seen as a part of that larger commitment by the members to assist one another in the performance of their religious duties. As already mentioned, this is one way in which they affirm themselves as a community. Helping to make a minyan is perhaps the most common type of such religious assistance. Coming to shul on the occasion of a friend's yartzeit is one instance of this practice, but there are others.

According to the halacha, for prayer to qualify as tefilah sheh be tzibbur, at least six of the minimum ten people present at a minyan must be actively engaged in prayer. Yet this law also implies that some who do not pray may still be counted. They must, however, respond to certain obligatory prayers during the course of the service, and so they are necessary participants. This allows people to come to a minyan in spite of the fact that they may already have prayed elsewhere. Such persons manifestly come to aid those who have need of a minyan to perform the rite of public prayer. As suggested earlier, there may be other, concurrent, reasons for attending (as in the case of Housmann); but at least on a manifest level of participation, some of the people come only to help others get a minyan together.

Another variation of this kind of aid occurs when persons stay in shul because their exit would mean that only nine others would remain and the minyan would be destroyed. Thus, during morning weekday services, several members pray more quickly than the rest because they must leave earlier to catch a train or get to work. When there are not enough people present to allow such exit without destroying the minyan, these members will stay in spite of the inconvenience. Indeed, no one comes to the minyan if he cannot, in a pinch, make such sacrifices. Here, again, the manifest explanation is that the members stay to aid others in the performance of their religious needs; latent sociological explanations flow, as already suggested, from the collective attachment to the minyan as symbol.

One member, in offering me his reasons for coming to a minyan even when he does not need it for his own spiritual satisfaction, explains, "I just wanted to, you know, set an atmosphere of *achrayus*." *Achrayus* is a Hebrew word denoting "responsibility" and connoting a religious responsibility in particular. This sense of achrayus does not seem to extend to other congregations; Kehillat Kodesh members do not as readily aid the Happiton and Ram Sholom congregations with their minyans. Only if one's friend is a member of these other shuls will one help in getting a minyan together there for a chiyuv.

Assisting at the mikva is another way in which members help one another perform the rituals that are important to them. Immersion requires the assistance of another person, who must watch to see that (1) the immersion is, as mandated by halacha, total and (2) that it does not result in drowning. Normally, a woman hired by the Sprawl City Orthodox Jewish community aids individual women in the performance of their ritual duty. At one point, however, this woman had to be hospitalized for an extended period of time. The responsibility of assistance fell back upon the community, which met the need by sending out a corps of volunteers, who took over the task on a rotating schedule. No one questioned the importance of helping another Jew in the observance of halacha.

In similar vein, a *chevra kadisha*, burial society, assists individuals in the preparation and burial of their dead. Here, too, at least one of the underlying concerns involves aiding another in the exercise of his religious duties.

Money may also be given for such ends. When at Passover time the president announced an appeal for funds in order to send *matzah*, the dietary staple of the holy day, to Soviet Jews, who had no other source for the unleavened bread, the congregation responded generously, exhibiting, among other things, a concern with helping the Russian Jews in the performance of religious ritual.

In summary then, Kehillat Kodesh members are prepared for and accept the responsibility to band together to minister to the religious and ritual demands of others. Those who give and those who get help in part serve to define the parameters of their community. Some persons deserve a generalized kind of help— perhaps money or public support—simply as members of the larger Jewish community, while others receive more intensified aid, as in the case of shul members. The more extensive and effortful the aid, the more communally linked are the individuals. As Schmalenbach has pointed out, "Community, then, can be characterized as that order of social coherence which develops on the basis of natural interdependence."[23] For Orthodox Jews, assistance in ritual performance constitutes one of the bases of such interdependence. While ritual demands place such interdependence in broad outline here, it is in fact subject to multiple restatement and reaffirmation in other contexts of Kehillat Kodesh life, as will be detailed later.

The Rabbinic Authority

The rabbinic role deserves some discussion. This role, which at one time in history was primarily that of teacher and scholar, has in contemporary times become enlarged (or decreased, depending on one's perspective) to include preacher, halachic arbitrator, and sometimes even symbolic model Jew. Along with such formal role characteristics has come a host of informal, yet equally important, expectations. A detailed description of the substance of the role must, however, be preceded by some attention to the issue of rabbinic authority. It is his legitimate authority—ordination—that transforms the learned, articulate, and observant Jew into "rabbi."

Ultimately, the source of rabbinic authority is halachic expertise.

At its highest levels of discipline, this understanding of halacha brings with it ontological apprehension (in both senses of the term); coupled with Orthodox Jewish ordination (that is, anointment by another Orthodox rabbi), it makes one a rabbi. For the rabbi who would assert an additional authority as spiritual leader of a synagogue congregation, political sagacity and pleasant personality are informal, yet no less mandatory, prerequisites for successful role enactment. Nevertheless, scholarship remains the nub of Orthodox rabbinic authority. "Historically, traditionally, ideally learning has been and is regarded as the primary value"; even in the face of "economic pressures and outside influences," which have, over time, somewhat eroded the emphasis on scholarship as a prerequisite for rabbinic authority, Orthodox Jews (perhaps because of a relative isolation from outside influences) have maintained respect for, and ideological conviction about, the importance of learning, especially for their rabbis.[24]

The rabbi, as the epitome of learning, shares in the strength of that ideological belief and thereby commands and receives respect. This respect may be displayed in various ways: from the relatively minor deference exhibited in the chazanic wait for the rabbi's prayer cue to such homage as standing upon his entrance into the room, from the dramatic granting to him the most prestigious kibbudim to following mention of his name with acronyms of blessing.

Among Orthodox Jews, authority cannot be separated from respect. The latter must regularly affirm the former. In the house of prayer, respect becomes translated into kibbudim, of whose regular receipt the rabbi in authority may be assured.

Of course, not all rabbis receive the same respect, nor do they hold the same degree of authority. Furthermore, not all are equally learned and hence do not equally fulfill the demands of the role. Thus, in spite of the fact that, in matters of religious concern, rabbinic authority is final, the authority of particular role incumbents is not. Rabbis' scholarly reputations both rise and fall. In America the chief or town rabbi with absolute authority no longer exists. In the contemporary religious panorama, persons are free to choose almost any rabbi to be their guide and arbiter on religious matters. To be sure, the choice is limited to Orthodox rabbis. Even with that limitation, however, there is a complex hierarchy of rabbinic authorities to whom the members of Kehillat Kodesh may appeal.

This hierarchy ranges from the local *de facto* authority, Rabbi

Housmann, to the more renowned international leadership of such rabbis as the chief rabbi of the State of Israel. The Orthodox Jewish community, being both highly endogamous and closely knit (relative to other Jewish sects), finds no rabbi so distant that he cannot be appealed to legitimately in one way or another—either as kin or acquaintance. Like members of a royal family, many rabbis are either related to one another directly or by marriage; however, their families are large enough (perhaps because of strict adherence to the dictum "Be fruitful and multiply") to enable many lay Jews to share, or at least claim to share, kinship with them. Appeal to such outside authorities makes it possible to circumvent a local decision with another more to one's preference. Thus a member may disregard a local halachic interpretational ukase with the response, "I know that Rabbi Gutman decided that the halacha [requires thus and so], and I always follow his opinions."

To better comprehend these possibilities of choice in rabbinic authority (a choice which, once made, must be adhered to consistently), one must understand that rabbinic responsa may be divided into two categories: *machmir* and *maikail*. Machmir denotes very strict interpretations of the law, often requiring difficult personal adjustments for their fulfillment. Maikail refers to the more lenient and liberal interpretations which seek out and find legal loopholes, using, rather than overlooking, legal ambiguities. The modern Orthodox Jews of Kehillat Kodesh seem to prefer the rabbi whose responsa qualify as maikail. Of course, what is considered maikail for one may be machmir for another. Be that as it may, regardless of the actual substance of the rabbinic decision, the accepted way for a shul member to characterize his choice of rabbinic authority is "maikail."

Accordingly, when a rabbi from outside the Dudley Meadows area was invited to Kehillat Kodesh to respond to halachic questions pertaining to the upcoming Passover holy days (this episode will be reviewed in greater detail in chapter 8), he was enthusiastically received because his decisions were lenient and in tune with the members' style of Jewish observance. As he spoke, members turned to one another smiling, and one or two whispered, "He's good; he's maikail."

The nature of these halachic questions (*shailos*, as they are traditionally referred to in Hebrew) is not manifestly theological or philosophical but rather practical, dealing with the everyday implementation and application of halacha and resolution of its legal gray areas. This is not to say that such questions (as will be seen later) have no theological significance for either the inquirers or the respondents. On the contrary, the ability to apply halacha to even the most mundane realities of everyday existence is precisely the way in which Orthodox Jews may experience theological truths. Halacha enables such Jews to sacralize everyday life along the lines suggested by their theology.

Halacha is the rabbi's stock-in-trade. If authority is at the heart of the rabbinic role, then halachic virtuosity is the sine qua non of authority. Yet halacha may very often carry its own authority, without rabbinic interpretation. Such is the case at Kehillat Kodesh, where halachic virtuosity among the members is by no means uncommon. Accordingly, for the members of this shul, a rabbi—to paraphrase Gershwin—is a sometime thing. Or, as one member put it, "In America everything has a season; so there's a season for rabbis too."[25]

The congregation, since it employs no full-time rabbi, makes its way through the everyday demands of halacha by calling on the virtuosity of its members and the traditions which are part of the institutional structure of Orthodox shuls ("They do it thus and so at other Orthodox shuls"). When particular needs cannot be met in this manner, the Sprawl City Yeshiva often supplies a willing rabbi to take on the temporary mantle of religious leadership. In this role he preaches on special Sabbaths and holy days of the Jewish calendar, arbitrates major halachic questions, and sometimes acts as model Jew.

In addition to such situationally specific needs for a rabbi, structural elements of tefilah sheh be tzibbur, such as those cited in the discussion of quasi-chazanic activity, demand some sort of everyday rabbinic presence. Here the "rabbi" need not be one who fulfills all the demands of the role; rather he must be one who can stand for a full-fledged rabbi. It is in this everyday task that Rabbi Housmann serves. He helps in affirming the ad hoc and spontaneous halachic decisions which must be made in the course of everyday shul life: Can such and such a prayer still be said, now that it is past twilight time? Does such and such a liturgical omission constitute a transgressive act? Such questions, which in their situational context have an almost rhetorical nature, are answered by Housmann. Invariably his decision is the one upon which the majority has already agreed, but Housmann can offer the authority of rabbinic affirmation.

In addition to these needs, Housmann fulfills many of the informal institutional expectations of the rabbinic role. These include soliciting charity, giving out alms to the poor who appeal directly to the shul, visiting the sick and bereaved, and, perhaps most important, acting as religious representative of the congregation at ritual events. This last responsibility explains the regular invitation of Housmann to circumcisions, bar mitzvahs, weddings, and funerals of members.

In return for fulfilling these responsibilities, Housmann is allowed to call himself the *moreh d'asroh* ("congregational guide"), a title traditionally reserved for spiritual leaders. Not all members, however, feel that he fulfills the minimum demands of the role; some complain that he wants more than he gives. This feeling has led some members to talk about hiring a full-time rabbi in his place. Others quietly challenge his title of rabbi by innuendo, suggesting, for example, that they have never heard the name of the institution which ordained Housmann as a rabbi.

While Housmann treads a dangerous line, often exploiting his prerogatives, he is able to maintain his rabbinic authority by strategic retreats, already exemplified above. For his services, he receives payment in the form of kibbud. Like money, however, one cannot simply amass kibbud for its own sake without incurring the wrath of the community which both dispenses and gathers it. As Housmann's "salary" becomes higher and higher, the membership looks for replacements. As teacher, he has been already replaced by a series of guest teachers. In the house of prayer, he has been restricted yet still manages some hold on kibbud, a measure of his residual rabbinic authority.

Housmann is by no means the only rabbi who is subject to the criticism of his congregation. Few if any rabbis succeed in living up to all the expectations of their congregations. Paradoxically, they thus fulfill what is perhaps the most taxing of rabbinical role requirements—to be the group's whipping boy. When a rabbi holds authority over the religious lives of some group, he is liable to castigation as much as praise for his halachic decisions. The same interpretation of the law may satisfy some members' religious sensibilities and disturb others'. As an embodiment of religious life, the rabbi frequently becomes a focus for the modern Orthodox Jew's ambivalence about his religion. While sharing in the power of his congregants' faith, he is also apportioned a measure of their frustration over its inhibitions and restraints against modernity. While advising his followers what Judaism has to offer, he reminds them, too, that they may never fully pass into that modern secular world around them, which so much and so often intrudes upon their consciousness. One can thus easily understand the temptation of the "modern" rabbi to underplay the interdictory dimensions of the faith.

Strangers and Guests

Another prominent role-player in the house of prayer is the outsider. His role may be further divided into those of stranger and guest. Let us consider this pair first, for through them we may better comprehend the role of the outsider.

As described by Simmel in his now famous essay, the stranger is a wanderer: "his position in the group is determined, essentially, by the fact that he has not belonged to it from the beginning, that he imports qualities into it, which do not and cannot stem from the group itself." Yet, while the stranger is an outsider of sorts, he must be considered as "an element of the group itself. His position as a full-fledged member involves both being outside it and confronting it."[26]

In the shul three types of strangers exist. First is the stranger who knows, and is known by, no one. He is simply a new face, an unaccompanied Jew who has wandered into the shul. Second is the stranger who is strange to the setting but not to the people who participate in it. He is essentially a visitor, coming at times from elsewhere in the city and often greeted with the surprised salutation, "What are you doing here, stranger?" Third is the stranger who comes as a mendicant. He is a stranger because no one knows who he is or where he is from, but everyone knows why he has come.

All three types of strangers (let us call them foreigner, visitor, and mendicant) qualify under the terms of Simmel's analysis. They are outsiders, wanderers, who have not always belonged to the group, import new qualities into it (e.g., gossip, stories, jokes, talent), and become an element of the group which inhabits the house of prayer.

The guest is a stranger of sorts, too. Yet, unlike the strangers discussed above, the guest is not alone. He has come *with* a member and so shares in the host's insider's rights. He is introduced to the president, is welcomed publicly during the announcements on Sabbath mornings, and in general is gathered into the group. To honor the guest is to honor his host as well.[27] It is not only the guest who may become insulted over a kibbudic slight; his host is offended as well. The guest, by virtue of his attachment and allegiance to his host, can be trusted to live by the rules of the group. The host implicitly vouches for him and thereby neutralizes the threat of his strangeness. In short, the guest may be trusted, while the stranger may not.

To make guests out of strangers describes the essence of the Kehillat Kodesh response to outsiders. (Of course, there are always some guests whom one wishes were strangers instead—but that problem needs no explanation.) Toward this end, the stranger may be given a kibbud; as one member put it, "If a stranger came in, I guarantee you he'd get an aliya [i.e., kibbud] the first day." In return, he is expected to offer information about himself, either voluntarily or in answer to inquiry. This information inevitably exhibits some common ground with others present, even if it is only that the person has been in an Orthodox shul before—which usually leads to story-swapping. Such affinity is a necessary component for a sense of communion, which Schmalenbach defines as being "bound up with ... one another on the basis of characteristics ... naturally held in common."[28] It is to be *en rapport*.

Frequently the effort leads to foreigners being invited home by shul members; then, when they next return to shul, they come as guests. Ultimately the entire congregation becomes host to the stranger if, continuing to return as a wanderer, he becomes at one time guest of one family and at other times of others.

The foreigner who wishes to become a native is assisted by the group. The group, after all, is as much threatened by his strangeness as he is by its. The situation at Kehillat Kodesh is complicated by the Dudley Meadows neighborhood. Situated in the midst of a growing neighborhood of black Gentile strangers, who for obvious reasons cannot enter into communion with and be assimilated into Kehillat Kodesh without destroying its essential religious and social identity, the congregation finds itself confronted by an uncompromising strangeness from without—a strangeness which serves as a constant reminder of the limits of the group's embracement capacity, its reach. In the face of such reminders of its weaknesses, the group dares not neglect to welcome Jewish strangers, who, although different in some respects, are fundamentally like the insiders. Through the assimilation of such strangers, the group once more asserts its grip on individuals. Inability to transform not only the black Gentile but the Jewish stranger as well would perhaps raise the group's anxieties about its integrity and continued existence to intolerable levels. Those anxieties, coupled with the familial spirit expressed by the president and affirmed by the members, add an element of urgency to the collective effort at stranger/guest metamorphosis.

Despite all such welcoming efforts by the group, strangers do, at least for a limited time, exist as a situational phenomenon in the shul. Visitors are first to leave that status; foreigners are next. Of mendicants there will be more to say later on.

The visitor need do nothing to move from stranger to guest. Inevitably he will be beckoned by an acquaintance to sit near him and thereby become—at least in the confines of the setting—this member's guest. For the foreigner, the effort is a bit more complex.

The first problem encountered by the foreigner as he enters the setting is where to sit. As stated earlier, he chooses a seat nearest his point of entrance, an area near the doors, which seems reserved for him. (The existence of such an area for strangers suggests their special marginal status in the group, intimated by Simmel. They are neither completely inside nor totally outside the group.) Next, he must determine how to act so that he maintains a "coherence among setting, appearance and manner."[29] The ideal adaptation for the foreigner in the house of prayer becomes that of "worshiper enveloped in prayer." As such, the stranger/foreigner is assured that he is acting according to the formal demands of the house of prayer. He may engage in an inordinate amount of quasi-chazanic activity in this adaptation, often making sure that everyone around can hear him. He accomplishes several things by this: he (1) transports himself into prayer; (2) displays his familiarity with and knowledge of prayer; and (3) sometimes exhibits chazanic ability.

These messages may spark the first steps toward embracement. A good quasi-chazan is asked to become chazan, a role which marks the insider. A stranger who calls notice to himself by his prayer demands attention. At Kehillat Kodesh such attention implies embracement, expulsion in general being a thing of the dark past.

Some strangers may, either by silence or ineptitude, exhibit their unfamiliarity with the setting. Here are included the many new-comers to Orthodoxy. These too are embraced, for their interest in practicing religion is a confirmation of everything the members have done with their own lives. As one member pointed out, "These guys [i.e., newcomers to Orthodoxy] prove that American Jews are beginning to see that this is the only way to live." For the Orthodox Jew, who has long felt himself an outsider, if at times a camouflaged one, in the American secular world, dominated, as it seems, by non-Orthodox Jews, the return—as he sees it—of such Jews is the sweetest of all triumphs.

Mendicants

Although the third type of stranger, the mendicant, is, like the others, a wanderer and outsider who has become an element of the group, unlike them he seems to have come only to exploit and take from the group rather than to join and give of himself to it.[30] Insofar as his mendicancy is recognized, he is, in the middle-class cultural perspective of Kehillat Kodesh, socially blemished by his financial difficulty and morally tainted by his expressed reliance and apparent total dependence upon others. In both a real and a symbolic sense he *appears* to be an uneconomical addition to the group. Since he has come for money, all other activity in the setting is for him secondary. For him the house of prayer is a house of opportunity whose open door stands as an invitation for solicitation among a captive congregation—captive both by their physical presence and by their commitment to the Jewish imperative of charity.

A few words are in order here about the tradition of almsgiving among Orthodox Jews. The giving of charity is and always has been an integral part of the religious life of Orthodox Jews. To give of one's wealth to another Jew in need is an imperative, commanded both by the laws and the traditions of Jewry, and no man may consider his religious obligations completely fulfilled without his having engaged in some charity-giving. The synagogue, an institution manifestly organized for the fulfillment of communal religious obligations, is thus an ideal place for the communally oriented act of charity. Accordingly, the custom of including some act of charity in the context of communal prayer became an institutionalized part of the daily services. When no mendicant to whom charity could be directly given was around, money—often only a token sum—was dropped into a pushke (charity box), where it would be held in reserve for the poor. Although in contemporary times the fulfillment of this imperative of charity has been largely relegated to collective giving by large Jewish formal organizations, face-to-face almsgiving still takes place in many of the relatively small Orthodox congregations, like Kehillat Kodesh, which exist on the American scene. The encounter between mendicant and donor is, however, not without strains and tensions; at least that is the case at Kehillat Kodesh.

Since the mendicant's primary task is to collect money, any other activities he may engage in are perceived by those who recognize him as a mendicant to be motivated by and corollary to this primary effort. As a mendicant, he is interested in making friends and in joining in the activities of the collectivity only insofar as this helps him to collect money. While he may seem to become involved in what is going on in the setting—most commonly, prayer or conversation—the moment he asserts his mendicancy and solicits funds, his other actions are all seen in the light of that effort and are perceived as strategies rather than as expressions of sociability or communion. Thus his prayers become little more than strategic retreats, useful for devising plans for approaching one or another congregant for money; or his prayers become a way of expressing his commitment to Jewish observance and thereby minimizing his status as complete stranger.

The removal of an air of strangeness is an important dimension of the mendicant's effort. By it he establishes a rudimentary basis for common feeling between himself and the others; by showing that he too is an observant Jew, committed to prayer, and familiar with the way one acts in an Orthodox shul, he seeks to kindle sentiments of communion.

Recognizing that "economic ... arrangements ... become a part of a communal routine," the mendicant, if successful in asserting such embryonic social bonds, will try to strengthen and draw upon them, "transforming [these] obligations of mutual loyalty into definitely binding expectations" of alms receipt.[31] The acquisition of such alms does more than get him money. As Mauss has suggested, "[gift] objects are never completely separated from the men who exchange them; the communion and alliance they establish are well-nigh indissoluble."[32] The proficient mendicant understands the steps he must take to build such relationships and realizes that they, and they alone, will serve as conduits through which his financial help will flow. Contradistinctively, the shul member, who also understands the obligatory and coercive power of the social and communal bond, is careful *not* to bind himself to another if to do so would incur too great a financial or social expense.

Mendicants, whose presence in the house of prayer is frequent almost to the point of regularity, may be divided into three distinct types: *beggars*, *schnorrers*, and *meshulachim*. For all three the house of prayer is the primary arena of activity; each, however, has a different status and is responded to in kind.

Beggars

Of the three types, the beggars are the lowest in status. In their appearance, demeanor, and actions these men kindle few if any communal feelings among the members. They are Jews—that much is assumed—and in need; little else about them seems to matter. One never tries to make guests out of them, never asks their names, their point of origin or destination, or even why they beg. These men (they are always men—as are all mendicants in the house of prayer) are the derelicts of the city's skid row, who regularly visit the synagogues in the area each weekday morning, hoping to gather loose change from the congregants or from the congregational charity box. These donations are the only means by which members bind themselves to the beggars. But it is a bond which is offset and contradicted both by its substance and by the manner of its donation. When beggars do receive money, they inevitably receive the smallest amounts of any of the mendicants. Moreover, they receive it with a minimum of sociability and a maximum of status-degradation ceremony. Nevertheless, the beggars are the ones who come back most often.

At Kehillat Kodesh, such men seldom if ever stay for the prayers. Instead, they enter, receive their portion, and leave for the next stop on their route of supplication. They remain essentially outsiders in spite of their regular appearance in the setting. On the one or two occasions when a beggar has tried to stay and pray (and thereby latently exhibit something of his union with the members), he has been discouraged from doing so by various jokes made at his expense or even by outright suggestions that he leave, since his continued presence is not necessary.

The fact that such beggars are not enlisted as part of the minyan is a point of congregational pride. It is a sign of strength that the minyan can be gathered from within the community and need not be "bought" or exchanged in return for alms. At Kehillat Kodesh, even when one or two men are needed to make up the necessary quorum, beggars are overlooked, treated as nonpersons. As one member explains, "Buying a minyan like that would be terrible; I mean, it would be like paying off a bunch of people to make *your* minyan." Another declares, "If you start asking these guys to come to the minyan ... it won't be your shul any more—just a bunch of beggars." As a sign of collective strength, the minyan must not be defiled by dependence on nonintegrable strangers for its existence. By excluding the beggars, the group keeps them nonintegrable and limits the establishment of social bonds with them. Not only the collectivity, but also individual members minimize the bonds between themselves and the beggars.

In the substance and manner of almsgiving, members also minimize, if not completely deny, any hint of such a bond. Giving the beggar a small amount—the usual donation is less than a dollar—serves as a symbolic indication of the tenuous and limited nature of the link. If, as Mauss suggests, "to give something is to give a part of oneself,"[33] a small donation is to give very little of oneself—to be bound to the recipient only minimally and by the most slender of social threads.

As if to assure that the bond will remain weak, almsgiving is accompanied by status degradation of the recipients. Paradoxically and ironically, this activity lays the basis for a rudimentary social relationship based upon exchange. To say that the beggars are not asked to pay for their alms by participating in the collective activity of the minyan is not to say that the members and congregation make no demands in return for their acts of charity to beggars. On the contrary, in return for money, these men are subjected to a kind of social and spiritual extortion. Although such reciprocity is of the variety which Gouldner describes as "heteromorphic," where "the things exchanged may be concretely different but should be equal in *value*, as defined by the actors in the situation," the return is no less a recompense.[34] Consider, for example, the following entry from my field observations:

A beggar enters the sanctuary during the morning's prayers. As he enters, he directs his steps toward Rabbi Housmann, who, having come in a few minutes before, is still in the process of putting on his prayer garb. The man waits respectfully and silently, eyes lowered, hands by his side, while Housmann and everyone else seem to ignore him.

As the beggar stands near Housmann, Lonsky steps forward, presses a coin into the beggar's palm, and says, "O.K., good-bye," signaling the beggar that he is not needed or expected to stay for the minyan. All this activity goes on as the others pray.

The beggar swings around to leave, looking down into his palm in the process. Evidently it is not enough, less than his usual share. He redirects his steps toward Housmann, who has, like most of the others, continued to ignore him. The beggar turns toward Velvel: "I usually get a couple of quarters so that I can bet . . ."; the rest is inaudible. Velvel shrugs him off. The man's eyes search the room for others who will respond to his appeal. He finds, instead, heads buried in prayer books, avoiding him. The people have already made their deposits in the faceless "pushke" (charity box) and will not respond any more to this beggar.

Suddenly the beggar is leaving, jingling some coins, his quest successful, someone having stuffed more into his palm. No signs of graciousness or acknowledgement. The beggar simply leaves silently, not invited or allowed to stay, not bade farewell.

Not all beggars receive their alms with this relatively minor abuse of silence. Such ignominious silence on the part of Jews, who place such a high value on words, is no doubt a high price to exact for charity. Nevertheless, other beggars must pay for the receipt of charity with embarrassment far less oblique. Included is joking at their expense, as when one member pays a beggar and announces for all to hear, "I hear you've got a seat on Wall Street." Moreover, some beggars must tolerate invasions of privacy to which no other stranger in the synagogue would be subjected (except children, who, as nonpersons, can be playfully abused—and sometimes not so playfully). Thus, for example, one member says to a beggar, "Why are you always so dirty? Why don't you take a haircut and a bath?" Throughout all such abuse the beggar remains passive, responding only rarely with some half-hearted remark.

Yet one begins to see that the beggars are as important to the shul as it is to them. While they receive mistreatment at the hands of their benefactors, they also receive a small but steady supply of money that *encourages* them to return. Manifestly, their existence gives purpose to the daily charity deposits in the community charity box and gives the members a chance to fulfill the religious imperative of almsgiving. Yet their presence seems to have a deeper-rooted, latent meaning as well. When the beggars fail to come for several days, the same members who revile them are among the first to inquire after them. The observer begins to realize that the presence of the beggars on a regular basis is a testament to the strength of the minyan and all that it implies about the staying power of the group. When the beggars come, including Kehillat Kodesh on their daily route, they imply that the minyan there can be counted on to exist, that the group can marshal its collective strength in the form of this quorum. The beggars' failure to come, like rats deserting a sinking ship, is an ominous sign to the members that the reliability and stability of the minyan—the group—is in question. Beggars cannot afford to take a chance on a nonexistent or dying minyan.

Furthermore, the individual member, in seeing that he has given a gift which could not possibly be returned in kind, in realizing that he has engendered in the beggar a dependency, gains ascendancy over the recipient—giving the latter what Simmel has described as "a taste of bondage" and enhancing his own status. It is the presence of the poor (to say nothing of their dependency) which makes the rich realize and affirm their own wealth. In exchange for alms, the beggar seems to be upgrading the status of both the group *and* its members. That symbolic exchange—status affirmation and upgrading in return for steady supplies of money—coupled with the religious need to find recipients for one's charity, creates at least a rudimentary alliance or social bond between donor and recipient. Schnorrers, the next type of mendicants to be considered, illuminate this relationship even further.

Schnorrers

The schnorrer is not a mendicant by choice, like the beggar, nor is he a person of such low-class standing. Rather, he is a middle-class Jew who has, through some misfortune, come upon hard times. The death of a wife which forces him to take care of his many children rather than work; illnesses which keep him from making a living; recent immigration, which has not yet allowed him to find a job; and unexpected family expenses are all typical of the reasons the schnorrer offers to explain why he has turned to the Jewish community for help. When the schnorrer comes to shul, he must be prepared actively, energetically, aggressively, and sometimes even frantically to volunteer a great deal more information about himself than the beggar does—lest he be treated like the latter. Indeed, the schnorrer must wear his biography on his sleeve, so that it will be near his solicitous palm. Careful not to be overly solicitous, like the beggar, the schnorrer proclaims that mendicancy is a *temporary* state of being for him (although, all too often, such a "temporary" state has a way of becoming endless).

The schnorrer always tries to present and exhibit himself as an Orthodox Jew (like the potential benefactors) who, in spite of his hardships, has kept strong his commitment to Jewish life and observance. His efforts to hide his ultimate financial aim, however, at times seem half-hearted. When he enters the shul, he may ostentatiously involve himself in prayer or religious study by picking out the proper volume from the bookshelf and perusing it. Yet the attentive observer finds that involvement in such tasks is in fact subordinate to other aims. The schnorrer's eyes begin to wander and search for prospects, a conversation is struck up with someone nearby, an opportunity is found to tell the tale of hardship and woe. When such opportunities do not occur—in part because the members have learned to watch out for the potential mendicant—the schnorrer asserts himself. He is not the self-effacing beggar, as the following example from my notes indicates:

With the end of the prayers, the schnorrer steps forward toward the *bimah* [the pulpit in the center of the room]. He holds in his hand two letters of reference, which he calls to our attention. They are his credentials. But this money-collector will go beyond the letters; he will tell his story.

He speaks in Yiddish (perhaps because he has seen a copy of the *Jewish Daily Forward* in Velvel's pocket, perhaps because he wants to emphasize his Jewishness, or perhaps because he speaks no English). He explains aloud to all those assembled that he has worked hard all his life, as they have, but he has now come upon hard times, especially because he suffers from "arthritis" (the only English word he uses). In his hand he holds a cane. He has a family to support, as we all do, and if we could give him some financial help, he says, he would be most appreciative.

The man's forthrightness has frozen the participants in their places. No one has sneaked out the door or even tried to leave. No one can claim ignorance of this stranger's needs. He has shined a spotlight on all of us by putting one on himself, knowing that, if he can tap one or two people for money, the rest will feel impelled to give in domino-like fashion. A few of the men begin to take out their wallets, looking at the others' actions. All the donations are bills, and all are handed to Rabbi Housmann. Some members ask Housmann for change—something that could not be done without embarrassment were the money being given directly to the schnorrer.

While Housmann is collecting the money, those who have already given wait and talk. The ritualized giving is evidently not yet complete. Some members complain aloud about the need to give, one man saying, "I don't understand. In these times of social security benefits and all. . . ." But the grumbles are hardly as abusive as those made to beggars, and everyone who grumbles still donates. In response to some complaints about the need for giving, Velvel says, "It's a *mitzva* [positive and mandatory ritual commandment] to give him [that is, the schnorrer] some money." Giving is a religious responsibility, as important for the donor as for the recipient. The others agree and add, as one man puts it, "God forbid that we should ever need it," a comment never heard in the presence of any other kind of mendicant.

The schnorrer receives the money from Housmann and thanks the people aloud. Then, as the people shuffle out, the schnorrer approaches some directly, shaking their hands and offering words of blessing. Finally, he approaches Harwood and asks for a ride to another synagogue nearby, the next stop on his journey. He gets his ride.

In all that the schnorrer does, he tries to establish some basis for common feelings between potential donors and himself. Even in his appearance, the schnorrer is careful to come dressed and groomed in a manner which indicates middle-class status, not unlike that of his possible benefactors. If his coat is a bit threadbare, it is still a good coat—one, which, like its owners, has come upon hard times but was not always in its present unhappy condition.

In his presentation of self, the schnorrer leaves the image of beggar behind and approaches the other end of the stranger scale—the guest status. While he never fully becomes a guest, he is able to make claims on the members, ask for rides, demand attention, and keep the group assembled. It is he who dismisses the congregation with words of thanks, handshakes, and blessings. He may touch the donors, physically and symbolically. In his blessing, he seems to invest himself with the power of heaven, in part compensating for his apparent lowly status as mendicant. The schnorrer draws on his strengths, on his bonds with the members, and translates his efforts into dollars.

The manner and substance of the members' responses to the schnorrer reflect the degree to which his efforts at communion have succeeded. In one visit he may gather more money than a beggar makes in months (he therefore makes sure to visit a place only once or very seldom, in order to avoid the contempt bred by familiarity). Gone is most of the abuse that accompanies gifts made to beggars. Even the demeaning position of having money placed in one's hands by a benefactor is minimized because only one member collects the money and serves as a buffer between donors and recipient. The presence of the intermediary also helps assure that the schnorrer will not establish too close a tie with any one member, turn this member into his host, and then demand more from him than from the others.

Efforts at limiting the bonds between members and schnorrers are less concerted than those surrounding the member-beggar interchange. This is in part explained by the fact that schnorrers, while passing as simple strangers, have already established relationship and bonding even before they ask for money. The money reflects that bond instead of primarily creating it, as it does in the case of the beggar. However, should a schnorrer reveal himself and his purpose before he has had a chance to establish communion, exhibit Jewishness, or tell his sad story, he loses his audience and is treated shabbily. If he does not receive abuse and undergo status degradation, he nevertheless receives very little alms. The proficient schnorrer is therefore quite careful and attentive to the preliminaries to his pitch.

As was the case with the beggar, the relationship between schnorrer and donors can be understood as having certain latent qualities of an exchange relationship. In return for money, the schnorrers, even more than the beggars, attest to the presence, stability, and importance of the shul community. These mendicants, some having come not merely from other cities but from other states and countries, have risked more and traveled farther and longer than the beggars to arrive at their destination. The costs of travel, both in time and in money, make only a few shuls worthy stops on the schnorrer's route. For such a small group as Kehillat Kodesh to be chosen is an affirmation of its wealth. The proficient schnorrer realizes the implicit affirmation in his choice and in his tale never fails to mention the travail he has had in arriving at the present location. Often he uses this detail of his story as a way of enlisting aid in moving on to his next stop, as in the case cited.

In addition to such payment of status affirmation in exchange for his money, the schnorrer makes another payment—this one unique to him. In return for a sizable donation, the schnorrer volunteers to give up a part of his informational preserve, "the set of facts about himself to which a person expects to control access while in the presence of others."[35] He reveals parts of his own biography, subjecting his life and actions to the evaluation of people whom he may not expect to offer him similar bits of themselves in return. Here the schnorrer stops short of being a guest, for a guest would have the right to expect a return of information in exchange for what he has revealed. Instead, the schnorrer must be satisfied with a return of money rather than whole-hearted communion, sociability, and informational exchange. Ironically, while he keeps telling the story of his life, not only to exhibit his troubles but also to show that he once was—and to some extent still is—one who shared a life and world view with those who are now his benefactors, his efforts to be embraced by the group are doomed. For all his efforts, he remains a mendicant and outsider, stigmatized by his plea for money.

Rather than friendship, the relationship between schnorrer and donor is closer to what Wolf describes in the patron-client model, with donor as patron and schnorrer (indeed, to some extent, all mendicants) as client. Wolf explains that

> The two partners to the patron-client contract do not exchange equivalent goods and services. The offerings of the patron are more immediately tangible. He provides economic aid.... The client, in turn, pays back in more intangible assets. These are ... demonstrations of esteem, a strong sense of loyalty to his patron ..., information on the machinations of others.... The client is duty-bound not merely to offer expressions of loyalty, but also to demonstrate that loyalty.[36]

By returning again and again to the shul, or by having come to it in the face of difficulties, by confessing his problems or exhibiting them, mendicants in general demonstrate esteem for their benefactors and exhibit loyalty to them. This heteromorphic recompense supports and buttresses the social bond between mendicants (in this case, schnorrers) and the people of Kehillat Kodesh.

Meshulachim

The third type of mendicant, the meshulach, is a client like the others. Unlike them, however, he collects money primarily for others rather than for himself. He is a money-collector by occupation, a professional. The word "meshulach" is a derivative of the Hebrew verb "to send." Indeed, the meshulach is one who is sent by others to act as their agent in the collection of funds. Frequently he represents a religious day school or academy of higher Jewish learning (yeshiva). On rare occasions, he may be sent by a group of schnorrers who have decided to band together and send one man to collect for them, thereby minimizing their own travel and travail. Yet, no matter who has sent the meshulach, donors always know that the money he gets ought to be apportioned among many.

In return for his efforts, the meshulach usually receives a commission from his employers, who thus stimulate him to collect as much money as he can. Accordingly, the more money a meshulach collects, the further he removes himself, as well as others, from a status of mendicancy and poverty.

To talk about the social status of the meshulach is no simple matter. He shares in the prestige and esteem of those for whom he is an agent. At the same time, however, his appearance, demeanor, and behavior establish a separate social status of his own. This personal status in turn projects itself onto the institution or group he represents in either a positive or negative way. The most successful combination in this symbiotic relationship occurs when each enhances the status of the other. The meshulach with highest status and most prestige, representing an organization with like high status and prestige, can make the greatest demands upon his patrons.

Organizations, realizing that a meshulach with high status can gather more money, have gradually begun to rename and so upgrade their messengers. On one occasion a man visited the shul and described himself as "the executive director for student planning." Commenting later on this new title for a meshulach, one member said:

> They've got these new names now, but you can always tell a meshulach. I remember once a Rabbi Pagman who was a meshulach in America for many years before he moved to Israel and became a meshulach for some yeshiva over there. They sent him back to America to collect some money, but this time they gave him some fancy title—executive or educational director. You know they really built him up. I mean, they said this man was responsible for the education of forty thousand *talmidim* [students]. So naturally you thought, "And *this* man is coming to talk to us." So people really shelled out. But still you realized that the guy was a meshulach.

This ability to recognize a meshulach is a talent developed by the members through a lifetime of exposure to them. Although to the outsider the meshulach may look like nothing more than a pious Jew, sometimes in long black kaftan, beard, and broad black hat, at other times in relatively modern attire, the insider not only recognizes the meshulach but can also evaluate his relative status compared with others in the same profession.

Recognition is easiest with low-status meshulachim, who collect for small and little-known organizations. These are the men who arrive in frayed coats, disheveled, and lacking the posture or demeanor of dignity that characterizes one who sees himself, and therefore presents himself, as an executive director rather than a mendicant. The eyes of such low-status meshulachim are the eyes of beggars, searching only for a handout and looking down and away at the slightest challenge. Although men of piety and some learning, they are neither the most pious nor the most learned. Instead, these meshulachim are often expendables whom the scholars have sent out to "dig up some money." (The pious scholar is still of greater value than money to the "people of the Book." Only on rare occasions are the best students or revered teachers sent out to drum up funds. After all, the money is to enable these very men to engage in Jewish study; *that* is their task—not money collection.) The meshulachim who represent schools gain some social strength from the traditionally important role which Jewish scholarship has always played in Jewish life. They are buttressed not only by the religious imperative toward charity but also by the biblical commandment to "teach them [the laws and traditions of the faith] diligently unto your children" (Deut. 6:7). Thus, while a meshulach of this sort may act like a beggar, he is, if he collects for a school, more than a beggar. Moreover, the more important or respected the school, the higher is the status of its meshulach. Whether or not he represents a school, the meshulach is by definition a religious Jew. No matter how simple he may be, he is not so simple as to avoid the observance of religious rituals. He may not know, in any philosophical sense, why he does so, but that he ought to keep the laws and traditions is beyond question. In that sense, he is no different from even the most simple shul Jew.

Perhaps out of respect for the organizations of learning which they represent, or in recognition of their immersion in the Jewish world, these meshulachim are not discouraged from staying in the sanctuary during prayers.

The unsuccessful meshulach is one who spends little or no time in asserting his communality with his potential patrons. Even while he stays in the sanctuary, he roams around, looking for someone to "tap" for funds rather than exhibiting piety, learning, and other such aspects of high status—qualities which the members respond to with respect and often greater donations. The low-status meshulach allows his purpose to be transparent and so to taint his whole being. For him, as for beggars, prayers are but an opportunity to find a captive crowd. The following extract from my notes describes one such occasion at Kehillat Kodesh.

> The meshulach hung over everyone. Gone was the usual conversation among the members. Instead, all buried themselves in prayers, thereby shielding themselves from invasion, leaving the meshulach as an outsider. His surveying eyes met no one else's. He held an open prayer book but did not look into it very often.
>
> As some men finished the *amida* and waited for others to finish, they became subject to the meshulach's solicitation. He watched carefully for the three steps backward which signal a man's completion of his prayers.

For each man approached, the meshulach had a set procedure. First he would draw out from his briefcase (that sure signal that a stranger is a meshulach) a letter with a gold seal on it. This letter, his credentials, described a small yeshiva in New York City. Having shown the letter to a member, the meshulach asked if the member could spare some money for these students. The letter was mere formality, for no one had to read it; it was like so many they had read before.

When one man sat down to write out a check, the meshulach stood silently, watching him as he filled out the spaces on the paper. Now came the rest of the procedure. The donor was given another look at the letter, a handshake, and a nod, and, after a look at the size of the donation, a few words of blessing and a receipt.

No conversation, no sharing of stories took place—only a silent transaction. Throughout the procedure, each man's attention seemed elsewhere. The meshulach's eyes looked far away, the blessing formal and empty. For his part, the donor was not involved, either. Some donors even kept talking to someone else as they handled the almsgiving.

Now the meshulach approached me.

"Did you see this?" he asked, as he showed me the letter. His hands trembled. For both of us the encounter was painful. I gave him some money and got a handshake and nothing more. My donation was evidently not enough for a blessing, but I did get a receipt.

One man gave the meshulach money and was about to leave without receipt, handshake, or blessing.

"Where are you running? Wait a minute," the meshulach called. He did not want to accept the money without a proper response. He was not like the silently accepting beggar. The pocketing of a check or bills did not complete the encounter. A receipt and handshake were necessary and, at times, a blessing too.

The meshulach folded his letter and put it away. He had collected all he could here. Now he turned to a member and asked if he could come home with him for a talk. The man responded with another donation, saying, "Here, I haven't got the time."

If the low-status meshulach is not treated to the same status-degradation ceremony as the beggar, he is nevertheless treated like an outsider rather than a guest. He is met with silence and relative disregard. And, one avoids taking him home, lest he become a guest.

The high-status meshulach is much more circumspect in his

collecting efforts. At first he makes his appearance like a simple stranger. Neatly groomed and dressed, he is careful to leave his briefcase out in the coatroom. Once inside the sanctuary, he is a careful manager of impressions. He engages in prayer with great shows of piety and intense involvement. Before the beginning of prayers he involves himself in learned study, exhibiting his scholarship and Judaic activities. If he engages in conversation, he is careful to talk about matters other than his occupation. He exchanges gossip, tells about practices he has seen elsewhere. The minstrel qualities of his wandering are emphasized; he is the somewhat exotic wandering Jew come for a visit. He is, least of all, the odious mendicant.

But he is a mendicant, and he is after big stakes. He is not looking for the spontaneous or reflex donations of the moment. His snare is much wider. Only after he has made himself into a guest, an insider, does he reveal his purpose. Now he may ask to make a speech on Sabbath, or he may ask to visit each member at home—all in order to gather a respectable amount of money for his institution. This is the "executive director," who carefully builds a bond between himself and his potential patron and then exploits it fully. Once he begins to do so, he must act quickly, before members realize the purpose underlying his friendliness. If he is too slow in his timing, the members will disengage themselves from him, and the relationship which he has worked so hard to establish will fade away before it is confirmed in the gift of alms.

Donations made to the successful executive-director type of meshulach are the most generous, both in substance and manner of bestowal. They are subject to little or no visible interactional tensions. Any status degradation that occurs does so in subdued ways and only if the stranger emphasizes his mendicant-meshulach status. When this happens, the members, especially those who have already been financially tapped, may grumble among themselves and see to it—via gossip, often loud enough for the meshulach to hear—that the stranger quickly loses his guest status and is seen for the mendicant he really is.

This meshulach must remain wary, since even a seemingly innocuous remark, such as a passing mention of a yeshiva with which he is associated, may reveal his mendicant-meshulach stigma. Members' openness toward strangers becomes transformed into a kind of social distancing as soon as the ultimate intent of financial exploitation becomes publicly obvious. Thus when, on one occasion at Kehillat Kodesh, an executive director began to give himself away, the members who had been conversing and gossiping with him, offering information about themselves and the community, began silently to slip away while he spoke with the president. It is only when the alms pitch comes as a kind of afterthought to interaction, as an apparent surprise to both giver and getter, that the meshulach completely succeeds in his efforts.

Besides such subtle interpersonal techniques for collecting money, more logistical strategies are used. Thus, meshulachim divide the Jewish world into territories. Much like salesmen, they agree not to encroach on one another's territory. Accordingly, not more than one meshulach representing the same group will tap a particular congregation. This practice is absolutely essential in order to avoid such dodges as, "Oh, we already gave to your yeshiva (or group)." The written receipt is also a part of the strategy. A copy is always kept by the meshulach, ostensibly for the records, but also for sale to the mailing-list compilers, which various other Jewish institutions utilize.

In the executive-director meshulach we find mendicancy in its most developed form. The successful meshulach seems to display an intuitive, if not explicit, understanding of the reciprocity underlying face-to-face almsgiving. He realizes that greater communal feeling leads to social bonding, which in turn may be translated into a good donation made with a minimum of status degradation. The successful mendicant is one who can take another's money without feeling less important than or inferior to the donor and without making the latter feel cheated and exploited. By the time the executive director blesses his patrons, he seems to be enhancing their status and felt identity. He allows them to feel that they have become part of something important by affirming relationship to him and his organization by their monetary donation.

As suggested earlier, the executive director may make a sermon on a Sabbath, often mixing homiletics with pitch-making. In return for money, he returns homily, wisdom. He presents himself as a man of scholarship who honors the group with his presence in return for their presents. Not only does he affirm the group in its existence, he also elevates it. As he does so, he of course elevates himself as well, succeeding in his mendicancy more than any of his lesser counterparts, paradoxically because he makes himself appear to be less a mendicant than they. The bond suggested by the gracious and generous gift simply confirms an already expressed relationship based upon social status, religious concerns, and sociability.

As an interesting addendum, I should point out that nowhere do the distinctions among the various mendicants become as clear as in the dispensation of kibbud. While all members and guests may receive direct or indirect kibbudim, mendicants may not. Beggars receive absolutely none. Schnorrers and low-status meshulachim may at times receive perfunctory permission to perform some minor ceremonial duty. Only the high-status executive director, the man who has, at least temporarily, succeeded in distancing himself from the role of mendicant, may receive a full-blown kibbud—for example, the right to chant a portion of the Scriptures. To honor a man with kibbud is to dignify him, to make him a guest; and to make him a guest is to establish a social bond of some substance, which is easily transformed into a generous donation.

Children

One final role-player in the house of prayer must be considered: the child. According to halacha, the youngster below the age of thirteen (for boys) or twelve (for girls) is not eligible for kibbud in the synagogue. For girls this is a moot point, since, no matter how old they are, they will not have such prerogatives and responsibilities in the shul. Little boys, however, would seem to rank as low as beggars and women. Such, however, is not the case. In an ingenious way, the congregation has found a way of dispensing kibbud to little boys even in the face of halachic imperatives to the contrary.

Boys are potential men. This principle acts as the loophole through which the congregation can make the sociological adjustments that enable the male child to rise above his female counterparts. The boy is given kibbudim in preparation for his ultimate manhood. That is, he receives certain kibbudim as part of his Jewish training or study. It has already been suggested that study is ineluctably a part of prayer. On this pretext, kibbud for a young male becomes a form of study and is therefore permissible.

Accordingly, the members of Kehillat Kodesh have set aside certain kibbudim for small boys. These include being chazan for the last few prayers of Sabbath and holy-day morning prayers, opening the ark when another young boy is chazan, and, on occasion, chanting the haftora portion from the prophets on Sabbath.

These kibbudim, however, are not invested with the same status-enhancing power as the ones received by adult males. Although kibbudim modify one's public identity, their symbolic meaning is inextricably bound up with the community's general evaluation of the recipient; and no kibbud, in and of itself, can make the group socially (as opposed to ritually) evaluate a boy as a man. Of course, just as parents (the woman, whose honor is reflected in the honor of the males in her family, is included here) value their own kibbudim, so they value, albeit in a diminished sense, their children's. Moreover, in the world of children kibbudim are particularly important, because boys become more or less esteemed as a result of receiving or failing to receive them. In fact, the boys imitate their parents in their stress on kibbudim. The training which the receipt of these kibbudim offers is thus social as well as religious, since it acts as a means of initiating the young male into the world of the shul. By the time a boy becomes bar mitzva, he understands and is fully prepared to use the medium of exchange of the setting—the kibbudim—and has begun to value them in the same way that his father and mother do.

Besides their assessment and use of kibbudim, boys imitate their fathers in other, more concrete, ways. The mimicry in the way they dress has already been described. Other parallels appear in their observance of sexual segregation, their shifting involvements, and even, as will become clear, in their concern with gossip.

With the cast of characters now presented, we may return to the action in which they play their roles.

4   *Shifting Involvements*

> Underneath apparent differences,
> we shall be able to glimpse a
> common structure.
>
> *Erving Goffman*, Behavior in
> Public Places

Tefilah sheh be tzibbur, the central activity in the house of prayer, can be generally defined operationally, that is, in terms of liturgy. Yet, if one analyzes the components of the term, one finds *two* key elements: *tefilah* or prayer, and *tzibbur* or collectivity. The convergence of these two elements suggests an interaction between the liturgical and the social in communal prayer. Moreover, the words hint that the relationship is reflexive—that while prayer transforms the collectivity, the collectivity can also in some way transform prayer.

From the liturgical standpoint prayer is meant to be something "which modifies the conditions of the moral person who accomplishes it."[1] Communal prayer, in theory, moves persons closer to one another and to their god and changes them through that communion. In these terms one speaks of "a holy people sanctified by prayer."[2] Yet, tefilah sheh be tzibbur is more.

Because it is worship engaged in with others, performed in public, it is, like all other public behavior, subject to the "ground rules and associated orderings of behavior that pertain to public life."[3] Moreover, because communal prayer is habituated collective behavior, conventions arise to facilitate its performance. Accordingly, one way the collectivity transforms prayer is by conventionalizing it. The same words are repeated with identical intonation. Standing, sitting, bending, and singing all become codified and routinized. No word or moment of prayer contains a liturgical surprise. While making the practice of tefilah sheh be tzibbur easier by removing ambiguity from the art of praying, such public conventions also turn it into a craft, with the result that the imaginative, personal element in all prayer, whether individual or communal, is inevitably diminished.

Second, the various roles played in the context of the house of prayer delimit and affect the tefilah. As Douglas has put it "people's behaviour to their god corresponds to their behaviour to each other."[4] Nowhere could this statement be more true than in the house of prayer. While all shul members broadly define their activity in the house of prayer as tefilah sheh be tzibbur, various role-players interpret and understand the performance of that activity in various ways. Each, playing out his part in the web of action that comes to be defined as communal prayer, sees the process from his own perspective. For the mendicant, in addition to being a spiritual pursuit, tefilah sheh be tzibbur is viewed as an opportunity to exploit communal feelings for financial gain. For the chiyuv, it is a chance to prove his allegiance to the faith and respect for the dead. For male children, going to the house of prayer is more than simply praying to God; it is a chance to exhibit one's coming into adulthood. For the gabbai, it is an exercise in social banking, where the debits and credits of kibbud must be sorted and disbursed in such a way as to allow the collectivity to hang together with a minimum of friction. For the president, tefilah sheh be tzibbur offers a chance to survey those whom he leads and to reaffirm his leadership. For the rabbi, it is an occasion to exercise moral leadership, halachic judgment, and authority. Finally, for the members, tefilah sheh be tzibbur is an opportunity to reaffirm their relationship with other individual members and with the collectivity.

In spite of these different perspectives, a generalized definition of the situation is sufficiently strong that the entire group can join together in tefilah sheh be tzibbur without experiencing the dissonance of rival definitions which would force its members to question not only their unity of purpose but also their congregational union—not only what they are doing but why they are together. Beyond the various perspectives which emerge from shul roles and their expectations, and "preliminary to any self-determined act of behavior,"[5] is a collective, intersubjective definition of the situation which has moral authority over any individual participant's view of the setting and of any activity in it. Any behavior or assertion of a situational definition that would repeatedly challenge or discredit the collective definition of tefilah results in the perpetrator's being defined as an outsider, one not familiar with the claims of the setting. In short, the collective definition of the situation as perceived by the participants acts to control or at least coordinate individual behavior in the setting.

In prayer, the liturgical format, made up of prayers, hymns, and biblical readings, constitutes the thematic element of the collective definition. But liturgy cannot and does not totally constitute *communal* prayer. In such public activity social involvements play an equally important part. Included are role involvements and involvements associated with the public assembly within which communal prayer occurs. These latter involvements include conversational engagements of sociability, machinations of collective control and maintenance, and gossip, joking, and information exchange as well as discussions of kibbud and liturgical format. These involvements are characteristic of the shul as house of assembly. Also present are involvements typical of the house of study, such as discussions of Torah and the reading of sacred or scholarly texts.

Finally, in addition to all these main involvements, there are side involvements, which may occur simultaneously: the donning and removal of prayer garb, the dropping of coins into the pushke or into the hands of beggars, the arrangement of ritual articles; then there are the less ceremonial moving of chairs, the occasional pacing back and forth in the shul aisles by some men during prayers, and—in the case of young boys—the playful punching of one another in a kind of "I-got-you-last" game. Viewed thus, tefilah sheh be tzibbur is a series of involvements in which members shift among varying legitimate definitions of the shul (as house of prayer, study, or assembly) while simultaneously maintaining liturgical prayer as the keynote of this sociological harmony. A comprehension of the allocations of involvement within the setting helps the observer make sense out of what otherwise appears to be a chaotic blend of activities.

The collective definitional situation and the limits it places on the shifting of involvements are always clear to insiders. They know that the only legitimate involvements during tefilah sheh be tzibbur are those consistent with the definitions of house of prayer, study, or assembly. Thus, for example, doing calisthenics would be an illegitimate involvement, negatively sanctioned because it is not consonant with any of the institutionalized definitions of the shul. Only involvements which *can* be fitted within some primary framework of meaning associated with the shul may occur during prayer.

To say that the participants "are engaged in tefilah sheh be tzibbur" is simply to particularize, to explain situationally, the phrase which the members use to describe all activity in the synagogue: "being in shul." At some times "being in shul" means basically tefilah sheh be tzibbur; at other times it may mean "learning" (the core of study), and at still others it may refer primarily to sociability. Yet in each case "being in shul" is a combination of all three.

Tefilah sheh be tzibbur is thus more than prayer. While it remains the basic involvement, to which there is constant return, prayer is by no means the *main* involvement, the one that "absorbs the major part of an individual's attention and interest, visibly forming the principal current determinant of his actions"; nor is it even the *dominant* one, "whose claims upon the individual the social occasion obliges him to recognize." A man may become primarily absorbed in the study of a volume of the Talmud even as he is secondarily engaged in moving his lips in prayer "in an abstracted fashion without threatening or confusing simultaneous maintenance of a main involvement."[6] Moreover, if he becomes so deeply involved in study that he becomes oblivious of the prayers and perhaps even stops whispering them, he at that moment indicates that he does not recognize the claim of prayer as the paramount reality. A moment later, however, prayer will once again become his main involvement as he lifts his voice in hymn infused with kavannah; then his eyes will skim the page of the Talmud in "abstracted fashion." Similar shifts occur between conversational sociability and prayer. Because of their frequency, such serial involvements appear to be almost simultaneous.

While every context contains these series of legitimate involvements, which take turns in dominating the action as well as the individuals' attention, each context reveals a unique pattern. In tefilah sheh be tzibbur, one discovers a frequent return to prayer as both main and dominant involvement; similarly, study-period serial involvements are always marked by a preponderance of study, and assemblies by a preponderance of sociability. Within any series, activities of prayer, study, and sociability all have equal claim and equal situational legitimacy; no matter what the context, each of these belongs properly to "being in shul." In any particular context, the participants, like jazz musicians jamming together, each going his own way, expressing variant legitimate melodic or harmonic involvements, must at certain times come together, and it is that union that constitutes the basic involvement, the formal definition of the situation.

The social dimension of tefilah sheh be tzibbur expresses itself also in terms of time. Liturgically all morning services are alike, having many of the same structural components. Evening services, although different from morning ones, are liturgically and structurally similar to one another. Temporally, however, the lines of categorization must be redrawn. Workday morning services, no matter when they begin, end promptly at 7:30, in time for the regulars to get to work. On Sundays, when only some members work, the same prayers last longer than during the rest of the week, and on Sabbaths they last the longest. During the week the time spent at evening services, after dinner, may exceed the time spent on morning services, even though morning services are longer and liturgically more complex. What explains these otherwise mysterious temporal variations is that longer services include more social involvements, which, although not appearing in the liturgy, are an integral part of the occasion. Thus the evening assembly for prayers is the occasion not only for the recitation of mincha and ma'ariv but also for a recapitulation and discussion of the day's events. Moreover, in their routinization of such procedures, the actors imply the definitional legitimacy of both pursuits as part of their gathering for prayer. Indeed an evening service without *shmoosing* (conversation), even though liturgically perfect, remains structurally incomplete.

Though not all involvements occur at every service, the repertoire of involvements which constitute communal prayer begins even before the formal beginning of prayers, during a period of preparation and anticipation which may be called the *warming-up period*. Although all congregants engage in shifting involvements, not every participant's series is alike. Some have more varied series than others. The involvements during warming-up periods reflect these differences. They also reflect the length of the services which are to follow. Thus, workday morning services have shorter warming-up periods than those of the evening; those before Sabbath prayers are long, while those on Sunday are shorter than Sabbath and longer than workdays, and so on.

Some people fill their warming-up time with sociability, emphasizing their tzibbur orientation to institutionalized public prayer. Like its subsequent expression during the tefilah sheh be tzibbur, sociability here becomes expressed in conversational exchange. Such interchange is, in Goffman's terms, "supportive," aimed at letting participants show one another that among them an "affirmed relationship actually exists"[7]—here, that they are part of the same tzibbur. The participant warms up not only by indicating his awareness of the others' presence (i.e., by saying hello) but also by citing some common element which can be shared in conversation, often a joke or a bit of gossip. One might speculate on this need to express communal feelings before beginning to pray with another; however, all that can be stated with assurance is that some people warm up with exhibitions of interpersonal solidarity.

Other ways of displaying the social emphasis of communal prayer may occur in the warming-up period. Among these is the summoning of a minyan. Membership lists are produced and telephone calls are made. Before the actual calls, however, members may discuss and evaluate each name on the list as a potential minyan participant. While manifestly concerned with planning the minyan, latently such conversation offers a way to indicate insider status. Only the native knows whom to call or can predict who will come. The fathering of a minyan thus implicitly forecasts a social rather than a religious exercise.

Some members may warm up with a combination of activities, some of which emphasize tzibbur (i.e., social matters), and some of which emphasize tefilah (i.e., prayer matters). In anticipation of a minyan, the same members who are making conversation may also appoint a potential chazan, begin some prayers, open siddurim to the proper page, or start to don prayer garb. These latter actions forecast the tefilah dimension of the forthcoming event.

Just as there are some who fill their warming-up time completely with social emphases, there are others who restrict warming-up to prayer-oriented action. Rabbi Housmann exemplifies the latter. He may spend this time in preparing the ritual items to be used in the upcoming service: rolling the Torah scroll to its proper place, opening the chazan's siddur to the right page, placing the pushke on the bimah, and sometimes beginning to recite preliminary psalms. Others may mix such involvement with study, picking up a volume of the Talmud or a copy of the weekly reading from the Torah scroll, after having made all preparations for prayer. They may mix sociability with these activities by discussing the Torah or prayers with others who are present. Commonly, those who spend the warming-up period preparing for prayer will also engage in study, thereby connecting two religious acts.

In still another kind of warming-up, the participant does not engage in acts of sociability, tefilah orientation, Torah study, or any combination of these but rather acts as if he had not *fully* arrived at shul. He is in the setting but not yet of it. This kind of warming-up may be accomplished in two ways: (1) by reading materials which manifestly have no legitimate place in the shul (e.g., magazines) and are therefore easily put aside or (2) by staring off into space. Both activities involve a kind of "inward emigration from the gathering" or setting.[8] Moreover, both imply that the person who engages in them is ready to plunge into prayer at a moment's notice and needs no special warming-up for what will momentarily occur; he is suggesting that for him the shul is solely a house of prayer.

Decisions as to how to fill the warming-up period may vary under different conditions. The man who on one day warms up with an emphasis on tefilah may, on another, accent sociability. For example, on Friday night, surrounded by friends, he may warm up for sociability; on Thursday evening, however, if few of his friends are present, he may warm up for prayer and little else.

If the shul happens to be filled with many mendicants, sociability among the regular members, which might otherwise arise during warming-up, is curtailed, and "involvement shields," designed to avoid solicitation, are raised.[9] These are established by involvement in prayer or study, activities which are harder to intrude on than conversations; for the latter, occurring in sociability spots, are often open to all comers. Nothing thrusts the members into prayer and study more quickly than an outsider who has come to exploit their sociability.

Those who come to shul before the formal beginning of communal prayer can warm up slowly during a preparatory period when no formal activity competes for their attention. By the manner of their warming-up, they may set the tone for the subsequent early moments of the tefilah sheh be tzibbur. The latecomers (as long as they remain in the minority) have few such luxuries in warming-up. Forced to catch up to the congregation's pace of prayer, they are limited both in their warming-up and in their power to change the tone of the gathering. The setting appears to have a built-in mechanism for negatively sanctioning the latecomers: they must begin prayer with a minimum of warming-up and must operate in an atmosphere not of their own making.

Nevertheless, some warming-up occurs even for the latecomer. It may consist simply of a rapid visual scan of the setting and its inhabitants, searching for nods of recognition and affirmation, words of greeting, and supportive interchange. Or a latecomer may simply thumb through the pages of the siddur, perusing the portions to be recited. Finally, the latecomer may sit in his seat and briefly stare off into space as if the prayers had not yet begun or he had not yet fully arrived.

For some latecomers, especially those who emphasize the social character of tefilah sheh be tzibbur, such brief warming-up, with its curtailed sociability, is insufficient. These persons may try to draw others out of their prayers and into conversational help in warming up. The expectation here is that, if the situation were reversed, the latecomer would provide the same help. Those who respond to this implicit request are usually the ones who consider the shul as essentially a place characterized by sociability. Should the latecomer try to draw out a member who defines the shul primarily or exclusively as a house of prayer or study, he will be met by smiles or nods but little or no conversation; the message is quickly passed that the disturbed participant is present not to converse but to pray or study. Of course, most insiders know who is and is not sociable, and only the former will be disturbed.

On Sabbaths and holy days, the sociable latecomer is aided in his warming-up efforts, for on these days handshaking and greeting are traditional and act as handy warming-up devices for sociability. As the latecomer makes his way to his seat, he may stop, greet, and be greeted by, others, with whom he shares short chats. By the time he reaches his seat, he has had abundant opportunity to express sociability and (incidentally) to reaffirm his membership in the group and thus be ready to pray with it.

Moreover, warming-up on Sabbaths and holy days may commence prior to arrival in shul. Since walking is the only halachically permissible way to get to shul on these days, members may turn their trip into part of their warming-up periods, extending the boundaries of the shul into the neighboring streets. People meeting one another often walk on together in sociable conversation. Indeed, this activity may become so engaging as to infringe upon the beginning of prayers. As the walking partners enter the sanctuary, they may have so warmed up for conversation that they may continue to converse until they are either shushed or enjoined or inspired by the example of others to pray.

The boundary-extending quality of Sabbath walks exhibits itself in other ways as well. Such journeys serve as warming-up periods for activity in settings other than the shul. For example, shul members who invite one another to Sabbath dinner begin the visit from the moment the host waits to escort his guests from shul to his home. Conversation topics thus commence long before the formal beginnings of sociability around the dinner table.

The subject of Sabbath dinners deserves closer scrutiny. Rather than serendipitous events, invitations to such dinners are subject to a whole set of unspoken yet unbreachable conventions and procedures. Like a prestation, each invitation is subject to repayment, although not always in kind. Members of the same clique usually repay dinner for dinner. For every invitation received, another is tendered, always in alternating order; each succeeding invitation ensures that host and guest will be tied together in obligation.

Repayment for invitations from members who are not within the same clique may take other forms. Thus, when a guest brings along a bottle of wine, flowers, chocolates, or some other gift, he is both repaying his host and signaling him not to expect a reciprocating dinner invitation. (Not all gifts guarantee this message; but gifts given by members of other cliques do.) In accepting the gift, the host acknowledges that the obligation has been paid off, with no other response expected.

The prestational quality of meals often requires one to take into account the menu. As Mary Douglas remarks, "Drinks are for strangers, acquaintances, workmen, and family. Meals are for family, close friends, honored guests."[10] At Kehillat Kodesh one might say: kiddush (cold meal, standup, an occasional hot hors d'oeuvre) is for all members of the shul; dinner (hot meal, several courses, sitdown) is for the members of one's clique. Repayment for an invitation to a meal may be made in the frame of a kiddush. No matter how lavish or filling the kiddush, it does not require repayment and serves to close an obligation that no material gift has closed.

It is interesting to note that kiddush is the sort of meal tendered to the entire congregation. When a member sponsors a kiddush in shul, he does not impose invitation obligations on all those present. The lengthy discussion of the menu of such a kiddush is the members' way of evaluating the respect shown the group by the donor. However, the kiddush has become so standardized that little room is left for individual expression. Kiddush at home still allows for some expression of relationship. Some kiddushes may express little more than minimum necessary repayment (a few crackers, an alcholic drink, a piece of cake); others express a closer bond between host and guest (a hot dish, herring, expensive foods); while, finally, the full-course meal expresses the closest linkage.

To return to the subject of walks to shul, not all encounters during the walk to shul provide warming-up periods for sociability. The expectation that people will walk together once they have met is, however, sufficiently strong that its violation requires some explanation. When persons of the opposite sex meet, such explanations come relatively easily. These meetings inevitably occur long after the start of shul prayers, since women do not begin arriving until about an hour after the first men. Accordingly, when a man overtakes a woman on his way to shul, both realize that the former is late and will have to maintain his more rapid gait. Both gait and time communicate an explanation for the violation of expectations. As the man passes the woman, he may account or apologize for his behavior, usually through some "remedial interchange"[11] like slowing his pace for a moment, greeting her, exchanging a remark or two, and then making some joke about being late, after which he once again speeds up—released by a nod or other gesture from the woman which signals her acceptance of his explanation. In the absence of such a courtesy explanation, one runs the risk of being characterized as a snob or a boor, an identity soon publicized through gossip.

The woman who wishes to avoid a man she meets slows her own pace so much that no male could walk with her without casting doubt on his desire to get to shul. No male, no matter how late, can afford to have it appear that he does not care about getting to shul on time. Rushing is a penance and price for being late, so a leisurely gait must be legitimately explained. The man who walks with his wife or child has such an excuse. Being with his family is more important than rushing to shul.

If one wonders why unrelated men and women seldom walk to shul together, one need only recall that sexes do not mix within the shul. On Sabbaths and holy days, when the shul's boundaries extend out into the street, meeting on the street is like meeting in shul, and under such circumstances males and females remain separate. Unrelated men and women sometimes do walk together, but only when a man and wife meet a second woman or man and all walk on together or when a man with young children walks on with a woman whom he meets. In both cases an intermediary exists to separate the sexes.

When a man meets another man, avoidance is not so simple. Unless one of them is forced to walk slowly because of some physical condition, the other can make no appeal to his need to hurry to shul. The only ones who manage to pass other men are those involved with the running of the service—for example, the gabbai, chazan, or chiyuv—or someone accompanying them. In short, only those who have some genuine reason for going slower or faster can avoid, and be avoided by, passersby. For the most part, however, this avoidance is not desired, for such meetings extend the period of warming-up and its helpful anticipatory adjustment.

In general, then, one must describe the process of warming up as anticipatory adjustment for a forthcoming primary involvement, an adjustment which in its substance reflects an individual's assessment and definition of the action to come. The anticipation may be for prayer, for socializing, for worshipful study, or for some combination of these elements. The notion of warming-up also implies that definitions of a situation, far from being generated only within the formal frame of a given situation, can also evolve from one's activities in an immediately prior situation. Very often one warms up for the primary activity by doing essentially the same things that one will later do with perhaps greater intensity. For the observer, such warming-up is the key to deciphering the nature and emphasis in individuals' serial involvements in the forthcoming activity. To know how a person warms up is to comprehend his future allocation of involvement and thus to decipher his definition of the situation.

One should not jump from this fact to the conclusion that such emphases are immune to influence. On the contrary, one of the qualities of communal prayer is its power to reorient and inspire one to pray, no matter what future activity is initially suggested in one's warming up. An uninspiring service, on the other hand, allows and often induces individuals to enter a pattern of involvement which stresses sociability rather than worship. A careful observation of the warming-up period enables one to trace the direction of influence, to determine whether the collectivity is transforming prayer into assembly or whether the prayer is transforming the collectivity into a people sacralized by worship.

The high holy days, the Days of Judgment and Atonement, are excellent times for observing and tracing such influences. Everyone arrives on time. Many respond to the tension of the time with a warmup that thrusts them out of loneliness and into sociability. Conversation among many—but by no means all—is not unusual. To the observer, the participants seem to be warming up for a great celebration of sociability. Yet, as the service begins, and even more as it continues, members stop talking, draw themselves inward, cover themselves with prayer garb, close their eyes, and one by one create an atmosphere permeated with kavannah. Indeed, even the young children sense the wave of change that has come over the collectivity.[12] Conversation stops as fewer and fewer people are willing to talk. The kavannah of one stimulates the rapture of his seat partners.

As an ethnographer, concerned primarily with the observable, I am forced to point out that kavannah and other spiritual states are not easily perceived, nor are they always correctly identified. The adroit shul Jew knows well how to appear to be immersed in prayer while in reality leaving his mind elsewhere. In an environment where displays of kavannah are requirements, albeit unwritten, such exhibitions are not unusual. The Kehillat Kodesh member, like so many other public persons, is a great manager of impressions.

Nevertheless, faking such rapture is not easy, for the faking may itself intensify one's spiritual state. The singing, swaying, and closing-of-eyes—all part of the image of kavannah—have the ability to overpower the participant quite quickly, and independently of his intent. This understanding is the implicit meaning of the talmudic dictum, "Ritual observances do not require kavannah" (*Pessachim* 114b). They need no prior kavannah, for the acts themselves produce it.

But kavannah and prayerful intensity are difficult to sustain. The longer the service, the more will tefilah be interspersed with other involvements.[13] The longer the prayers, the more difficult it seems for the participants to maintain peaks of religious intensity.[14] As the long service continues, the participants become increasingly aware of one another's presence and of their collective union. In no way is this more easily deciphered than in the growing amount of conversation and singing that occurs in the course of tefilah sheh be tzibbur. Let us first consider the talking, leaving singing for a subsequent chapter.

Simmel has described conversation as one of the "shadowy bodies" of sociability. Sociability does not, of course, characterize all conversations. "As soon as the discussion becomes objective, as soon as it makes the ascertainment of a truth its *purpose* (it may very well be its *content*), it ceases to be sociable."[15] People may, however, exchange information, gossip, and truths as part of sociable conversation as long as this is not the purpose generating the talk. (Of course, intent is a difficult thing to observe, much less document ethnographically.)

Simmel further defines the nature of sociable conversation as follows:

> talk is the purest and most sublimated form of two-way-ness.
> It thus is the fulfillment of a relation that wants to be nothing but relation—in which, that is, what usually is the mere form of interaction becomes its self-sufficient content. Hence even the telling of stories, jokes, and anecdotes, though often only a pastime, if not a testimonial of intellectual poverty, can show all the subtle tact that reflects the elements of sociability. It keeps the conversation away from individual intimacy and from all purely personal elements that cannot be adapted to sociable requirements. . . .
> The telling and reception of stories, etc., is not an end in itself but only a means for the liveliness, harmony, and common consciousness of the "party." It not only provides a content in which all can participate alike; it is also a particular individual's gift to the group.[16]

For the shul members, conversation during tefilah sheh be tzibbur is essentially an exercise in sociability.[17] The similarity and repetitiveness of the topics discussed reflect such sociability. They are for the most part adapted to sociability requirements rather than to relentless probes of personal life. Although personal concerns (for example, occupational pursuits, home squabbles) are not completely missing, since many of these people are close friends who in other contexts would share such inner, private selves, the conversation during communal prayer is primarily the small talk of sociability which Simmel describes. The jokes, the gossip, the anecdotes are vehicles for expressing and affirming sociability or, as we have called it, tzibbur.

Admittedly, not all shul conversations have equal significance. Like the hippies Cavan observed, shul Jews "may 'talk about something' in the course of talking, but that 'talk about something' is not necessarily separate and distinct; rather it is interspersed within the ongoing verbal activity."[18] Furthermore, as will become clear when we examine gossip and joking, conversation may for some persons maintain relations of sociability while for others it fulfills objective, purposive requirements.

Before saying anything about the substance of the conversations that occur during communal prayer, one must discover exactly *when* such talk can and does occur, since its practice is sometimes prohibited. Indeed, a closer look at tefilah sheh be tzibbur indicates three variables which affect the presence or absence of conversation: (1) the point in the prayers during which the participant enters the setting, (2) the participant's identity (whether he is, for example, man, woman, child, gabbai, or chiyuv), and (3) the nature of the prayer service.

These variables must be considered in light of both the liturgical and the social contours and benchmarks of communal prayer. The coordinates of these two are not necessarily the same, although they are never altogether unrelated. Someone may be late liturgically, having missed several parts of the service, yet still be on time socially, having arrived on time according to the expectations of the group. For example, men and women, as we have remarked, have different legitimate arrival times; yet, while all women are liturgically late, they are not all socially late. For the gabbai, on the other hand, liturgical and social time are identical, and he is socially expected to be present at the liturgical beginning of prayers because of his responsibility for cuing the service.

In general, one might suggest that a person's social timetable is directly related to the degree of his participation in the activity of communal prayer. The greater his ritual involvement, the greater the congruence between his social timetable and the constant liturgical timetable. Thus, while being liturgically on time universally means coming before the first prayer, for some members a particular arrival time indicates social lateness, while, for others, the same moment is defined as being early. While any Jew familiar with the siddur can know the liturgical timetable, only an insider knows both timetables and the relationship between them.

To better understand the issue of talking in shul, one must know something about the liturgical format of the various services. Each of the services making up the liturgy of prayer recited in the synagogue represents and is named after sacrifices made in the holy temple in Jerusalem prior to its final destruction in 70 c.e. Each service is organized around a central prayer called the *amida*, a recitation of nineteen benedictions (fewer on Sabbaths and holy days). To illustrate the importance of the amida, the rabbis also refer to it as "tefilah"—the same word used to denote prayer in general. Without an amida, no tefilah can be complete.

Each of the services—*shacharis*, the morning prayers; *musaf*, the additional prayers recited on Sabbath and holy-day mornings; *mincha*, the afternoon prayers; and *ma'ariv*, the evening prayers— is made up of a set of preliminary and concluding prayers surrounding the amida. Not all of these prayers are the same for the various services. Shacharis preliminary prayers may be divided into two parts: (1) *pesukay d'zimrah*, introductory hymns and verses of praise blended with scriptural quotations, and (2) the actual shacharis, a series of prayer stanzas leading to the amida. The concluding prayers of shacharis are short and few. Musaf, following, as it always does, the shacharis, has no preliminary prayers but consists primarily of an amida squeezed in after shacharis and before the conclusion of the morning service. Mincha has one preliminary stanza of prayer (on Sabbaths and holy days there are two) and a single concluding prayer. Although musaf is a shorter prayer, its closeness to shacharis makes it appear long. Mincha therefore is experienced as the shortest prayer. Essentially created as a short break from the mundane realities of the day, its brevity reflects an understanding that in the heat of everyday life little time can be set aside for prayer. Mincha is the prayer that most modern Orthodox frequently neglect to recite. Indeed, the shul has given up trying to get a mincha minyan during the week. Ma'ariv has seven preliminary stanzas of prayer and one concluding one. On Sabbaths, ma'ariv is preceded by a special set of hymns called *Kabbalat Shabbat*, literally, "receiving the Sabbath."

In addition to such liturgical division of the various services, a ritual distinction may be made between those prayers in which one is either permitted or prohibited to be *mafsik*. "To be mafsik" (coming from the Hebrew "to stop") means to discontinue or disrupt one's involvement in any ongoing activity. "To be mafsik in tefilah" thus means that one has stopped being involved in prayer and has thereby challenged prayer's status as the dominant involvement of the social occasion. More concretely and operationally, the term is defined as speaking any words other than those of the actual prayer during the period of its recitation. Finally, in practice the definition has come to be even more precise: "being mafsik" means speaking English (or any vernacular) in the course of (Hebrew) prayer.

One need not be mafsik oneself to cause another to become so. One need only draw the other into conversation during portions of the prayer when to converse is halachically prohibited. Consider the case of a latecomer, busily catching up[19] to the chazan in his prayers, who, while reciting prayers during which being mafsik is prohibited, is drawn into conversation by his seat neighbor, who, being in pace with the chazan, is by now involved in prayers during which being mafsik *is* permitted. The seat neighbor may speak, but the latecomer may not.

In its unfolding, a service formally moves toward increasingly more stringent prohibitions against being mafsik. For example, while one may be mafsik during the pesukay d'zimrah, one may not speak during the actual shacharis. With the advent of the amida the prohibition on any other involvement reaches its apex. Not only speech but movement as well is limited. The proper way to recite the amida is standing erect, feet touching one another at the instep, and facing toward Jerusalem and the site of the former temple. Nothing is allowed to challenge one's involvement in the amida. While the restrictions on other involvements are strict, deviations do occur. Openly defiant deviations (e.g., boisterous conversations), are both halachically and socially illegitimate, for they publicly undermine the devotion to prayer called for by the occasion. Less obvious ones are commonly ignored. Finally, prayer with kavannah forbids even the hidden inner wanderings of the mind and heart; but these deviant involvement shifts, since they are easily disguised, can readily occur.

Although all prayers nominally require kavannah and full attention, they do not all include prohibitions against being mafsik. The absence of this prohibition implicitly encourages open involvement-shifting during many prayers. Consequently, the prohibition against being mafsik has therefore become, in practice, a boundary separating portions of the tefilah sheh be tzibbur in which tefilah is the dominant involvement from those in which it may be but is not necessarily dominant. Moreover, along with this kind of division has come the unstated but commonly understood notion that the prayers during which one may not be mafsik are more important than the others.

The participants in tefilah sheh be tzibbur are aware of these distinctions. The more prohibitions against being mafsik within a particular service, the more will sociability—and the conversation which carries it—be inhibited and hampered. If the prayer service in session is defined by many such prohibitions, and if a person has entered the sanctuary during just such a solemn period, very little conversation will take place, and the situation will seem primarily defined as a house of prayer. If, however, a service has few such prohibitions, the set of involvements and associated situational definitions will be broad-ranging.

The longer the liturgical format, the more periods there are when it is prohibited to be mafsik. These periods are not only obstacles to involvement-shifting but are also emotionally very taxing. They require a sustained high level of kavannah for extended periods of time. Faced with these massive demands of prayer, shul members have *in practice* redefined the prohibition against being mafsik. Thus there are prayers during which absolutely no other interrupting involvements may legitimately occur (e.g., amida); there are others during which some sort of side involvement is still possible, including limited kinds of conversation which eschew English but permit the use of gestures, glances, Hebrew phrases, Yiddish expletives, and a host of grunts and inflections whose meanings have become part of the syntax of conventionalized shul communication; and there are still others where mafsik prohibitions are simply disregarded. This Kehillat Kodesh practice has greatly decreased the period of time when prayer is the universal paramount reality and collective definition of the situation. Concomitantly, the period of prayer requiring universal kavannah has become quite brief but, at the same time, more easily fulfilled. The fewer demands one puts on the tzibbur for devoted prayer, the more one can be assured that the required portions of devotion will be achieved. Such conventionalization may limit individual flights into ecstasy, but it at least assures regular moments of kavannah at every service, usually during prayers like the amida.

Some of the prayers during which being mafsik is absolutely prohibited have the power to claim the full attention not only of those in pace with the chazan but also of others who for some reason are out of step—for example, latecomers who may be talking or catching up in their prayers. They also prevail for people who are simply helping to fill out the minyan and may already have prayed elsewhere. Able to demand such universal attention, these prayers are in practice judged the "most important."

Consider, for example, the kedusha, the prayer of sanctification recited during the chazan's repetition of the amida (a repetition occurring at every service except ma'ariv). Like the amida, it must be recited with feet together and without any interruptions. The moment the chazan begins the words of the kedusha, all other activity ceases and the people are drawn back to tefilah. No matter what they were doing at the moment, they all proceed to pray together, their movement frozen. Anyone who walks in through the door at that moment will stop, turn toward the East, and begin to pray the kedusha. The individuals are thrust into and frozen by the prayer. No other paramount reality exists which can legitimately claim the involvement and attention of the worshipers. While another involvement may have been legitimate a moment before the beginning of the kedusha, to continue to engage in it now would constitute deviance. The conversation before kedusha was permissible; during kedusha it is a sin. Yet, a moment later, at the conclusion of the kedusha, the conversation may resume as the entire unity again dissolves into the diverse involvements which make up the tefilah sheh be tzibbur—a situation earlier likened to the alternation between the unison playing and individual choruses of jazz musicians.

"Most important" prayers, like the kedusha, help maintain the underlying theme of tefilah, which serves as the basis for the series of other involvements in tefilah sheh be tzibbur. Implicit in such prayers' importance is their ability to define the situation, shift context, and thus serve as what Bateson calls "context markers."[20]

Generally, context-shifting, the social reconstruction of reality, occurs in one of two ways. In the first type it originates from the individual who, by shifting his involvement from one activity to another, places (or, to use Goffman's term, "keys") himself into a new frame of meaning or context.[21] This kind of context shift, which is limited to actions which may legitimately become dominant involvements, has been called the process of "shifting involvements." Here, it is the actor who is responsible for the context shift and by his own actions modifies the definition of the situation. He may do so in order to conform to the collectively defined context or for other reasons. Yet he, and he alone, is responsible for accomplishing the shift. Moreover, the greater the number of others whom he draws into his particular involvement, the greater is his influence on the group's situational definition.

The second type of context-shifting occurs independently of the actor but nevertheless changes the definition of the situation.

Commonly the result of a liturgical change, as when the kedusha begins, such context-shifting makes the act that was completely acceptable in one moment and context deviant in another. The man speaking to his seat neighbor the moment before the beginning of the kedusha was acting properly in that context. With the first words of the kedusha, the same conversation becomes improper. Yet the actor has not changed his actions; rather, the context in which those actions are taking place has changed in such a way that they must be interpreted differently.

The adroit participant in tefilah sheh be tzibbur learns to synchronize and adjust his activity with the changing contexts of the liturgical format. If no one in the setting challenges an act, trying to restrict or change it, it may be considered a legitimate expression of context. If this is not the case—if talking members, for example, are asked to be quiet—the actor runs all the risks of the deviant and illegitimately involved. The artful participant, however, knows when and how to adapt his activity so that he will seldom if ever be accused of patently illegitimate involvement.

In short, context-shifting is adaptive activity. In the first type of shifting, the context becomes redefined or adapted to conform to the action of the individual. If he talks, for example, the shul becomes a place for sociability and little else. In the second kind of context-shifting, the individual must adapt to the context which has redefined his activity. He must remake and alter his action if he wishes to remain properly in context.

To be sure, forms of adaptation may be worked out prior to the actual context shift so that individuals are prepared for the change; for example, people begin to terminate conversations when they hear the chazan approaching the kedusha. But such adjustment presumes a high degree of regularity in the context shifts. Such regularity exists when the shifts are liturgically based, but it is not the case for context shifts, which—although independent of the individual—emerge from the fluidity of social interaction within the collectivity. One never knows just when the group will ask one to adapt one's actions—change one's step, as it were—to be in context.

The question which seems naturally to arise from this analysis is how and why the actor can in one case have the power to change the context through his own actions while in another he must adapt his actions to conform to a context created independently of his will. To answer the question, we must take a closer look at the actual ethnographic data on the phenomenon.

I have already pointed out that individual context shifts occur within the larger context of the shul as a place for prayer, study, or assembly. Furthermore, in tefilah sheh be tzibbur the underlying thread of liturgy ties the action together. Portions of it, during which one is prohibited from being mafsik, assertively represent that liturgy. A blatant contextual challenge by an actor may disrupt the activity and shift context, but it runs the risk, like all challenges to established orders, of failure, which discredits the challenger and not the context. When most of those around one are maintaining a single definition of the situation, a discrepant action, intending to change the context, runs the greatest chance of discrediting the actor. Accordingly, it is under such conditions that the participants will be most likely to conform to the context and to adapt their activities accordingly.

The following entry from my field notes illustrates this point:

> Szaczes and his brother are talking during the kabbalat shabbat portion of the service. They, like all others, are interspersing their prayer with conversation. Neither of them need hide this conversation in the context of the kabbalat shabbat. As I look at them, my action is not interpreted as a threat to their conversation but rather as simple curiosity. Suddenly, however, the context changes. With the opening benedictions of the ma'ariv, this same talk must either cease or be hidden. Now the Szaczes brothers are the only ones talking, and my look is suddenly interpretable as a warning glance, requesting them to cease talking and not be mafsik. The acts have not changed, but their meaning has. The brothers stop talking.

Other situations exist when individuals may successfully change the context in defiance of the existing frame of meaning. Consider the following example from my field notes:

> During the Torah scroll reading many people talk with one another. The gabbais are trying to shush them, but small cliques and klatches defy this shushing and keep on talking. Indeed, in one or two cases the people being quieted engage the gabbai in conversation. They succeed in making listening deviant and talking acceptable.

These two episodes support the following principle for determining when context forces adaptation from the actors and when actors may change the context. One may say generally that, when he can, a person will "try to re-create the world; to build up in its stead another world in which its most unbearable features are eliminated and replaced by others that are in conformity with [his] own wishes."[22] As long as an actor can control his context—remain omnipotent in his world—without discrediting himself, he will try to do so. In the first episode, the participants saw themselves threatened with exclusion and discreditation and therefore desisted from what might have become a challenge to the contextual definition. Certain liturgical moments, periods of study, or periods of sociability have this kind of unchallengeable power of situational definition, but in other cases the context can be successfully challenged—as in the second episode. Only the insider knows which challenges to the context have a chance of success and which are doomed. Outsiders and total strangers therefore decorously adapt their action to the formal context, that being the only situational definition they perceive. They are consequently also the ones who feel most alienated from the action. The presence of a large group of outsiders always makes for a more formal service. Only the insider challenges context; the outsider adapts and, in doing so, clearly identifies himself as an outsider.

In tefilah sheh be tzibbur, the most frequent challenge emerging from the flux of participatory action comes in the form of talking. As I have suggested, such talk is sometimes for pure sociability and sometimes has an ulterior purpose as well. What appears to one man as small talk is for another a very shrewd and planned effort at achieving something. Nowhere does this point become clearer than in an analysis of the major topic or type of conversation overheard in shul—namely, gossip; and gossip will now become the focus of our ethnographic and analytic discussion.

5

Gossip

From a man's mouth, you can tell
what he is

The Zohar

The more common a behavior, the more it piques the sociologist's
interest. At Kehillat Kodesh, gossip is such a behavior. One cannot
be long in the setting without being struck by the intense involvement and interest of the members in this activity. Accordingly, no
study of the shul would be complete without an investigation of
gossip, first with regard to its general social significance and then
with regard to its situationally specific meanings. Such a task
requires one to decipher the social and psychological meanings that
emerge from the action of the participants, to discover the social
functions of the activity, and, finally, to describe an ethnography
of practice. Let us begin with a general discussion of the meaning of
gossip.

To begin with, the word gossip itself is ambiguous, since it serves as both verb and noun. It refers not only to the act of transmitting information but to the information itself and, finally, to those who pass it. The "gossip" is one who "gossips," and the substance of that communication is "gossip." This linguistic character suggests, perhaps, that gossip has a way of totally consuming one's being and identity.

While the dictionary defines gossip as "small talk and idle talk or rumor, especially about the personal private affairs of others,"[1] the sociologist may try to add greater precision to the definition. Let us begin by noting that gossip is information which is specialized. It is not necessarily of objective importance; its significance, in fact, is limited to a specific set of individuals. One person's gossip is easily another's trivia. Moreover, the information always concerns a particular, easily identifiable person or group. As Paine puts it, gossip is, "1. talk of personalities *and* their involvement in events of the community and 2. talk that draws out other persons to talk in this way."[2] While written communications may serve (e.g., gossip columns), gossip remains primarily spoken.

Finally, the facts contained in such "talk" may, but need not always, be accurate. Indeed, gossip may be subdivided into: (1) reports—accurate and approbatory information; (2) false reports—inaccurate, though approbatory, information; (3) scandal—accurate, though derogatory, information; and (4) slander—inaccurate and derogatory information.[3]

The accuracy of gossip is not only determined by the actual facts. Innuendo, communicated either explicitly through accompanying evaluations of the fact (e.g., "But I don't really believe this" or "Isn't that slanderous?") or implicitly through nonverbal glosses (e.g., the raised eyebrow or shrugged shoulder), may be enough to undermine confidence in the accuracy of the information—but not necessarily enough to suppress the gossip. Indeed, the obvious exaggeration and patent falsehood may be precisely the stimulus for a long discussion about the "real truth" as perceived by the community of gossipers, as is often the case at Kehillat Kodesh.

On the related matter of gossip and the definition and regulation of social reality, Thomas offers two useful principles: (1) if people define situations as real, they are real in their consequences, and (2) "society attempts to regulate [reality] by persuasion and gossip."[4] A synthesis of these two principles suggests that persons have only to believe in the facts they learn and in their significance in order to treat and respond to them as gossip. In this sense, gossip seems to differ essentially from more formal types of communication (e.g., the relaying of technical directions or the handing-down of orders), where the need for accuracy is an inherent feature of the information. Gossip, rather, is a social construction of reality which may or may not be grounded in indubitable fact. Indeed, one might suggest that its primary characteristic is that it is a social construction, with substance remaining necessarily secondary.

In being a member of a particular group, one is able to appreciate the significance of gossip in a way that no outsider can. As Gluckman suggests, "the outsider cannot join in gossip" because "gossip does not have isolated roles in community life, but is part of the very blood and tissue of that life." Moreover, while persons may have to belong to a particular community in order to appreciate the significance of its gossip, once such membership exists and is organized around "the fairly successful pursuit of common objectives," an interest in the gossip may itself become a factor of communion. Put simply, the relationship between gossip and a community seems to be symbiotic: if "friendship leads to gossip," gossip also leads to friendship, since only one's "friends" (i.e., fellow community members) are interested in one's gossip.[5]

To the principle of the relationship between gossip and community membership another must be added. An interest in gossip and an estimation of its significance may not be shared equally by all who pass or receive it, in part because not all individuals share equally in the community of which they are nominally members.

This working definition requires elaboration and substantiation, for it raises a crucial question, one which has troubled students of gossip almost from the beginning. To suggest that gossip has significance, albeit socially circumscribed, still leaves open the question why, in spite of its possible inaccuracy and in face of its limited relevance, people are sufficiently interested in gossip to make it one of the oldest and most sought-after sorts of communication.

"The most obvious function of gossip is the spreading of news or information ..., a direct means of communication among a group."[6] However, unlike more formal communications, which have regular and patterned *modi operandi,* "gossip is an unregimented spread of information."[7] Furthermore, not only is gossip "a very general, and important, way of obtaining ... information: sometimes it is the only way,"[8] since data about the personal qualities of persons in the community, and about relations among persons, are seldom, if ever, part of other sorts of communication.

(A notable exception is joking—to be discussed in the next chapter
—in the course of which much information is revealed and
transferred.)

Beyond such strategic significance is a social-psychological one,
based on the postulate that persons seek to present themselves in
ways protective of the self. That is, interaction, the public interplay
of selves, presents risks as well as satisfactions. People wish to
minimize the former as they maximize the latter. In the effort, the
individual attempts "to control the conduct of others, especially
their responsive treatment of him."[9] Gossip can help in several
ways.

One of the self-endangering possibilities of interaction concerns
disharmonious conduct on the part of the individual. For those
who wish to guide their behavior so as to be in tune with
community standards of acting and thus above reproach, gossip has
a strategic and tactical value. As Stirling argues, "gossip acts as an
upholder of traditional standards," since it is "a reflector of public
opinion."[10] Furthermore, as Szwed asserts, "Not only the facts of
gossip are important here, but also the evaluations." Together,
facts and evaluations provide individuals with a "tally sheet for
public opinion" and thus a means for determining what self-
presentation is publicly laudable and what is socially reprehensible.[11]

With every bit of gossip comes the unspoken refrain suggesting,
"So you had better do thus" or "Beware of ever doing thus." As West
explains in his report of gossip in Plainville, and as one might
reiterate of Kehillat Kodesh, "People report, suspect, laugh at, and
condemn the peccadilloes of others, and walk and behave carefully
to avoid being caught in any trifling missteps of their own," thereby
protecting their selves at the same time that they point to the
liabilities of others through gossip.[12] "By deprecating the acts or
practices of others, the gossiper thereby raises his status in his own
eyes [and, one should add, in the eyes of others, who learn implicitly
and sometimes even explicitly that the gossiper would and does act
otherwise], adding to the security of his self-image."[13]

Not only may one gossip about others in order to present oneself
in a favorable way by comparison, but one may even offer gossip
about oneself in a kind of self-initiated/self-focused gossip. Such
gossiping may be seen as a defensive gesture, designed to retain for
the ego at least some measure of control over what facts and
attendant evaluations become part of the gossip about him. The
interpersonal sacrifice or offering may be anxiety-provoking but far

less so than information over which one has no control by virtue of having no knowledge. Most gossip remains, after all, behind one's back.

The tactical significance of gossip goes beyond being defensive, for it becomes at times a *primarily* offensive act of aggression which only secondarily provides for security of one's self-image. To perceive this possible significance of gossip, one must realize that to know something about another which is not universally known is to share a part of the other's own power over his self. It is to have made an incursion into his informational preserve, "the set of facts about himself to which a person expects to control access while in the presence of others."[14] Once the territory of another's self is violated and invaded, as it may be through gossip, power is wrested from the other, whose hegemony over his self is correspondingly diluted. To know, for example, that Derfler does not pay full shul dues is to be able to weaken his self-presentation as a full-fledged member.

Information thus gathered is then subject to strategic management by its possessors and distributors, who may select and edit it in order to present impressions of others which negatively affect their public faces. "Gossip is in this sense," Cox suggests, "a special case of Garfinkel's 'status degradation ceremony.' "[15] As Gluckman puts it, "Gossip . . . is one of the chief weapons which those who consider themselves higher in status use to put those whom they consider lower in their proper place."[16]

Gossip is also capable of positively affecting the perceived impressions of both gossiper and target. The nature of the effect seems to be variable. Several combinations exist:

1. *Approbatory information auspiciously transmitted.* Both gossiper and target manage to have their status enhanced by the gossip; the manner of transmission and the content both yield a positive charge.

2. *Derogatory information inauspiciously transmitted.* Both gossiper and target have their status degraded by the gossip, with an overzealous gossiper becoming gossipmonger and the target also suffering because of the unquestionably calumnious facts of the gossip.

3. *Derogatory information auspiciously transmitted.* The gossiper manages to enhance his social status, while the target is degraded; the transmission of information is circumspect, but the information itself remains ineluctably damning.

4. *Approbatory information inauspiciously transmitted.* The

gossiper suffers status degradation, while the target enjoys status enhancement; the information is clumsily passed, yet its substance serves to enhance the status of the target because of the undeniably flattering facts it embodies.

5. *Neutral information inauspiciously transmitted.* Here the target remains unaffected, but, because of his clumsiness, the gossiper is stigmatized as an overzealous gossipmonger.

In contrast to more blatant forms of attack (for example, public shaming), gossip is a surreptitious aggression which enables one to wrest power, manipulate, and strike out at another without the other's being able to strike back, since he can never be sure exactly who has generated the offensive against him. While one may at times, with considerable difficulty, learn the substance of gossip focused on oneself, learning the identity of the gossiper is next to impossible. Indeed, were such discoveries easy, one might suppose that gossip would soon be much curtailed. The social and psychological benefits would be more easily offest by the interpersonal risks of discovery and retaliation.

Gossip thus provides the gossiper (as well as the enthusiastic and willing recipient) with a means of expressing aggressive feelings toward another with a minimum of interpersonal risk and anxiety. "In this case," as Stirling says, "gossip may have a therapeutic value to the gossiper."[17]

Consider the following incident at Kehillat Kodesh, paying special attention to the way the members seem to defuse their anger:

> Rabbi Kinorg, a young bearded bread salesman, recognized as active in Jewish observance, has been standing in front of the bimah during the Torah scroll reading of Jimmy Kaufman, the young boy who regularly reads. At a certain word, Kinorg calls out a mistake he alleges Kaufman to have made and which he therefore asks to have read correctly. (Halacha demands that the reading be heard exactly as it is written.) No one else seems to agree with Kinorg's hearing, and Kaufman is motioned to continue.
>
> Kinorg repeats, "I demand that you repeat the word. I will not let you continue unless you correctly read the word."
>
> The congregation is now hushed as Kaufman stops. In a moment others begin to shout as well as Kinorg, but they are insisting that Kaufman continue. Kaufman remains silent, waiting for a decision to be reached.
>
> To several people who suggest that the word was read properly, Kinorg replies, "I know. I was standing right here [in front of the bimah], and he said the word wrong!"

The arguments are repeated. Velvel ends the talk, citing the halachic principle, *Achray raabim lehatos* ("Follow the decision of the majority"). The arguments are over. The reader continues. The whole interchange has taken less than two minutes.

The tension still remains, but it is obviously being expelled by gossip. I overhear the people sitting near me talking. Babblisky starts talking about the fact that Kinorg is not welcome in any shul he goes to and has no right to decide what is right and wrong here. The issue is not the word-reading but Kinorg's authority to decide.

"Only the gabbai should correct," Babblisky maintains.

Harwood begins telling me about Kinorg, explaining that the man is deaf and therefore stands near the bimah. His testimony about the reading of the word is thus highly suspect. "Besides," Harwood adds, "the guy's under all kinds of pressures. He lost his job. I mean, you can't take a guy like that seriously. He's a mixed-up guy."

Now I notice that Kinorg has walked over to Zinger. They speak softly to each other, and I can just make out the substance of their conversation from phrases overheard. Kinorg is now smiling and explaining that he is sure about Kaufman's mistake.

"I caught the guy with this before, but I didn't say anything," he says to Zinger. "This time I got fed up."

At the end of the service, much of the tension from this argument will have been dissipated. For about ten minutes after the actual episode people gossiped about the principals. In the process, all sorts of slanderous and semislanderous points were made. Yet, by the end of the service, handshakes, smiles, and amity were all that was left. Kaufman's father and Kinorg were smiling. Kinorg explained that he meant no personal attack against the boy, and Kaufman agreed that at times the noise in shul is such that no one can be sure of anything. The argument has passed, with no small assistance from gossip.

Gossip may further offer the ego-supportive qualities of scape-goating and projection. According to Stirling,

> Making the other person suffer [via gossip] and pay for his nonconforming to various inhibiting edicts of the group also acts as a justification for self-denial on the part of the gossiper; the target is used as a symbolic outlet for hostility toward the inhibiting cultural edicts in general.[18]

That is, gossip aids the rationalizing process which is a necessary part of any successful repression of ego-oriented, antisocial desires. More precisely, when individuals feel themselves bound and firmly held by a community, for whatever reasons, and when withdrawal is neither possible nor desired, gossip becomes an important (because successful) way to express antisocial feelings without seriously endangering one's group membership. Hence, one is not at all surprised to find that apparently tightly knit communities like Kehillat Kodesh are often the very ones which seem inordinately engaged in gossip or that Velvel, the most inexorably tied to the group, gossips the most; it constitutes his only release from the conciliatory burdens of his office.

As noted earlier, the outsider cannot join in gossip. The reasons are complex. In the first place, joining in is limited by the outsider's own (acquired) considerations of what is important and relevant. If he does not know or care about the events and personalities touched on in the gossip, he is bound to withhold himself from participation; and, even if he should want to talk, he would have nothing in particular to say. Moreover, because he may not know or share community values and objectives, he cannot have a guideline for acceptable and socially legitimate evaluations.

If the outsider cannot join in gossip, then, one begins to see that gossiping provides persons with a way to exhibit, both to themselves and to others, their status as members and insiders. Gluckman, drawing upon Colson's word among the Makah Indians, crystallizes the point when he writes that men mark "themselves off from others by talking about one another."[19]

Not only gossiping but also being its target may be a hallmark of membership. As Frankenberg discovered in his study of the community of Pentre, "Pentre people are those whom other Pentre people gossip with and about."[20] Indeed, in my own case, the longer I remained at Kehillat Kodesh, the more people seemed to talk about me and to me about others. This encompassing quality of gossip, as Thomas learned, is part of intuitive common knowledge:

> I asked a Polish peasant what was the extent of an "okolica" or neighborhood—how far it reached.
> "It reaches," he said, "as far as the report of a man reaches—as far as a man is talked about."[21]

The significance of gossip may further be discovered in terms of its usefulness in the exercise of sociability. The person seeking fellowship finds gossip, because it cannot be engaged in by the solitary individual, an instrumental means of achieving union with others. As Stirling puts it, gossip "is also a means of passing time, and as chit-chat, it offers a means of recreation and tends to solidify group-member identification."[22] While people may come together ostensibly to gossip, this activity may serve as a starting mechanism for purer forms of sociation. The gossip invariably occurring in the various sociability spots within the shul often constitutes the most intimate of interpersonal encounters among the members. One senses that being together may be as important as learning the gossip—perhaps more so. As such, then, the individual may engage in gossip as a ticket of entry into the state of being that Simmel calls "sociation"—togetherness. That is why the lonely newcomer, in shul as elsewhere, in order to facilitate his becoming an insider, so desperately seeks out gossip.

Like the individual psychological significance of gossip, its individual social significance is discovered in the service which gossip provides for the self. In the former perspective, gossip emotionally supports and protects the self in ways that for the most part remain unconscious to the individual. In the latter perspective, gossip locates the self in society. Here gossip helps place one inside or outside the group, enhances one's status as an insider, allows for characterization which is prestigious and potentially powerful, and generally supports the social position of the gossiper.

However, if gossip provided benefits exclusively for individuals, its pleasures, like all other ego satisfactions, would at best be merely tolerated and at worst would be repressed and resisted by the collectivity. Instead, one discovers the abiding presence of the group behind gossip. While persons do in fact gossip in self-interest, "the individual operates . . . within a system of institutions and groups."[23] That is, individuals do not gossip alone but *with* others, within the domain of the group, which in turn places restraints on individual self-interest.

One has only to try to overstep, for purposes of self-interest, the implicit boundaries of public propriety to feel the until-then-hidden restraints surrounding gossip. Under such conditions, the gossiper may find himself made to feel anxious, insecure, low, and insignificant as a result of the same gossip which, when done properly, yields opposite results. This propriety in essence marks the difference between the gossiper and the gossipmonger.

Because one finds that the group sets clear though unspoken rules and norms governing gossip, one must assume that the group either tacitly approves or openly encourages it. Indeed, if the case were otherwise—if the group's interest lay only in preventing gossip—one might find the activity as rare as incest or other widely prohibited forms of behavior. Instead, one finds gossip to be universal in both time and social space, occurring always and everywhere. Why?

Groups, like individuals, may be thought of as having selves or personalities, and, like individuals, groups guard, protectively present, and care for their egos. As Durkheim stated it, "There can be no society which does not feel the need of upholding and reaffirming at regular intervals the collective sentiments and the collective ideas which make its unity and its personality." He continued: "Now this moral remaking cannot be achieved except by means of reunions, assemblies and meetings where the individuals, being closely united to one another, reaffirm in common their common sentiments."[24] While Durkheim's primary interest in these remarks was in deciphering the relationship between society and religion, his conceptualization may be used for understanding the collective psychological significance of gossip.

Reunions, assemblies, and meetings are of course not held for religious reasons only. Even if the manifest purpose of such get-togethers is religious, persons also come together to gossip. Kirshenblatt-Gimblett offers an example:

> By far the most frequent times for telling stories in the round form were the hour of twilight each day and the afternoon of the Sabbath. In the *bes medrash* "prayer or study house" or shul "synagogue," storytelling was a favorite daily pastime before and after prayers, but especially at twilight after the afternoon prayers had been said during the hour the men were waiting for the evening prayers to begin.[25]

Where Kirschenblatt-Gimblett found folktales, I, at Kehillat Kodesh, have found their counterpart—gossip. No shul gathering may pass without discussions of "community matters," latent reaffirmations of community sentiments, beliefs, and values.

The group, whose emotional hold over its members depends upon their holding on to common sentiments, reflecting some common psychic characteristics, must therefore encourage any and all mechanisms which serve this end. Gossip fills the bill. Thus, even in the face of the halachic prohibition against all forms of gossip, the shul members gossip because to do so "is a reaffirmation of the solidarity and indeed the existence of the community as such" and a way to "maintain themselves as a group—an elite—in the wider society in which they live."[26]

In short, not only does gossip provide particular information, as manifestly it must; it also offers the individuals in the group a chance to find out whom they are among, what is thought there, what the "we-group" believes, and the ways in which its members act. And, in offering individuals an opportunity to learn and relearn, affirm and reaffirm, these collective truths, gossip offers the group a means of self-control and emotional stability.

The dynamics of such collective self-control, and its correlate, emotional stability, may be understood, further, through the notion of the *informational preserve*. I have already mentioned the individual self-control and protection offered by the ability to invade another's hegemony over his self. Yet there are emotional implications for the group as well. The realization that control over the facts about oneself is limited by the presence of gossip creates a sort of universal hegemonic weakness which cannot help but foster communal interdependency. There will be at least a show of mutual good will when no one risks too aggressive a challenge against another for fear that the other will mount a gossip-generated counterattack. Only when each person knows qualitatively the same sorts of things about others as they know about him is any sort of strategic balance achieved, is any hegemonic security conceivable. The difficulty both of evaluating the quality of gossip and of knowing who knows what about whom serves to perpetuate gossip. In turn, the continued presence of gossip assures efforts to preserve mutual good will and communal interdependency, because it forces individuals to keep building defenses around their own selves instead of mounting offenses against the selves of others. The balancing act goes on and on, helping in a latent way to maintain a dynamic balance between individual interests and group needs. For a group like Kehillat Kodesh, whose fragile existence demands a spirit of conciliation, this dimension of gossip is crucial.

Finally, as suggested earlier, gossip offers the individual an outlet for aggression. Moreover, it does so without forcing an individual into an overt and disruptive show of force. The interpersonal advantages for the individual have already been cited. However, the benefits of this sort of outlet for aggression accrue to the group as well. In allowing, indeed encouraging, gossip, the group allows individuals to find a way of living within the collectivity, to let off steam, while minimally threatening the stability and security of the group. Gossip helps to avoid the kind of divisive outburst of anger that often leads to collective disintegration. (Recall here the case of Rabbi Kinorg.) Members maintain manifestly friendly relationships while in private they gossip actively and intensely.

Thus one finds that the collectively oriented psychological significance of gossip lies in its provision of support for the collective ego's needs. It is a way of affirming and asserting communal sentiments, solidifying group-member identification, maintaining cohesiveness, and emotionally controlling the collectivity and the individuals which give it its life.

If the individual sociological perspective of gossip reveals it to be a means of socially locating a person, from the collective sociological perspective it may be seen as a means of locating the group vis-à-vis other groups. As indicated earlier, gossip serves to distinguish individuals as either outsiders or insiders—a matter of significance to the collectivity as well. Indeed, "There is no easier way of putting a stranger in his place than by beginning to gossip; this shows him conclusively that he does not belong."[27]

Gluckman puts forward the principle that "the more exclusive the group, the greater will be the amount of gossip in it."[28] Groups for whom exclusivity is identical with survival can thus be expected to be intense and frequent gossipers. This is confirmed by Cox, who found that the Hopi, threatened by the prospect of cultural assimilation, maintain their separateness by active gossiping, and by Frankenberg, who discovered that in Pentre, a Welsh border village in danger of becoming another faceless English working-class suburb, gossip is the stuff of life. And we, in our examination of Kehillat Kodesh, a group imperiled both by the exodus of Jews from Dudley Meadows and by the destructive tendencies of modernity, find gossip a common and an absorbing pursuit.

One might add, as a further principle, that the greater the corpus of information which makes up the store of gossip exchanged within the community, the more there is to being a full-fledged participant and member. At Kehillat Kodesh, as elsewhere, gossip is by no means restricted to the latest news; it embraces the whole history of personalities and events. Hence, the newcomer has much to learn. Moreover, the technical problems of gossip-gathering and transmission (as will be elaborated shortly) act as a substantial barrier "to exclude parvenus"—those who would assert insider status too easily.[29] Hence, gossip serves the group as a fence of words within which the population may remain safely corralled.

From the collective as well as from the individual sociological perspective, gossip may be viewed as wealth. A community's gossip is the wealth of information about its members which is stored within it. Like folktales, many of the same gossip items may be told and retold year after year and time after time with all the freshness of a new report. To learn the gossip is to share in communal wealth.

Finally, as implied in many of the other points raised here, gossip not only differentiates insiders from outsiders and parvenus but can also be used to distinguish various strata of insiders. Gossip may act as a vehicle for classifying the membership, distinguishing intragroup cliques, and affirming various sorts of relationships, from the most transient to the most intimate. In its content and patterns of exchange, gossip "reflects the relational structure of the individual's social world." In the simpler words of one of West's Plainville informants, gossip "shows how people are all connected up."[30]

How gossip may act as such a vehicle must now be analyzed and ethnographically described. First, however, it is necessary to say something about the nature of gossip exchange; for it is through exchange that gossip serves to differentiate between members and cliques within a larger collectivity.

Gossip: Exchange and Accessibility

By now we have various perspectives on what gossip is, and in particular we have an idea of its significance and benefits. Without question, to know and to be able to engage in gossip is something of value. Like anything else of value, gossip—and the ability to engage in it—is subject to exchange, very much like a gift. And, as Mauss pointed out, "a gift necessarily implies the notion of credit."[31] Associated with all gifts is a series of interactions which generate obligations that must be discharged. Mauss lists three among these as primary: giving, receiving, and repaying. Moreover, because gossip possession and transference have emotional as well as social consequence for everyone who is directly or indirectly involved in the transference, it is a gift of no small importance.

Indeed, pursuing the gift metaphor offers a useful way of understanding something about the passing or exchange of gossip. To begin with, gossip seems to qualify as a *prestation*, "any thing or series of things given freely and obligatorily as a gift or in exchange; and includes services, entertainments, etc., as well as material things."[32] Moreover, "prestations which are in theory voluntary, disinterested and spontaneous . . . are in fact obligatory and interested."[33] Like such prestations, gossip at first glance appears to be casual, idle, somewhat spontaneous chatter, of little account. Upon closer observation, however, it reveals itself to be part of a tight system of obligatory exchange. No one can consistently be a recipient without sometimes being a donor. To do so, to try to take in more than one gives out, is to risk being classed as a "busybody" or a "snoop" and to be excluded from a good deal of gossip activity; this presents a problem for the participant observer–researcher, who unobtrusively wishes to get more than he gives.

No one can consistently refuse to be a recipient of gossip, either. To do so, to be only a donor, is again to chance being classed as a "busybody"—in this case one whose primary interest is in spreading information about others. As Vidich and Bensman found in Springdale, the "bad folks" were the ones who "wantonly spread gossip around town."[34] In shul such "bad folks" are called *yentas.*

Finally, the person who scorns gossip completely, declining to be either donor or recipient, at the very least risks stigmatization (ironically, through the very gossip he scorns) and at the worst excludes himself from a central activity of collective life and sociability. As with prestation, "to refuse to give . . . like refusing to accept . . . is a refusal of friendship and intercourse."[35]

Like other forms of wealth, gossip enhances the prestige of the person who has the ability to acquire and disburse it as well as simply to possess it. Moreover, as already suggested in the discussion of the individual perspectives on gossip, it offers emotional and strategic benefits as well. Indeed, so great are the advantages of being in the know that individuals may be willing to "enhance their prestige by *pretending* to have access to 'inside information,'" that is, by dealing in less-than-reliable information, with all the attendant social risks of being found out.[36]

Donorship thus reflects the etiquette of interpersonal relations, but a "pecuniary" insight into donorship might be offered as well. If gossip is wealth, it must, in Veblen's terms, be made "conspicuous,"[37] its ownership publicized: "The only way to demonstrate [one's] fortune is by expending it."[38] One gossips, shares information with others, because that is the way to exhibit how much one is in the know.

However, as suggested in the gift metaphor, the prestation of gossip is not made manifestly, and strictly speaking, as something to be exchanged. On the contrary, for the donor to derive the fullest enhancement from his wealth, he must be able to engage in conspicuous waste, to have so much information that he can afford to be quite generous in handing it out to worthy recipients (although not so lavish as to overwhelm them and make repayment impossible; for worse than to receive no gift is to receive one so large that, since repayment can never be made, one is left forever beholden and inferior). He must *appear* to be giving out information without expectation of return. Various means of accomplishing this show may be utilized. One may, for example, not only speak swiftly, allowing for no interruption during which a return could be made, but also abruptly change the subject once the transmission is complete. Or, with a similar sort of self-presentation in mind, the gossiper may present his information in an apparently offhand manner, introducing it, perhaps, by such linguistic qualifiers as "by the way," "incidentally," or some other tag line which indicates a degree of purposeful disinterestedness.

The same sort of veneer of unconcern for repayment which characterizes gossip prestation is described by Mauss in connection with gift-giving in general: "Pains are taken to show one's freedom and autonomy as well as one's magnanimity, yet all the time one is actuated by the mechanisms of obligation which are resident in the gifts themselves."[39] If repayment can be made, it must be.

Despite all the shows of generosity, both donors and recipients must realize, if they are to continue to be involved in gossiping, that all information received incurs an obligation of repayment. When once, early in my observations, I tried to solicit gossip without any significant return, one member finally asserted in hardly disguised anger, "Look, I'm not gonna make it that easy for you. Find out for yourself and then tell me."

Implied in my informant's remark is another means of comprehending gossip in terms of exchange. As already suggested in the examination of gossip from the individual psychological and sociological perspectives, gossip is wealth and power. To engage in gossip is to exercise power. Moreover, to enable another to engage in it is to empower, to enfranchise him, as it were, as a gossiper. But to remain solely a recipient of power is to imply that one has nothing more than what one has just been given. Only a return of gifts of equivalent or superior value will redeem the original recipient from the relatively lower status which the donor has implicitly handed him along with the manifest prestation. "Such a return will give its donor authority and power over the original donor, who now becomes the latest recipient."[40] Thus, even though gossip is wealth—and so one might suppose that men would be interested only in accumulating it—the desire for status one-upmanship, and the need to herald one's wealth serve to keep the exchange of gossip going.

The prestation metaphor, however, suggests yet another possible way of explaining the exchange of gossip. Friendship, as we saw, leads to gossip, and gossip in turn supports friendship. Moreover, "to give something is to give a part of oneself," and "to receive something is to receive a part of someone's spiritual essence."[41] One might synthesize these points and reach a new hypothesis: the nature of friendship, communion, and intimacy is such that each party wishes to offer the other the best of what he has. And because friendship, communion, and intimacy all imply emotional and communal support—precisely the sort of asset attached to the ability to partake of and participate in gossip—friends share gossip with and about each other. To put it somewhat differently, one might say that friendship enables a person's intimates to share in his social construction and discussion of reality; or, as Berger and Luckmann phrase it, "The significant others in the individual's life are the principal agents for the maintenance of his subjective reality."[42]

While one must agree that "gossip . . . will not contribute to the cohesion of a grouping of persons, unless these persons are united by a sense of community which is based on the fairly successful pursuit of common objectives," nevertheless, "gossip and scandal are . . . generally . . . enjoyed by people about others with whom they are in a close social relationship"; indeed, "gossiping is a duty of membership of the group."[43] If one wonders how one can be friends in the face of gossiping, one need only remember that gossip and scandal represent transformations of aggressive impulses that, otherwise expressed, would be far more injurious. Indeed, gossip with its implied restraints is precisely for friends; others less dear would perhaps be subjected to far less restrained and concealed malice. That is why one gossips only among friends. As one member of Kehillat Kodesh put it, "We don't wash our dirty linen in public."

As if to underline the communal nature of gossip, one recalls that the outsider cannot join in the gossiping, for he is one who can take gossip and manage it as he pleases, completely for his own benefit and without any regard for the restraints, the checks and balances, which members of the community observe. He does not have to temper his wealth and informational power with considerations of communal responsibilities of sociability and solicitude precisely because he is an outsider. Accordingly, one finds that those who are not responsible members of the collectivity, either because of social position or personal failing, are excluded from gossip exchange (although not necessarily from becoming the *subject* of gossip). One finds, for example, as I did, that both the unaccompanied stranger and the child (or childlike adult) are seldom if ever persons with whom one gossips, since neither of these persons feels himself bound by communal restraints. The group implicitly realizes that "the more [a person] becomes a trusted member, the greater may be his concern about ... betrayal."[44] That concern is precisely the restraint that the collectivity can count on from the insider. Only when a person may be expected to hold a commitment to the group greater than, or at least equal to, his commitment to himself, may all sorts of gossip from all segments of the group be shared and exchanged with him. Only then may he discuss social reality.

Prior to exploring the exchange model as a vehicle for comprehending the transmission and flow of gossip, I suggested that all collectivities are made up of various strata of insiders as well as certain types of outsiders. If such is the case, then each of these secondary collectivities may be identified by its association with a particular sort of gossip exchange. Such exchange, one might hypothesize, would generally be characterized by the common rules of exchange in the collectivity at large but would also display particular qualities with regard to exchange and accessibility which would be characteristic of each stratum. In both content and patterns of exchange, one might expect the gossip to reflect (and incidentally offer the sociologist a tool for deciphering) the relational structure of the gossipers' social world.

The types of gossip and gossip exchange which I propose here must be seen as theoretically tentative, suggested in part by my experiences in the shul and offered as a means of deciphering the observed practice of gossip.

Types of Gossip

Closer examination of gossip reveals what should be experientially, if not intuitively, obvious to anyone who has ever been a party to gossip: not everyone is exchanged with equally, not everything which is exchanged is available to everyone in the community, and not all gossip is alike. Rather, information is divided between items to which there is relatively easy access and items surrounded with substantial restrictions. The former, prestations of low value, are easily traded, the latter quite the opposite. As one advances in status from outsider to neophyte and then to full-fledged insider, one gains increasing access to all types of gossip, including the highly restricted. As one moves into the society, one may increasingly discuss and hence play a principal role in social-reality construction. The purpose of the following typology, which is graded from least-valuable and most-accessible to most-valuable and least-accessible types of gossip, is to provide us with a possible means of tracing the relational structure of a community, a structure hinted at by Kierkegaard when he wrote, "With gossip . . . everything is reduced to a kind of private-public gossip which corresponds more or less to the public of which it forms a part";[45] the typology is also intended to provide a means for determining individuals' roles in the reality maintenance which gossip assists.

One preliminary warning is in order: like all such classifications, this one must be considered as an ideal type, which reality—even as it suggests it—at best approximates. Actual examples which I shall cite as illustrations of one or another type on the gossip continuum would, perhaps with some justification, be placed elsewhere on that continuum by someone else; that is always the difficulty in interpreting real life. Nevertheless, the following typology offers, I think, useful ways of generally ordering matters of gossip.

News

To begin with, there is the gossip which one might call *news*. Like all gossip, news identifies the persons associated with the facts in question, but it need not be composed of particularly secret or titillating information. Rather, news items are reports of the events and acts which constitute the everyday life of the community, notes and comments on life in progress. Who came to shul on Sunday, how many people so-and-so invited for a party, the date of a forthcoming marriage—all qualify as news items. The news may be part of a larger corpus of knowledge, or it may be a single piece of gossip, with no apparent connection to anything else.

Such gossip is news (that is, of interest) "to a relatively small number of persons who know [or know of] one another."[46] To the outsider, who has no connection whatsoever with the group or any of its members, the newsworthiness of the information is nil. While he may know the information, he would not under normal circumstances *want* to know it. Accessibility to news seems limited only by interest. While outsiders may share in it, they are not expected to exercise their prerogatives of access (unless, like newcomers, they hope to become insiders).

In "pecuniary" terms, the more easily obtainable an item, the lower are both its socially regarded and exchange values. So too is the case with gossip: the greater the number of people from whom the gossip may be garnered, the lower is its value in exchange. The more people who know something, the less likely it is that the information will retain strict restrictions on wider accessibility. This general realization about the pervious nature of news creates and fosters a self-fulfilling condition under which those in possession of this kind of gossip feel little constraint to hold onto it or to be cautious about passing it on. This circumstance in turn assures that news will remain readily available and accordingly of low value.

To suggest that news is of *low* social or exchange value is not to suggest that it is of *no* social value. Having news in abundance and expressing an interest in the newsy details of everyday community life may serve as hallmarks of membership. A particular news item may be of limited value, but a mass of them has considerable social meaning and is subject to social restrictions, being limited to those who may assert insider status, "the permanent members of the attentive public."[47]

While news in and of itself may be neutral information, it has the potential of becoming socially charged with either positive (i.e., status enhancing) or negative (i.e., status degrading) effects. Knowing who attended the minyan, when coupled with other information—for example, that a yartzeit was missing—is far from neutral news. Thus, no matter how neutral the news may seem, the gathering and exchange of it is not.

In tacit recognition that news is not lacking in social consequence, participants may be expected to become wary of those who collect a great deal of it without making any sort of return. Hoarding is discouraged in the implied mutuality of conversation, the common medium of news exchange.

For the new member, news is the first gossip to which he is exposed. One quickly identifies the newcomer by the fact that he possesses little more than such news information. It is what he must save to exchange for more valuable gossip. In my role as participant observer, I gathered a lot of news about who participated in what. Indeed, the members, knowing I went to most affairs and had *written notes*, came to expect much news from this new "informed source." My news was exchangeable for more valuable items of gossip. Thus, after a period of time, when I had amassed enough credit by cataloguing and divulging participants at various shul functions, I began to be repaid for my news with more valuable gossip. Once, as I listed the members present at a masquerade party, the recipient of the news began to respond by telling me some gossip about each person I mentioned. Although I later learned that much of this information was public knowledge, at first hearing it had all the freshness of an exposé. Furthermore, receiving it served as a benchmark of initiation into full-fledged membership.

Public Knowledge

The episode I have just described brings up a type of gossip which is more valuable than simple news and less accessible: *public knowledge*. Such gossip is distinguished by containing facts whose social charge and significance are far less ambiguous than the facts contained in news. The details of public knowledge are often, although not always, embedded in a complex narrative which serves to frame and hence point out their social meaning; as a result, a social construction of reality is more patently a part of the social discussion of events.

Public knowledge is also distinguished from news by being strictly limited in accessibility to recognized members of the public. But here the "public" is confined to insiders; no longer, as with news, does it apply to any attentive public whose interest might be *temporarily* activated by special circumstances. Once information becomes public knowledge, it becomes part of the collective informational preserve. Public knowledge is frequently made up of the social history of the group in question; and, whether or not every member of the community actually possesses this information is definitely less important than the fact that any full-fledged member *could* possess it—that no restrictions to access obtain for those judged to be responsible participants in collective life.

While public knowledge may not always contain the latest gossip, and its secrets may long since have been revealed, those who would have themselves recognized as insiders must still exhibit a competent, abundant, and enthusiastic familiarity with this fundamental staple of communal gossip. "To be able to gossip properly, a member has to know not only about the present membership, but also their forbears."[48]

Indeed, the first substantial public knowledge that I began to receive, as my status as member solidified, were old stories about the early arguments and upheavals in the shul. In time each member offered me the gift of a story, almost as if such prestation were a token of welcome into the community. At first all the gossip I learned was about events that had occurred long before, and few of these items related to current and developing history. The quality of these gossip items revealed one of the characteristics of this type of public knowledge: it is the type of gossip which may and often does become transformed into folktales. Elements of the narrative seem with time to become codified and the listeners' responses predictable. In urban and contemporary settings, where transiency is so often a fact of collective life, folk tradition may perhaps be replaced by the not quite so historically distant public knowledge. Instead of trading old tales, people trade old gossip—public knowledge. At Kehillat Kodesh, where, in addition to the emphasis on modernity, one finds a congregation whose members are for the most part under forty and are the progeny of a generation ripped from many of its folk roots by the holocaust in Europe, the substitution of public-knowledge gossip for folktales is especially prominent.

For example, one story which had become a staple of public knowledge at Kehillat Kodesh concerned Brown's wife, who had given birth without ever realizing that she was pregnant. Each time the story was repeated, it was told in more or less the same way. It began with a mention of the member's last name, which brought forth laughs and chuckles from the insiders—outsiders immediately marking themselves off by their muteness and their uncomprehending expressions. Then came another mention of the husband, his response to the news of the birth of a child he was not expecting, a comment about the reason the woman did not realize she was pregnant, and a final joke about the story, usually something about how the member responded that he would probably name the child Jesus.

The story was repeated quite frequently, and knowledge of it was a sure sign that someone was an insider. When asked if I had ever heard the story of Brown, my affirmative response signaled not only knowledge of the story but also that I was something of an insider.

One of the more interesting qualities of this folkloristic type of public knowledge is its manner of exchange. Beyond serving to initiate the novice, the actual circumstances of such public-knowledge exchange very much resemble the exchange of folktales which Kirshenblatt-Gimblett describes in her study of a shul of old men.[49] Because public knowledge is the kind of gossip which is by

definition open to everyone who is a full member, it is the best kind
of gossip to exchange in public in place of the public telling of
folktales. The exercise remains the same; it is that of storytelling.
What has changed is that the stories are not legends of the shtetl but
gossip about the shul—that last vestige of the shtetl in the
contemporary American panorama. The telling and retelling, the
exchange of this public knowledge, occurs usually before and after
the services—like the folklore-telling Kirshenblatt-Gimblett describes—and in sociability spots, where everyone ought to be
allowed to participate. (I have already said that the presence of too
many outsiders keeps members away from such spots; thus the
problem of excluding outsiders from this kind of gossip is avoided.)

The exchange of folk stories can occur in four narrative styles,
according to Kirshenblatt-Gimblett: conversation, storytelling
round, storytelling solo, or monologue.[50] The exchange of public
knowledge occurs in much the same way. Because it is exchange, the
process often takes the form of story in conversation or in round,
where repayment or swapping can occur almost immediately.
Occasionally, the solo or monologue format occurs, very often
when members of the audience are initiates, who by definition have
very little to return. In essence, participants in such narration of
public knowledge are not only retelling a story of gossip; they are
also reaffirming their membership and involvement in the shul and
its social life. They are exhibiting the fact that they are not solitary
individuals but are part of a union of interest. Indeed, such
narrative events become very much the stuff of sociability, where
what is conversed about is not as important as the fact that people
are engaging in conversation. Such gossip becomes the common
ground which brings people together. In spite of their various
involvements in the secular world and elsewhere, as members they
have this public knowledge in common and may use it as a vehicle
for sociability. Like prayer, this gossip brings people together—and
perhaps that is why it has become so much a part of the
conversation that occurs during prayer.

Public-knowledge gossip becomes not only the recitation of
narrative events but also a declaration of normative behavior; it is
the *most*-public tally sheet of public opinion. Moreover, it contains
the crystallized characterizations of past events and of members'
reputations: that so-and-so is a big giver, lives beyond his means,
or is lax in his Jewish observance; that such-and-such was a
scandalous party, a financial flop, an exhilarating occasion. These
accompanying evaluations are as much a part of public knowledge
as the facts themselves. Thus, when members gossip about so-and-

so who has stopped attending the minyan even though he has the religious obligation to recite kaddish after a deceased kinsman, the norm and value of reciting kaddish religiously is thereby asserted. The public-knowledge gossip serves here to reaffirm principles of religious observance.

The facts of such gossip need not be completely spelled out; references may be quite oblique. For example, when a group of men stand together talking and one asks, "Was Barry in shul this morning?"—knowing full well that Barry is a chiyuv, realizing that everyone else knows that too, and that everyone knows that a chiyuv must attend shul daily—he is implicitly making a point about Barry and about religious observance.

The references made need not be degrading or scornful. For example, one group of women I overheard were talking about a young man in the shul who was making his fiancée Orthodox— watching out to see that she came home from work before the Sabbath, adhered to the laws of kashrut, and so forth. Their evaluation of this young man in the gossip exchange indicated that such behavior won their approval and could be emulated by others without incurring scorn.

A second sort of public knowledge exists as well. Unlike the first sort, the neo-folktale, which is "not news" but rather is made up of elaborations of events and acts of the past, this second variety consists of gossip which *ought* to be publicized—gossip which, although not yet a part of the corpus of public knowledge, seems to warrant inclusion in the public domain. Included in this category are accounts of novel events as well as those that have had forerunners in previous public knowledge; the latter then represent a continuation of an old story, a sequel.

This second type of public knowledge takes various forms. One of the more interesting has become institutionalized in the form of weekly announcements made by the president (or, in his absence, by another officer) at the conclusion of the Sabbath morning service, when the largest "public" is assembled. Although such announcements also contain news, they constitute public knowledge when their full significance is comprehendable only by insiders. Many of the items announced are not new to the members. Indeed, more often than not the president's announcements simply ratify information that has in the course of the preceding week become part of public knowledge. The announcement is the final ceremony, in which the entire community is notified and can make some sort of ritualized response to the public knowledge.

The announcements receive a great deal of attention; and, no matter how noisy the shul is a moment before the beginning of the announcements, silence is achieved within the first few seconds of Velvel's comments. Here is a public affirmation of those aspects of private and personal affairs which are the most respectable. This constitutes not only the announcement of the personal affairs of an individual but also the proclamation of those values and behavior patterns which the collectivity is willing to celebrate and publicize. As such, it is in a sense a reaffirmation and ratification of a social order that is characteristic of the group. Seldom is anything new learned; the known is simply celebrated and reviewed.

The announcements publicize such items as a member's engagement to be married, the birth of a child, the death of a kinsman, a farewell to someone leaving on a journey (with both destination and duration of trip identified and specified), the receipt of an academic degree or a new job, and the welcome of a newcomer into the community (including details about his or her occupation and place of origin). Such announcements are *legitimate* gossip. This is the kind of gossip which may be recited in front of the party who is its target.

For the most part such gossip is positive in nature. It shuns slander and, if it degrades, does so in such an oblique manner that the subject cannot make an openly aggressive response. It fulfills the minimum criteria of gossip and is therefore classified as such; namely, it is information about the personal affairs of others, identifies these others by name or in some other unmistakable way, is socially significant only to a specified group of others, and stimulates further gossip. Moreover, it satisfies the criteria of public knowledge because its information is available to any full-fledged member.

One final note. Like all gossip, no one may receive public knowledge without at times giving it. Anyone who is given a part of the public trust of gossip must somehow indicate that he already owns shares in that trust; otherwise, participation is prohibited. "To every one that hath shall be given, and he shall have in abundance; but from him who hath not shall be taken away" (Matthew 25:29). To be able to gossip about the events of public knowledge, one must be able to engage in commentary and narration as well as listening.

Outsiders mark themselves off immediately in both their inability to make the proper responses and their lack of a reciprocal gossip offering. Their presence, signaled by what they say or fail to say, may suddenly abort the full unfolding of public knowledge. Hence, as one watches people engaged in public-knowledge gossiping, one inevitably finds oneself observing the drama of communicants—insiders—intensifying and affirming their social reality and union.

Privileged Information

Of all the sorts of gossip thus far listed, *privileged information* is most limited in terms of public accessibility. Newsgathering and dissemination signal one's desire to be counted among insiders, and public-knowledge acquisition and donation confirm the achievement of that status; but the ability to get and give privileged information involves a quantum jump, since it asserts and affirms one as a *privileged insider*. Privileged information is the beginning of wealth and its attendant power, since it has greater prestational value than news or public knowledge.

The acquisition of such valuable information is no simple matter. Its high worth requires a return of equal or greater value. In homeomorphic terms, a return is adequate only if the exchanged gossip is also privileged information or is even more exclusive and hence more valuable. In heteromorphic terms, a return may require that the original recipient make the original donor feel enhanced in status. An obsequious display of having been impressed by the importance of the gift may be sufficient recompense. Consider, for example, the faithful servant who becomes the recipient of the most privileged information in return for shows of esteem and fidelity. For the most part, however, the exchange of privileged information seems, in a sense, to lend support to the axiom that the rich get richer while the poor stay poor, for it is shared primarily among those who have some sort of privilege to trade for it.

Admittedly, the gossip entrepreneur exists as well. The person who involves himself enthusiastically and frequently in all aspects of community life open to him will no doubt, sooner or later, witness (as this avid researcher did) events that qualify as the stuff of privileged information. With skill, by a carefully orchestrated effort at exchanging such gossip with privileged others (attentive insiders being able accurately to identify such people), a person may be able to trade one bit several times, capitalizing on his privileged information and amassing a wealth of gossip.

In contrast to the successful entrepreneur, who becomes one of the privileged, stand the gossip *nouveaux riches*—those who have accidentally acquired privileged information but do not know the proper way to handle or exchange their wealth. Not comprehending its value or its attendant responsibilities, such persons may blurt out the information in the wrong way or to the wrong person and thus devalue their new possession by "selling" it too cheaply. Once such devaluation occurs, reciprocity is affected. Gossip received from a *nouveau riche* often meets with the recipients' assertion of the low value of the goods received. One hears, "Coming from him, it's probably not true," or "I heard it from ———, so it's probably not worth very much." As such people prove, the possession of isolated bits of privileged information is no guarantee of privileged status.

In its content, privileged information is neither the essentially neutral substance of news nor the well-traveled (or traveling) announcements of public knowledge. Rather, this gossip is charged with an immediately apparent and unmistakable social meaning, since interpretations and attitudes develop along with, and become inextricably intertwined with, the facts. This combination of timeliness, inflection, and attendant interpretation make such gossip the stuff of a great deal of impression management. Privileged information may make or break reputations, enhance or degrade them. Moreover, by limiting access to privileged information, one may further orchestrate and affect general impressions of the reality to which the gossip refers. The same facts, after all, may have quite varying significance to different audiences, a point made abundantly clear in Goffman's essays on self-presentation.

Part of the "calculative, gamelike aspects of mutual dealings,"[51] privileged information is more likely to be used as a weapon than the previously mentioned types of gossip. Like all gossip, its use implies certain risks, many of which are intensified because privileged information is fresh, untested by time or public opinion. Those risks are in part responsible for keeping the gossip limited to a privileged, hence manageable, few among whom one dares make errors. The exchangers of this gossip are thus more intimate than those who trade news and public knowledge.

Nevertheless, privileged information is still very much *public* information, and its purpose remains tied to an effort to enhance one's public face, albeit among a selected public—the privileged. Admittedly, such privileged status is not identical with high status, in the latter's denotation as high social position. In large organizations those highest in formal social status often are privy to less gossip than lower-echelon operatives. More correctly, privileged status is akin to favored status, determined by informal rather than formal lines of stratification. Only where formal and informal lines of stratification are parallel—as is the case at Kehillat Kodesh—can one expect nominal leaders to be among those most in the know.

The greater the number of persons who are aware of one's possession of privileged information, the more likely one is to reap the benefits of possessing it—in, for example, a reflected rise in public esteem. At the same time, however, one must guard against too wide a public dissemination of the gossip, for this would devalue it and cause one to forfeit the social advantages its possession entails. Indeed, one finds that privileged information may at times be the sort of gossip whose existence people may know of without actually knowing its content; such gossip is also the information which everybody actually knows but which everyone at the same time still believes to be relatively exclusive; it is then a kind of border-line public knowledge.

Secret Gossip

A fourth type of gossip, *secret gossip*, is most restricted in terms of access. Unlike privileged information, such gossip is carefully protected from even the *de facto* publicizing which is characteristic of the former. Gone is the calculated leaking, so much a part of privileged information, and gone is the strategy of covert impression management. Instead, secret gossip is exchanged only within a small clique of people who already share a sense of trust. This intimacy guarantees that none of them will pass the gossip out of the collective informational preserve. One finds that statements of secret gossip "are never made in public situations."[52] Although one may hear such accompanying ritual remarks as, "This is just between you and me," or "Don't tell anyone else I told you," such warnings are, more often than not, superfluous, since the conditions of recitation as well as the substance of the gossip assume secrecy.

The smaller the clique which shares the secret, the more secure will the possessors be of maintaining confidentiality. Accordingly, one finds secret gossip the last sort of gossip to which the newcomer gains access. He must first become part of some tightly knit clique before he can share in the gossip dimensions of its existence. Once sharing in such gossip, the individual becomes linked to others, not only through the prestational obligations of gossip exchange; he is further bonded through mutual possession of a secret and all that that entails. The relationship is similar in many respects to what Simmel describes in connection with secret societies.[53]

Secret gossip is paradoxical in nature, since it seeks to conceal and reveal at the same time. "Secret" suggests concealment, while "gossip" implies revelation. As Simmel has said, "The intention of hiding, however, takes on much greater intensity when it clashes with the intention of revealing."[54] The ambivalence of secret gossip cannot help but strike the gossiper. He wishes to reveal and thereby cash in on the value of the facts he possesses; yet he is aware that the information must remain at what Vidich and Bensman call "the intimate level of gossip."[55] Simmel elaborates on this tension:

> The secret contains a tension that is dissolved in the moment
> of its revelation. This moment constitutes the acme in the develop-
> ment of the secret; all of its charms are once more gathered in it
> and brought to a climax . . . ; the moment of dissipation lets
> one enjoy with extreme intensity the value of the object. . . .
> The secret puts a barrier between men but, at the same time, it
> creates a tempting challenge to break through it, by gossip or
> confession.[56]

The temptations toward revelation may be "pecuniary." Secret gossip, that most scarce of informational treasures, has a high exchange value. Its possession marks one as having a wealth of community knowledge, while its donation guarantees a repayment of similar scale which adds to one's being in the know.

The advantages of such gossip may also be ego-supportive and strategic. The most concerted efforts to further one's own interests by discrediting others can be made within the confines of such secret gossip, where only a minimal display of aggression before a carefully selected audience is involved. Consider the following example:

> Fred and I are alone in shul waiting for a minyan to gather.
> The hour is late, and it is fairly apparent that no one else will
> come. The talk begins to get much more secret in nature, and
> Fred is talking about others in a way that he would never do were
> anyone else present.
> He starts to talk about Izzy Zinger. "Zinger's a faker, a real
> phony," he says.
> "What do you mean? Do you mean that he's not really as frum
> as he makes himself out to be? I've always seen him with a
> yarmulke [mandatory head covering for males] on the street."
> I point this out, passing Fred a kind of informational repartee
> and deposit for what is going to be some sort of revelation.
> "Oh no, I don't mean in that way," Fred replies. "He's a faker
> in other ways. Like, he always claims to be doing good for all
> these organizations around, but I know that I pay my full tuition
> to the day school and he never does—and it's not because he can't
> afford it, believe me. He's just a phony."

Gossiping in secret, Fred can directly and boldly overstep the group traditions of amity and unity without anyone else (except the gossip recipient) seeing the attack and hence without incurring the communal negative sanctions toward provocateurs. Once expressed, the frustrating anger which stimulates the gossip is for a time cathartically discharged. He is thus able to improve and support his own self-image by discrediting Izzy.[57] If the psychic satisfaction is not total, strategic ends are at least partially accomplished. Nevertheless, the secrecy is testimony to the strength of the group. Where no such collective force exists, secret slander soon becomes public insult.

Not unsurprisingly, one finds that members of the shul who see themselves as leaders are among the most frequent utilizers of secret gossip. They use it to hold on to their power and to peddle influence, often at the expense of their rivals' reputations. Realizing that open aggression and struggle would destroy the very substance of the group whose esteem and following they desire, the leaders must gossip frequently in secret. Indeed, the mistake made by the original founding leaders was that they permitted the battles and struggles for control to be fought openly, with catastrophic results. For the present leadership, tension is handled by means of secret gossip. Social wounds are more easily covered and healed that way. (This is not to imply that the leaders are the only, or even the primary, users of secret gossip. While it remains a useful tool for handling emotional tensions within the group, other types of gossip are much more helpful for large-scale information and impression management—a matter of interest for leaders—and are accordingly used.)

At Kehillat Kodesh the success of such behind-the-scenes gossiping became most apparent in the nominating and electing of shul officers. No candidate met any open competition; when two persons ran for an office, one of them either withdrew or else joked about his candidacy in such a way that all votes became unanimous. The politicking had gone on beforehand, much of it by means of secret gossip.

One should not jump to the conclusion that all secret gossip, whether evaluative or declarative, is necessarily slanderous; but all gossip is potentially injurious to the existence of the group and/or to its members. Any information that threatens to destroy the unity of the group is made secret, and its dissemination is strictly controlled. Implicit here is the understanding that he who harms the group is in danger of being harmed by it in return.

Although slander or scandal are the most obvious varieties of injurious information, other types of gossip may certainly qualify. Consider, for example, gossip which is highly speculative in nature.

Until its truth is fully established, it must be kept secret. The dispenser of such gossip knows that he has to be careful in his exchange; for if the information turns out to be false, or if its propagation turns out to be deleterious to the parties concerned, all that can be gained from gossiping may be lost. By keeping the gossip secret, the gossiper insures himself against such backfire. Here is an illustration:

> Jake has told me that Mel may be getting married. It isn't public knowledge yet, so I am not to tell anyone. "After all," he says, "if it isn't a hundred percent positive, we shouldn't spread it around—but, if it is, you're among the first to know."

On the chance that the information is true, the donor tells the recipient that he is "among the first to know." Such a declaration is also a statement of the gossip's worth and implicitly constitutes its prestational value. However, if the information proves not to be true, the gossiper has protected himself. Moreover, the recipient, seeing that the donor is willing to risk his gossip reputation in front of him, cannot help but be impressed with the strength of the relationship between them. That he should be among the select few whom the donor would trust with such speculative material suggests that something about him is trustworthy.

Moreover, by keeping such gossip secret, Jake also protects both the target, Mel, and the community. The target is shielded from the social anxiety of public embarrassment, while the community is protected from appearing unable to safeguard its members from embarrassments and from the disunity which the punishment of any insiders, even gossipmongers, may stimulate.

In passing on this speculative information, Jake has made reference to public knowledge. Indeed, such secret gossip is not necessarily destined to remain secret. It may become public knowledge. One may say, generally, that very often the natural history of secret gossip is that it becomes, after a time, privileged information (especially when those "in the know" get together to discuss and evaluate it); and sometimes it even becomes public knowledge (when the group knowing the information no longer keeps it from insiders in general).

The potential benefit of any disclosure stands face to face with its potentially damaging effects, and, in a standoff, the disclosure is made in the form of secret gossip. When the damage of disclosure seems to outweigh any possible benefits, one may guess that the facts are kept secret, never being expressed even as secret gossip. When the benefits of disclosure offset any possible damage, the information will inevitably lose much of its veil of secrecy. While the gossiper must determine what the case is, his decisions are no doubt affected by his position in the group. That is why secret gossip remains the prerogative of "intimate insiders," whose allegiance to the group and its membership is beyond question. Anyone who is not an intimate insider cannot be depended on to keep secrets with the same dedication.

Accordingly, one of the ways to discover those most intimately related is to find out who is exchanging secret gossip with whom. Within one's clique—a group of intimate insiders—in an atmosphere of trust and sociation, the most outrageous bits of gossip are passed. The closer the members, the more similar their values and beliefs, the less likely they are to be affronted or put off by the assessments and perceptions displayed in such gossip. Within such gossip cliques, members may together reconstruct social reality in ways not only in their own interests but even counter to the prevailing communal norm. It is here that even Orthodoxy may be criticized.

When secret gossip is exchanged in shul, it never occurs at sociability spots, where everything discussed is open to everyone present. Rather it takes place between seat neighbors, whispering at their seats, or among intimates huddled in a corner, away from all intrusions. Unlike other types of gossip, which, often occurring as part of narrative events, can occasionally be gathered without incurring obvious obligations, secret gossiping is a one-to-one encounter.

One final point. Secret gossip does not differ qualitatively from the other three types. Rather, it must be seen as the most intensified form of them—because all groups reconstruct reality in gossiping; even news selectively highlights the relevant. What secret gossip allows, however, is a theoretically total control over the reconstructions of gossip; this control provides security along with freedom—an intellectual and emotional paradise of no small consequence. Each of the other types of gossip offers increasing amounts of this paradise, depending on the degree to which they control accessibility. Moreover, the greater the scope of control over social reconstruction offered by a type of gossip, the higher is its prestational value. Accordingly, a bit of secret gossip remains the best and most valued gift of all.

Kehillat Kodesh Gossip

In the discussion thus far, I have by no means said all there is to say about gossip; that would require a book in and of itself. Rather I have tried to abstract certain aspects of gossip which the day-to-day practices at Kehillat Kodesh suggest. Beyond the general dimensions of the phenomenon are those particular to this setting.

It has been suggested that gossip is limited to insiders. And yet, in listening to shul conversation, one finds nonmembers at times discussed. A closer examination, however, reveals that such apparent outsiders are really insiders of one sort or another.

To understand this, one must first recall that the members have lives and involvements outside shul. They may have memberships in other groups, many of which, like the shul, are small face-to-face communities whose members, one must suppose, gossip for many of the same reasons that shul people do. Furthermore, quite a few of the shul members belong to the same outside groups. Thus, it is not unusual to hear several shul members who belong to the nearby academic community sharing gossip about that group, using the shul as a location which allows for the exchange. Such gossip is in the setting but not of it.

Members also share their status as modern Orthodox Jews with others in Sprawl City (and indeed in America) who are not members of Kehillat Kodesh. Modern Orthodox Jewry is a group of which all members of Kehillat Kodesh consider themselves a part, and accordingly one may find a great deal of gossip indicating that relationship.

If one looks at the frequency of certain topics of shul gossip, a clearer picture emerges. On the basis of my field notes, I found that most of the gossip I overheard or received concerned itself with shul members. Next in frequency was conversation about other Orthodox Jews—some nonmembers and some former members. Gossip about non-Orthodox Jews was quite occasional. Gentiles were at times talked about in general terms—especially the black residents of Dudley Meadows—but never was there any reference to the personal or private affairs of any identifiable and specific Gentiles.

Although individual members may and often do have relationships with Gentiles, these relationships are not stressed in shul gossip because they are a part of life which weakens attachment to the shul and its world. Relationships with other frum Jews may be exposed through gossip, since they buttress rather than threaten ties among the frum shul members. Exhibiting links with the rest of the Orthodox Jewish world by means of gossip helps put Kehillat Kodesh on the Orthodox map. Expressing links with less-frum Jews or Gentiles takes it off.

Gossip about other Orthodox Jews deserves more attention. A distinction can be made between people who were never shul members and those who once were but are so no longer. The latter group may be further subdivided into those who have died and those who have left, either by moving out of Dudley Meadows or by deciding to stay in the area yet affiliate with another shul. This last class, unlike the others, is in part stigmatized, for it is made up of persons who have by choice deserted the group. Such disdain is often responded to by active rejection, expressed at times as malicious slander. Where the rejection becomes most strong, such deserters are not talked about at all. Gossip is, after all, a sign of sociation; its absence affirms a breach of all sociation. To ignore another is to socially murder him in a manner which even slander cannot accomplish.

The dead and the involuntarily absent are frequently mentioned in gossip. Such discussion serves as a means of incorporating the missing into the community of the present. Talking about the deceased brings them socially to life once again; recalling the activities or qualities of those who are gone makes them once more present. Such gossiping becomes acutely important whenever the group feels itself threatened with disintegration, a constant fear at Kehillat Kodesh.

Gossip about former members sometimes has the quality of making the gossipers feel as if the group is larger than it actually is. Indeed, the newcomer is not always clear at first whether the person being gossiped about is an active or a former member of the shul. When I first began to partake in gossip, members would often talk about Billy Klitstein, and for a long time I thought this man was simply off on vacation or a trip but still part of the shul. Only after I specifically inquired did I learn that he had left Sprawl City two years before.

In short, gossiping allows the participants to reconstruct reality and even transmute space and time.[58] It can recall the dead and the missing. To paraphrase the Polish peasant: "A man's community lasts as long as the report of a man lasts—as long as he is talked about." Moreover, it can obliterate the living and the present.

One finds that the gravely ill who linger die in gossip long before actual death overtakes them, while the suddenly dead live on beyond the actual moment of expiration in the gossip of those left behind. By no means the only indicator of social life, gossip is nonetheless a useful guide in determining not only how but whether "people are all connected up."

Kehillat Kodesh insiders gossip not only about former members but also about all Orthodox Jews. Very often such gossip takes the form of cataloguing. Consider the following example:

> Pinchas is cataloguing the various people who have come tonight. Among them are quite a few nonmembers:
>
> "That's Chava Gerstenfeld, Noam's wife. They live in the Northeast. He's a butcher—does very well.
>
> "There's Yudiwitz's nephew; I think he's a medical student now—but I'm not sure. He's always changing his mind. The kid's mixed up.
>
> "That guy's Slivovitz, the crazy frum optometrist. He's a *baal teshuva* [a penitent, i.e., one who has become frum on his own]. I could tell you a lot about him."

Pinchas continued to list and evaluate each of the nonmembers present, thus indicating his connections in the Orthodox world outside the shul. By virtue of his information, Pinchas, and people in the know like him, link Kehillat Kodesh with other Orthodox groups.

In Sprawl City, where Orthodox Jews are in the minority, such connections help overcome feelings of isolation. Because Kehillat Kodesh stands in a "changing neighborhood," which many of its old-time members are leaving, it has a particularly great need to experience itself as part of a larger, more stable collectivity. Part of the effort to fulfill this need takes the form of exhibiting solidarity or at least affiliation with other frum Jews in the area. Knowing about the personal and private affairs of other such Jews is proof of some sort of connectedness. Keeping in the know about the other frum (nonmember) Jews of Sprawl City may be interpreted as an effort to remain in some communion with them. The gossiper who talks about them thus not only acts for his own benefit but also demonstrates the ability of the group to become linked to other like Jews through its individual members.

Accordingly, the group encourages such gossipers. It does so by valuing and showing interest in gossip about nonmembers as well as about members; nonmembers are, of course, less often a subject of gossip, since less is known about them. Indeed, reliable gossip about other Orthodox Jews, whether it is news or secret gossip or anything in between, is enthusiastically traded on the gossip exchange. Indeed, for some newcomers such information is the sum total of their initial gossip wealth—the basic capital with which they start. Moreover, guests (and strangers being made into guests) often find themselves generously offering information about their home shuls. The donation of such gossip can bring repayment almost as quickly as information about insiders. In fact, the guest who has presented a great deal of such gossip is often the one to receive the most valuable kibbud, although no one in shul would suggest a manifest connection between these two events.

Slander about outsiders may have another purpose: that of social control, especially over the religious behavior of members. In a sense, such gossiping is not fundamentally different from gossip about the religious behavior of insiders. However, what may be an oblique reference to improper behavior of a specific insider becomes in the slander about outsiders an obvious criticism and a clearer articulation of the opinions of the gossiper, who seeks to enunciate and proclaim the group's norms.

One is tempted to ask why opinions about outsiders cannot be expressed as outright insult or direct face-to-face criticism. In response, one must admit that in some cases they can. However, the small and relatively powerless group at Kehillat Kodesh has learned to avoid conflict, not only within itself, but also vis-à-vis the outside world. Gossip, as pointed out earlier, allows for the avoidance of open conflict.

A final point may be made here. Slander about outsiders may bind the gossipers in a countergroup, "sustained through gossip,"[59] in much the way that the holders of secret gossip information, described earlier, are bound together. This is certainly the case at Kehillat Kodesh in the talk about members of other synagogues in the area. Of course, gossip alone is insufficient for marking a group off from another, just as it alone "will not contribute to the cohesion of a grouping of persons, unless these persons are united by a sense of community which is based on fairly successful pursuit of common objectives."[60] However, the shul members, already bonded in other ways, may affirm, strengthen, and experience their own community by slandering outsiders.

Earlier, during the discussion of the impression-management possibilities inherent in gossip, the classification of a self-initiated/self-focused gossip was suggested. This concept needs further explanation. Included in it is information, disbursed to others, about one's own private and personal affairs which might be of interest to them. The speaker talks about himself to make sure that the information others have is consistent with the picture he seeks to present of himself and to correct the distortions present in others' gossip about him. By itself, such information is not, strictly speaking, gossip, since it is a revelation about the speaker himself. However, such information, because of its substance and the situational context of its presentation, has the potential to become gossip once it is passed on to others. For example, one member tells another:

> I keep some *mitzvos* [commandments] more than others—
> like, I went to the movies during *sefira* [a period of Judeo-national mourning when pleasures are to be avoided]. But, you know, I didn't go out of my way to go; you know what I mean? Like, if everyone's going to the movies, I go too; but, I'm not out to ignore a mitzva.

In this he is giving the other information about himself which the recipient may turn into gossip to a third party. Implicit in this kind of revelation is the belief that the recipient of the information will accurately and faithfully repeat the facts as he heard them.

But why call such self-revelations "gossip"? The answer emerges from an observation of the contexts within which many such self-revelations occur. When offered in the context and framework of gossip exchange, all such self-revelations seemed to conform to many of the same rules and procedures as gossiping. They often occurred, for example, as part of the payment for gossip; that is, participants might donate information about themselves which the recipient could use as gossip. Consider the following conversational episode, which seems slightly rambling unless viewed in terms of the above explanation:

> Silver and Kotsker are chatting. Silver tells the latter about another member's recent heart surgery, reporting that a pacemaker has been inserted into the man's chest. He further volunteers that the man will have to take great care of himself, because his heart is obviously in a very damaged state.
> Kotsker has exhibited interest in the information, eliciting added details with pointed questions. This is privileged information, since the operation has been very recent, and the report of its details is not yet generally known.
> The story over, Kotsker now speaks. He punctuates the report with the evaluative Yiddish closing, "Iss avadeh nisht git" [this clearly portends ill] and suddenly shifts topics, disclosing

that surgeons from a nearby university hospital have recently
come to watch him in the slaughterhouse. [He is a ritual
slaughterer.]

"They want to know from what comes clots," he explains.
He continues to explain how his work is more important than
one would guess, since doctors study it.

"I'm the head *shochet* [slaughterer], so you know I got to
take care of them," he explains.

If one analyzes this exchange as gossip, one finds several things
happening. First, privileged information is exchanged for privileged
information, with the qualification that in the case of Kotsker the
information is primarily about himself. In a kind of storytelling
round, the participants effect information management. While
Silver manages the impression of the man with the pacemaker,
Kotsker is managing his own impression. Moreover, Silver's response to Kotsker's information was similar to the latter's response
to his communication: he solicited more information, asked questions, and ultimately would probably tell these facts as gossip to
someone else.

At Kehillat Kodesh self-gossip occurs quite often in connection
with matters of religious observance and halachic obedience. For
example, during a conversation about a weekly study group, one
member volunteers suddenly and unsolicited a detailed summary of
his busy weeknight schedule. He thereby thwarts gossip about him
which might be critical of his laxity in observing the halachic
dictum of Torah study. Or, in another case, a man enters shul
during the mincha prayers and announces to his nearest neighbor,
in words loud enough for others to hear, that he has already prayed
mincha elsewhere that afternoon. He prevents the slander that he
does not really care to pray.

One more point should perhaps be made in connection with the
assertion that self-revelations may constitute gossip, namely, that
such disclosures can, like other gossip, be typed as news, public
knowledge, privileged information, or secret gossip. Moreover,
some self-revelations are approbatory, while others are derogatory. The approbatory or derogatory dimension of self-gossip, as
with other gossip, is often determined by the context of exchange
and the future course of the informational flow. Most self-gossip is
intended to enhance its donor, but it does not always do so.
Negative charges sometimes make for derogatory effects. Even the
most positive and flattering self-information may be turned into
scandal or slander in subsequent transmission. Self-gossip may be

taken by the recipient and subverted or distorted. While the relationship between donor and recipient sometimes militates against such subversion or distortion, no guarantees exist.

Moreover, the self-gossiper may inadvertently transmit derogatory information about himself. If the recipient of this self-gossip communicates his immediate reaction to it, the speaker may try some remedial action. Sometimes, however, even the recipient remains unaware of the derogatory quality of the information until he in turn passes it on and sees a third party's reaction. For example, a member tells me that he is giving up business and going back to get a Ph.D. Later I pass on this gossip and receive the response, "Yeah, the guy really envies his brother, who has such an easy life in academia." I had interpreted the self-gossip as an effort to present an impression of someone willing to go back to school and better himself, while the new recipient of the news saw the information in a much less favorable light.

Finally, because of what seems to be its calculative nature, it should be noted that self-gossip, like all other gossip, must be exchanged and communicated in a casual way. Such talk must not appear to be the sole purpose of a conversation but must rather emerge idly from the ongoing chatter of sociability. The calculations and strategies which have been emphasized and indicated are latent qualities of all such conversational interchange; they become apparent only when one looks at a comprehensive and detailed record of activity in the setting, as I have done in my field notes. Only because gossip has for so long been considered idle and meaningless has it seemed necessary here to accentuate its functional and structural aspects. However, to view the exchange of gossip as a conscious and absorbing activity of shul members, part of their paramount reality, would be incorrect. Indeed, it is because they are so often oblivious of the nature and consequences of their gossiping that they are able to engage in it so successfully. Like breathing, its operation is smoothest when it occurs with the least amount of self-consciousness.

Gossip cells have been mentioned in passing. Essentially the entire congregation may be viewed as one large gossip cell, distinguished from the rest of the Orthodox Jewry of Sprawl City, in which various items of news and public knowledge are shared and evaluated by the members. Such exchange, as we have suggested, serves as one set of associations which helps to bind the membership together into a community. Within this large cell, however, there are gossip subdivisions. These have been referred to as *gossip cliques*. (To an extent, all cliques are gossip cliques, just as all groups are, to one extent or another, gossip cells.) Such cliques are not necessarily generated by gossip, although they may be maintained by it; in the main they consist of persons who share other commonalities but find that gossip helps to buttress and maintain their distinctiveness from the rest of the collectivity. The gossip shared among these subgroups may or may not be identical with that shared with the congregation at large. Recalling the gossip typology, one might say that, while all members trade news and public knowledge, privileged information and secret gossip necessarily imply smaller subdivisions, or cliques, which are privy to them.

These cliques may be defined and distinguished in several ways. For some, sex is the definitive feature. Women and men do not trade all types of gossip. The sorts of things my wife and I might hear were often quite different. The conversation among the women when they are alone—concerning such topics as someone's recent miscarriage, how many babies someone ought to have, the scandal behind one member's first marriage—are never discussed in the presence of men.

Some cliques are divided by age. This factor is confounded by and mixed with other related factors: marital status, language, educational background, and situational context. I shall elaborate.

A young man or woman who is single does not enter the gossip cliques of other members of equal age who are married. Accordingly, upon marriage a member learns a great deal more about what is going on in the congregation as compared with what he knew before. As one member, recently wed, pointed out, "I was shocked about how much I didn't know that was going on. Getting married has really opened up things for me." Through wives, husbands learn a great deal about the female world, and vice versa. Indeed, if I have learned anything about the women in Kehillat Kodesh, it is only because my wife was able to report to me about them and because, through my wife, I was able to enter the couples gossip clique.

Not all couples associate with one another. Although there are no formal restrictions on interaction between various cliques, interaction between couples of different age is rare. For example, my wife and I once received an invitation to Sabbath dinner from one of the older couples in the congregation. Such dinners, when populated by members of the same clique, are the occasion for gossip of the most far-reaching kind; from news to secret gossip, little is left unsaid and unshared. In this case the scene was quite different. Along with us, another couple from our gossip clique had been invited. The age difference between the two young couples and their hosts was between twenty-five and thirty years. Nevertheless, the evening passed with little visible strain—but also with very little gossip. With the exception of an occasional piece of news and a single story of public knowledge (about the early days of the shul's existence), the conversation was limited to such general topics as the decor of the hosts' home, the best way to get kosher chickens, or the rising crime rate in Dudley Meadows—subjects that all Kehillat Kodesh members may share, regardless of clique membership.

Being married and of similar ages does not guarantee that members will belong to the same gossip clique. These are necessary but insufficient grounds for such relationships. Educational background, often closely associated with the male's occupational status, is also a factor in gossip-clique association. Thus, the clique of which I and my wife found ourselves members included only those who had some college education, and the husbands were pursuing professional careers of one sort or another.

Membership in such cliques is inevitable. As new members join the shul, they are invariably introduced to others of similar background. When a young doctor came to the shul and the neighborhood, he was soon guided over to the area of the shul where "other young professionals like you" were sitting. Indeed, seat neighbors are more often than not members of the same gossip cliques. Such proximity makes possible the relatively unrestricted exchange of gossip that occurs even during the public assemblies of prayer. At public gatherings where members of the shul appear, grouping will often occur along the same lines as shul seating, which by now is apparent as a reflection of much more than habit. As they enter the shul, the members—new and old alike—have little choice with regard to where each will sit or with whom each will become associated. Those who challenge such informally assigned associations, who fail to find their niche—both actually and figuratively—in the community (as one member did by sitting on the other side of shul, in the section provided for unaffiliated strangers) soon find that they never become fully integrated into the congregation. They are seldom gossiped about (though they are not completely overlooked, since they remain fixtures of the setting); and no one gossips with them. They are seldom invited anywhere for Sabbath dinner and are rarely seen at sociability spots.

Another factor which affects membership in gossip cliques is language. Some members of the congregation, mostly the older immigrants, feel most at home in Yiddish. This is their native language, the one in which they first learned gossip, and it is still very much their language. Those who do not speak or understand Yiddish are naturally excluded from their gossip cliques. This factor is of declining importance at Kehillat Kodesh because the great majority of the members are not only not immigrants but did not grow up in homes where Yiddish was the language spoken. Although some young members understand Yiddish, and almost everyone knows a few phrases or at least common terms, the speaking of Yiddish is fast disappearing. That the young speak it at all is a measure of the lasting influence of some of the older members over the group.

Gossip cliques may be considered from yet another perspective. They are linkages best described by Wolf's label, "emotional friendships"—relationships characterized by expressive needs and feelings of close rapport.[61] At times such friendships, instead of being ends in themselves, may become means for achieving something else. This becomes particularly apparent in gossip, where the cliques may be used as sources of information.

Interestingly, shul membership is an instrumental bond (based on joint ritual and religious needs) that may be turned into an emotional one, while clique membership is an emotional link that at times may be transformed into an instrumental one. Membership in the shul fulfills a blend of emotional and instrumental needs. In gossip cliques the emotional element predominates (yet is never absolute), while for the community at large the instrumental bond is of primary importance.

Final Thought

Berger and Luckmann conclude their essay on the social construction of reality by saying:

> Man is biologically predestined to construct and inhabit a world with others. This world becomes for him the dominant and definitive reality. Its limits are set by nature, but once constructed, this world acts back upon nature. In the dialectic between nature and the socially constructed world, the human organism itself is transformed. In this same dialectic man produces reality and thereby produces himself.[62]

Gossip, one might suggest, is one way to define and redefine social reality. These gossip creations are no longer directly limited by nature, for they are transformations of that nature, pure human inventions. In that sense, they are not altogether unlike prayer, a human invention which transforms nature and the nature of men. Like prayer, gossip brings people together, gives them something to hold in common in spite of their various other pursuits. Accordingly, like prayer, gossip is very much at home in the shul.

6

Joking

> ... many a drama will turn into comedy.
>
> *Henri Bergson*, Laughter

Gossip is by no means the only source of conversation among the Jews of Kehillat Kodesh. They joke as well, and no study of the shul would be complete without some mention of this phenomenon. My purpose here is not to pursue an exhaustive investigation of joking and humor or to delve into questions of the historical foundations of Jewish humor; such tasks would far exceed the scope of this study. Rather, I shall briefly outline some of the functions and microdynamics of shul joking.

A close affiliation between gossip and joking prevails in the setting. Each may serve as a frame for the other and is often substituted for it in the course of conversational exchange, gossip being answered with a joke or joking remark and vice versa. For example:

> Kosofsky and Bilansky are chatting. The one tells the other about Poker's new job in the Sprawl City school system. Bilansky laughs and jokes, "What kind of an occupation is this for a Jewish man—teaching *goyim* [Gentiles]?"

> Riken is making jokes about Velvel's announcements. Wintergarten has overheard the joking and mentions that Velvel will be going to another shul next Sabbath for a bar-mitzva of a friend's son. "He should try to make announcements over there," Riken remarks, laughing.

Like gossip, joking may serve as the starting mechanism or focus of an interaction, helping to stimulate or sustain a gathering. As such it is a vehicle for the expression and exercise of sociability. The participants need not be—and indeed, because of the casual nature of the interchange, often are not—aware that the joking (or gossip) serves in this way. More often than not, once such interchange ends, the gathering breaks up. This fact becomes particularly apparent when one observes gatherings at sociability spots before and after the prayers, during the warming-up and cooling-down periods. Only when all the gossip and joking banter have been fully exchanged and some reciprocal balance has been achieved will someone at the sociability spot suggest that the prayers begin. Similarly, at the conclusion of the tefilah, groups disperse only when a silence indicates that nothing is left to be exchanged.

Sometimes the conversations during warming-up periods are prematurely ended by the congregational start of prayers. This commonly occurs because some members who have been warming up for prayer are ready and, by asserting the manifest purpose of the gathering, successfully dominate the action. When such a disruption of talk occurs, conversation becomes more prevalent than usual during the prayers; and cooling-down periods—periods of residual action after the formal end of the primary activity—also increase in substance and length. As if trying to balance and complete exchanges, tie up conversational knots, or finish narration rounds, the disrupted members keep on talking. Joking plays an interesting role here; it may easily act as the capstone for a social occasion—and become a termination signal—because it may at times require little more than a brief ratificatory or reassurance display—often simply a quick laugh or slight smile.[1] It does not always demand the continuation of encounter and involvement.

Joking may, of course, also serve as the stimulus for further conversation and interaction, as the second extract above indicates. This is particularly true of joking that consists of formal narratives that are pointedly humorous. Such joking retains many of the qualities of gossip and so demands many of the same kinds of repayment. Joke stories, like gossip stories, have a prestational quality. Often they become stimuli for a whole series of exchanges and may become used by the recipient for a future exchange. Like gossip, such jokes, since they are "retellable by any recipient,"[2] are useful vehicles for interactive conversational interchange.

Joking, then, seems to have dual qualities, being at once a stimulus for interaction and conversation and a termination signal and finale of interchange. Such attributes are particularly useful in a context like tefilah sheh be tzibbur, where sociable conversations are likely to be disrupted at any moment by prayer and other legitimate involvements. Accordingly, one is not surprised to find a great amount of joking punctuating the services.

The phenomenon of shul humor may be divided into two large types: *jokes* and *joking remarks*. The former are formal narratives, in great measure repeatable because they are not situationally specific. The latter consist of glosses, quite often situationally hinged, which may be anything from complex verbal recitations to brief nonverbal signals, such as winks or sardonic grimaces. Both have a need for some ratifying response on the part of some or all of the participants. The proper acknowledgement consists of some form of laughter, from guffaw to fleeting smile. When no actual laughing response is made, some ratificatory substitute is called for which will explain the apparently passive response. Such ratification is consistently provided by one's friends, those who share the emotional responsibilities of communal existence. When there is no such link—as when, for example, a cabaret comedian faces a hostile and unappreciative audience—responses need not ratify, nor need silence, both verbal and nonverbal, be explained. Among shul members, joking is seldom if ever ignored.

Although everyone in shul engages in some form of joking behavior, an ethnography of its practice reveals distinctions, not only between jokes and joking remarks, but also with regard to who jokes with whom and about what. The latter distinctions are in many ways parallel to the categories of shul gossip discussed in the preceding chapter. Moreover, joking exchange follows many of the same lines as the exchange of gossip. Finally, these categories reflect particular relationships among the jokers, just as the categories of gossip do.

The most general type of joking behavior—open to almost anyone who enters the shul—may be called the *formal joke narrative*. While not everyone may recite such narratives, everyone may listen to and laugh at them as they are being told. Since there are few opportunities for mingling of the sexes within the setting, such jokes are most frequently recited in groups consisting of either all men or all women.

Narration of such "funny stories" about fictional characters is, in practice, restricted to insiders; for though outsiders may on occasion tell such jokes, the gathering of the necessary audience is more easily accomplished by insiders. Furthermore, the outsider may not always realize the proper occasion for a joke (although outsiders who have had experience in modern Orthodox shuls frequently display a sense of when and how to joke). The exchange and recitation of jokes tends to be prestational in character. One joke deserves another.

Some kinds of jokes merge with gossip. This occurs when the characters of the story are no longer fictional but are people whom everyone knows. Such joking is no longer open to outsiders. Indeed, beyond the formal joke narrative, all other joking in the Kehillat Kodesh setting defines progressively more restricted types of in-jokes—jokes which can be recited and whose humor can be appreciated only by insiders. (In-jokes will be holistically considered later in this chapter.) In its most generally accessible form, in-joking may be termed *public joking*. This category of joking, analogous to public gossip, is the kind of banter that may and does occur among all the insiders in the congregation. Here one finds the recitation of the so-called "old jokes"—those long-known and oft-repeated narratives about insiders—along with the offering of joking remarks, repartee, and so on. The "public" here, as with public gossip, is restricted to persons who are considered insiders. Such restrictions are often imposed by the fact that the humor is comprehended only by insiders, who, being in possession of the necessary background information, are sensitive to all the implications of a particular remark. Public joking is perhaps the most prevalent type of humor heard in shul, for it cuts across age lines and, at times, sex lines as well. Here, as in the subsequent categories, words or phrases may become formulaic symbols of jokes or joking remarks and thus part of the private language of the group.

Included here is the ritualized joke, which, no matter how often it is told, brings forth the ritual response of laughter. Various events, for example, always bring forth the same jokes and ensuing laughter. Thus, around Passover everyone always makes a joking remark about the constipating qualities of the matzah diet, and others laugh in agreement. The ritual of symbolically throwing one's sins into a river at the New Year inevitably stimulates the remark, "You ought to throw yourself into the river," or something of that order, always followed by the obligatory laughter. Such ritualized jokes and responses serve as signals that all is going as expected. They reveal the smooth and relaxed atmosphere of a world in order.

Having little conscious, objective purpose, such joking serves easily as a vehicle for sociability, and so it is frequently heard at sociability spots. As men stand around the bimah, for example, they engage in an exchange which blends public knowledge and public joking. That, in essence, is the substance of traditional *shmoosing,* the Jews' "ideal form of intimate communication."[3]

While public joking acts to separate the insiders from the outsiders, *privileged joking* makes an even further distinction. Here the division is between insiders, turning some of them into outsiders. Persons who are privileged may be so in two senses: first, in a particular context they alone have license to joke without risking negative sanctions from the group; second, they alone are privileged to comprehend the humor in the joke or joking remark. The young boys at the back of the shul frequently engage in such joking, often breaking into open laughter and leaving the rest of the membership mystified outsiders.

Because of the privileged character of such joking, it may be engaged in in the presence of the nonprivileged and even in front of the objects of its humor. Certain restrictions related to the maintenance of group amity and unity do, however, obtain. In the first place, the jokers must be careful not to arouse tensions by overstepping the informal boundaries of good taste; furthermore, since they must not flaunt their privileged character and the discrimination it implies, they are often forced to disguise their laughter; finally, they must make sure that, when the object of a joking remark is present, the pronouncements are sufficiently controlled that they will not stimulate anger and argument, both of which are anathema to community life. This control can be achieved either by mitigating the deprecatory nature of the joke or by so disguising it that only the privileged are aware that a joke has been made at someone else's expense. The same restrictions do not, of course, hold with regard to public joking, for real outsiders need not be treated with such circumspection.

One more point must be made with respect to this type of joking.

Those involved in it do not constitute an established group. Rather, the privileged differ from one moment to the next, with the result that those who are privy to one joke may not be privy to the one that follows it at some later time.

The final analytical category, *secret joking*, does reflect an established clique who alone may engage in it. This, the most socially restricted form of joking, includes the humor that severely and crudely satirizes identifiable others. Because of its vitriolic nature, this joking must be kept secret both from its targets and from others not in the clique so that the jokers will not be stigmatized as socially disruptive. Sitting near one another in shul aids such jokers in keeping this kind of joking secret.

Those who engage in secret joking are *usually* intimates; if, for some reason, they are not already tightly bonded, this activity will in time help bind them together. Like conspirators, they are united by their "crime."

In terms of the distinctions already noted, one can say that most of the joking that occurs during the fluid context of the tefilah sheh be tzibbur consists of public joking. The other varieties, although by no means absolutely excluded during communal prayer, are more prevalent during moments in which the shul is primarily a house of assembly—for example, during the warming-up or cooling-down periods or prior to meetings.

Joking remarks have already been cited as starting and terminating mechanisms for interaction. They also emerge in other forms. One of these is the aggressive joking remark. Its substance may be a peculiar blend of friendliness and antagonism.[4] By taking the form of a joking remark, aggressive feelings may be expressed and exorcised (as they are by some kinds of gossip) without the risks of open conflict. The most biting remark, penetrating criticism, or personal slur can, when carefully couched in humor, be expressed without manifestly tearing the fabric of the community. (Only the crudest joking need remain secret.) For small groups, like Kehillat Kodesh, whose tenuous survival depends on amity, joking, like gossip, serves as a social and psychological safety valve, allowing the group to maintain unity and display friendship even in the face of the normal antagonisms and tensions of collective existence. The joking remark maintains a show of friendship even as one expresses hostility to another. A few illustrations are in order.

On Sabbath or holy-day mornings, when participants in the service constitute a captive audience, Rabbi Housmann is fond of giving a sermonette at some point during the prayers. The imposed presentation of these "words of Torah" is, however, resented by some in this captive audience, many of whom would prefer such speeches to be canceled entirely. Although a tacit understanding has been reached to restrict the number of these sermonettes, Housmann still speaks more often than many people prefer; he often simply stands and speaks up during lulls in the action, which may occur when an unwary chazan has paused too long between stanzas of prayer. In spite of the widespread antagonism to Housmann's speaking, no one will tell him openly and directly to stop, "because," as one member put it, "we don't want the guy to get insulted and leave." Alternative means for expressing antagonism to the speeches include joking remarks. Ernst, Housmann's son, is often the conduit for such aggressive joking: "Tell your father that I'm really hungry today and, if he speaks, I might faint." Although humorous in its exaggeration, the remark is expected to be transmitted by Ernst directly to his father, minus the humor.

The joking remark may be addressed directly to the person concerned—in this case, Housmann. For example, the word "amen," commonly recited as ritual affirmation at the end of a prayer, blessing, or section of study, has come to be used as a congregational response to all sorts of statements that can bear a religious interpretation. The ends of speeches are always marked with calls of amen from the congregation. Often, in the course of Housmann's sermon, one or two members will choose to yell "amen" during any pauses that occur. Such calls are met with audible titters and snickers from other congregants, and these reinforce the signal for Housmann to stop. Enough ambiguity and humor remain so that Housmann may ignore the signal and continue speaking without undue embarrassment. Nevertheless, the call—much like quasi-chazanic activity—is a cue for him to get on and finish. The antagonism is perceptible but not overbearing. Such joking, much like the joking insults which Ben-Amos and Enobakhare found among the Igbogie, "functions to release . . . tensions without violence, to prevent and avoid conflict and manifest aggression in a cultural [sic] permissible and . . . harmless manner."[5]

In the event that one is the recipient of an openly aggressive remark, joking may serve to defuse the tension of the encounter. Wishing to avoid open conflict, one may make light of insult and injury and thus allow the aggressor to retreat behind a cover of humor. The members of Kehillat Kodesh, who once easily took umbrage at even the most oblique aggression, now tend to joke their ways out of confrontations. When sudden bursts of anger between two members seem to be getting out of control, third parties often step in to heal the breach with humor. Here the joke is used to aid in overcoming the growing disharmony by abruptly changing the thrust of the discussion.[6] Thus, for example, at the end of a heated discussion between two members about current American politics, a third member joked, "The galitzianers [Jews coming from Galicia] have it all sewn up." This non sequitur made everyone burst into laughter. Behind the cover of this joke everyone could retreat from the oncoming argument. Indeed, the joke did not *happen* to come at the end of the conversation; it terminated it.

When a single joking remark is too weak to diffuse growing hostility, it may be followed by other jokes, or even by gossip, to drain off remaining tensions. Velvel is particularly skillful at alleviating tensions in this way. More than just a personality characteristic, Velvel's sense of humor is an important tool of leadership.

In addition to allowing antagonism to be harmlessly expressed, joking remarks may serve both to reveal normative behavior and assure its continuance, acting in this as a means of social control. Unlike the control of gossip, which often occurs by means of oblique references to third parties, joking often aims directly at its target. In the control over public religious practice and observance, this quality becomes most apparent.

Consider, for example, the joking remark about one member's prayer cloak. Two types of cloaks exist: a short linen scarf that hangs around the neck of the wearer, and a long woolen one which, draped over the shoulders, covers more than two-thirds of the wearer's body. The second is the one approved and worn by most Orthodox Jews. At one morning's service a novice member wore one of the short linen types. As he was called to the Torah scroll reading for a kibbud, one member called out, laughing, as the former touched the scroll with the fringes of his talis, "Why don't you get a talis instead of that *shmateh* [Yiddish for rag]?" Everyone, including the target, laughed. Next time he appeared in a woolen talis.

The joking remark may be used to make points of criticism about another's actions without embarrassing him.[7] For example, Velvel had just finished explaining, amid much laughter, how he had tried, illegally, to evade responsibility for causing a car accident. Upon completing the narrative, he looked around for some sort of ratifying response from his audience. One member replied, "I don't know if we should allow you to be president!" Again laughter. Yet amid all the jesting was the clear point that such action might be overlooked this time but was not something to be repeated too often, for it reflected unfavorably on Velvel's right to (moral) leadership of the group. After this remark, the subject was changed.

The humor inherent in these situations is not necessarily intrinsic to the words. Rather, "the speakers, the relationships between them and the speech situation . . . are decisive contributing factors to the interpretation of the message" and its humor.[8] That is, such jokes are situational; they depend on one's recognizing all the dimensions of the situation and of its participants. When people laugh at the remark, they laugh at the entire situation of which the remark is simply the marker. Consequently, quoting the actual remark can give the reader only an inkling—based on similar circumstances in his own experience—of the humor of the situation.

Joking remarks may be either isolated communications or part of a stable pattern of relationship. In the latter case, such remarks make up much of the substance of what Radcliffe-Brown calls the *joking relationship*, "a . . . relation between two persons in which one is by custom permitted, and in some instances required, to tease or make fun of the other, who in turn is required to take no offense."[9] The relationship may or may not be mutual (i.e., with both parties taking turns at making joking remarks at the other). That such relationships exist not only between individuals but also between groups may be suggested by the descriptions of the relationship between Kehillat Kodesh and some of the other congregations in the area. Condemnations of other Jews are often expressed as joking remarks. The potential divisiveness in such criticism is moderated by the joking format. Although one can only guess the reasons for such restraint, one is tempted to think that a heritage of malevolence from the outside has made Jews wary of public conflicts among themselves.[10] If one adds to that the particular dangers of a dwindling Jewish community in Dudley Meadows, one may perhaps have some hint as to the reason for the development of a joking relationship between Kehillat Kodesh and its less Orthodox neighbors.

Aware of the power of the joking remark in actuating disesteem, some members may engage in self-deprecatory joking as part of a strategy of defense. In a quasi-Socratic way, the self-deprecatory jokester controls criticism by generating it himself before others have had a chance to articulate it. (This kind of joking is analogous in its purpose to the self-gossip discussed in chapter 5.) Such self-deprecation allows the person to emphasize the most minor negative aspects of his persona and thus maintain hegemony over those aspects which at first appear beyond his control. Moreover, by presenting the self-deprecation as humorous, the jokester limits the injury of the remark. He also escapes the negative sanctioning of the collectivity, showing that he does not need others to tell him of his faults, since he knows them himself and is sufficiently in control of them that he can make jokes about them. As one member put it, "If you can still joke about it, it's not so bad."

An illustration can perhaps elucidate the point. According to halacha, or at least according to Ashkenazic Jewish tradition (which may at times have greater legal imperative than halacha), all adult males *may* wear a talis during morning prayers, but only the married ones are *required* to do so. By wearing a talis, unmarried men may hide the stigma of their single status. Of course, in a small community interlinked by gossip, as Kehillat Kodesh is, no member can really conceal his marital status. For all of his or her positive qualities, the unmarried member is inevitably subject to disapproval by the group, which places premiums, both ritual and social, on marriage.

Mendel Wintergarten is such a person. His reputation is constantly shadowed by the fact that he is unmarried. His self-deprecatory joking remarks reflect his awareness of this. For example, when his talis is slipping off his back during the services and another member replaces it for him, Mendel remarks, "They say if a woman doesn't put the talis on your back, it doesn't want to stay." Everyone, including Wintergarten, laughs.

Through his remark, Mendel, by admitting his failing, has in some way compensated for it. He displays his tacit acceptance of the legitimacy of communal standards which label him deviant. In accepting that status, he honors the group, winning at least partial indulgence from it. Indeed, because of Mendel's artful use of self-deprecating humor, he, unlike other adult single males in the shul, has managed to retain a position of respect in spite of his unmarried status. His joking is not, however, a source of respect (his scholarship is) but rather a device by which he minimizes the disapproval of others. Joking remarks may, then, be defenses and strategies for the self.

Such joking may also serve to expiate previously committed sins of deviance. By offering a disapprobatory image of oneself in a joking format, one accepts a limited penalty of degradation instead of a more injurious one. Moreover, the group, represented by the audience present, by recognizing the humor of the remark signals its approval of these limited confessions of guilt. In short, self-deprecating humor is a compromise between the conformist demands of the group and the defiance of individuality.[11]

Groups may also employ such joking as a strategy of defense against defamatory assaults. Jews have become craftsmen in this type of self-deprecatory humor; some even make a profession out of it. Perhaps more than any other people, modern Orthodox Jews have developed a talent for such joking, for they have special need of it when they step outside their world of parochial tradition to face the often harsh inhospitality of the contemporary world. Although minimizing public self-deprecation, such Jews may, among themselves, engage in a scathing self-mockery which seems to coopt the criticism of the outside world and make it manageable. The stigmatization of Orthodoxy becomes the stuff of such humor. When one can joke about what should be hurting one, the power of the pain is somewhat diminished.

For shul members such joking self-deprecation is a frequent group activity, concerning not only Jews in general but also Orthodox Jews in particular, for it allows the members to cope with the character assaults which they perceive to be directed against them by and in the Gentile and "ex-Jewish" world.[12] Such joking at times requires the speakers and auditors to assume the perspective of outsiders. The victims, in a kind of imitative magic, play at being attackers.

Consider, for example, the joking about one of the complicated rituals surrounding the Passover holy day. During the eight days of Passover, halacha demands not only that Jews refrain from eating leavened goods (*chometz*) but that such goods (e.g., dough) be removed from Jewish ownership. According to the specifications of the law, any chometz which is not so removed is prohibited for use by Jews not only during Passover but for eternity. For Jewish owners of bakeries, this law creates particularly complex problems. Like all Jews, these bakers must meet the requirements of halacha, especially if they wish to retain their Orthodox clientele after Passover. Since actual disposal before the holy days of all his chometz would be both economically and logistically burdensome for the Jewish baker (he would have to sell and replenish his entire stock in a very short time), he satisfies the law by means of a legal fiction: he closes his shop during the holy days but beforehand "sells" all his chometz to a Gentile (whose Passover-chometz is not prohibited for use by Jews *after* Passover) for the duration of the holy-day season—all the while keeping the actual goods in his closed bakery; after Passover, the Jewish baker buys back the chometz, opens his bakery doors, and resumes business as usual.[13] Commonly, because of the complexity of the law, a rabbi acts as an agent between the Jewish baker and the Gentile.

Two members, in talking about this Passover procedure in reference to a local Jewish baker, are joking about how strange it must seem to the uninformed. One man mentions that his wife called the local bakery to find out whether it had "sold" its chometz for Passover and received a perplexed answer from the owner, who said he always sells his bread—all year. "She should have asked him if they went through some mumbo-jumbo with a rabbi?," the other jokes. In the joke, the exquisite complexity of the legal fiction, which these Jews strictly observe, is satirically labeled "mumbo-jumbo."

Such joking about religion and ritual seems particularly indigenous to modern Orthodox Jews. While their Orthodoxy requires involvement in and fulfillment of the ritual demands of their religion, their modernity and experience in the modern world encourage a show of detachment from the parochialism of Jewish observance. Joking about that observance is a handy way of maintaining this front of detachment. Moreover, one finds that the more traditionally Orthodox members of Kehillat Kodesh are those who least often (and some never) joke about ritual or religious observance. The professionals—cosmopolitans whose careers have propelled them outward and away from the total Orthodox environment—are the most frequent jokesters of this sort. Yet, even to the latter group, such joking on the lips of true outsiders would be taken as insufferable defamations of Jewry and of Orthodoxy. Coming from insiders, it is funny.

No aspect of Jewish life is immune to such joking. A discussion of Jewish education, the historical mainstay of Jewish survival, is punctuated with the scoffing remark, "Look, if Jews had a bell in their synagogues, there would have been a whole *gemara* [volume of the Talmud] on it." Even the sacrosanct corpus of talmudic literature, to say nothing of the ritual of study, is open to ridicule by the same people who revere it, although the ridicule is always blended with a sufficient tinge of humor to make the slur ambiguous.

Physical characteristics and economic success, the two most

frequent subjects of vilification by outsiders, are also included in self-deprecatory humor. Consider the following two examples:

Lemberg and Fiedler are joking about Shonsky's appearance. "Did Shonsky have a nose job?," said Fiedler. One look at Shonsky's nose made it apparent that Fiedler had to be joking.
"If he did, he ought to get a refund," Fiedler said.
"That's just what I was going to say," said Lemberg, laughing.
" 'Course, I'm not one to talk," Fiedler allowed.
"That's all right, none of us are," Lemberg answered.
"Except for Ronald. He's got a nice nose," Mel piped in, commenting about his seat neighbor.
"Yeah, but his body's a bomb," I joked. We all laughed, and Ronald hardest of all.

Lemberg and Riken are talking about the Sprawl City Yeshiva's need for able lawyers. "We really don't need 'em," Riken says; "we're all con artists. We can get outta taxes on our own." Both men laughed.

Such joking is not limited to general characteristics of Jews but is often directed by members at the shul itself, as the following example suggests:

The shul has been having some trouble in recent weeks in gathering a minyan for the services. Now, for the past week, we have been having a good turnout. Riken is commenting on the matter and jokes.
"It's not good," he says. "We're getting too many. I mean sixteen—that's a bad sign. We should *just* be making it. Velvel, don't announce anything about this. Say [that] we're barely making a minyan. Say that at seven in the morning we didn't have a minyan. Don't tell them [it's] because people are coming in at seven ten." Riken and the others are laughing.

If the minyan, that sign of the community's strength or weakness, is not immune from deprecation, then the very central concerns of group existence are not immune. Indeed, this suggests that a good way to find out what people or groups are most concerned to protect is to look at the substance of their self-deprecatory humor.

Self-deprecatory joking is associated with another quality of joking at Kehillat Kodesh: its use as evidence of community membership. Deprecatory humor directed at the group is permissible only to insiders. Should outsiders make similar remarks, the response would be not laughter but resentment. Only when I had been completely reintegrated as an insider after revealing my role as an observer was I able once again to make deprecatory remarks in my joking. Such jokes were made cautiously at first, since I realized that the very activity which at one point could mark me as an insider might, at too early a juncture, stigmatize me as an outsider.

In essence, self-deprecatory joking is simply a specific form of the joking that enables one to exhibit insider status—the so-called in-joke. Such jokes are for the most part situational joking remarks, occurring often in the midst of conversation. They may be deprecatory but are by no means necessarily so. In both their recitation and reception, in-jokes may be seen as exercises of "unity in plurality"—vehicles for marking one as separate from some and included by others.[14] When the content of in-jokes is sufficiently esoteric, it tends to guarantee secrecy and limited accessibility, so that the conditions for the in-joke's transfer need not be meticulously restricted.

In-jokes may also latently communicate norms, expectations, criticisms, and public knowledge. In these functions, in-jokes, perhaps more than any other kind of joking, most closely approach gossip. As criticism, the in-joke, by keeping evaluations at the level of humor, enables the speaker to criticize without appearing to be involved in a pointed effort at discreditation. Such purposive evaluations would too easily subvert the atmosphere of sociability in which the in-jokes usually appear. Thus, for example, in the congenial context of Velvel's public announcement that a particular couple has become engaged, one member comments to another, "They've both done a *mitzva* [good deed] for each other." The remark receives laughter, since everyone knows that neither of the betrothed pair has been very popular with the opposite sex.

In-jokes may consist of epithets which classify a person or activity:

> Zenmount has been the chazan today, and now it is the point where a youngster usually concludes the service. No boy is around to take over, and Zenmount simply steps away from the bimah, commenting, "I don't care. Get someone else to daven [pray]."
> "He's getting to be a Caleb Goltner," one member says, referring to a former member with the reputation of a prima donna when it came to being chazan. Those hearing the comment laughed.

Here the in-joke requires one to know Caleb Goltner and what he has come to represent. Such in-joke epithets, like other joking remarks, may serve as insiders' signals that they are able to catalogue all members of the collectivity. In this cataloguing sense, epithets are similar to gossip.

The issue of gossip brings to mind the function of joking as a framework for gossip exchange. In their efforts to acquire and maintain a store of gossip, members often find themselves having to solicit information about the personal and private affairs of others. Blatant solicitation marks one as a busybody; to cover such personal inquiries, members therefore often resort to the ostensible concealment which joking allows. While this manner of deliberately casual inquiry is not always successful, it does offer certain impersonal and structural advantages. For example, upon my earlier-than-usual arrival in shul one Sabbath my seat neighbor satisfied his curiosity about this violation of my timetable with the joking inquiry: "What happened, did the heater go off in your apartment or something?" Without overstepping the bounds of propriety, the member found a way of signaling his interest.

Joking allows for the exchange of gossip without the donor appearing to be a gossipmonger. Velvel, making his usual visits with members during the course of a service, is jokingly asked, "Where did you put Riken today?" In answering the quip, he may harmlessly display his store of community information.

Finally, the joking nature of the inquiry helps both the inquirer and the person he questions to avoid the tension of information denial. One who wishes to keep information secret can respond with another joke without obviously insulting the questioner. Newcomers, not yet adept in the gathering of gossip, are frequent users of such joking inquiries, which signify both their interest in community affairs and their patience with the initiation process. In joking replies, insiders do not scornfully put them off.

Personal inquiry may be straightforward as well. The inept gossiper usually uses such an approach, and the joking reply may then (just as after joking inquiries) be used to avoid truthful or direct responses. In this case (1) the respondent's information remains undisclosed while he avoids appearing stingy with his information or callous in his refusal to answer; (2) the inquirer is emotionally protected and discreetly put off, even though he has exhibited himself as unduly curious; and (3) the community is spared open conflict and tension. For example, to the question, "Did Sidney get divorced again?," the nonanswer is, "Are you keeping scorecards?"

In order for a personal inquiry to be made in a joking way—whether it is addressed directly to another about himself or to a third party about another's personal affairs—the actual substance of the remark need not necessarily be funny in its own right. By surrounding his inquiry with laughter or by using vocal and nonverbal glosses in which curiosity appears unimpassioned, the speaker can maintain enough distance from his remark so that he can disown it at the slightest sign of risk. The following incident is a case in point.

> There has been a great deal of joking about attendance at the minyan. Everyone is laughing or smiling as we stand and sit around the bimah. Now, in the midst of all this, Riken asks, "I wonder why Zinger has been coming to the minyan every day?"
> Zinger, sitting nearby, easily avoids the seriousness of the question's substance by saying, "I want to get into Sam's book [i.e., *this* book, for which, as everyone present knows, I am gathering data]."
> We all laugh again, and Riken chortles, "Yeah, yeah, that's good."

A member's religion and ritual observance are quite often the substance of joking inquiry. Except in the environment of the gossip clique, most solicitation of such information is engaged in with the circumspection which humor allows. It is religious observance which has brought the people together in the first place. Too close an inquiry into the private religious life of the members could be—as it was in the early life of the shul—a stimulus for disintegration. By jokingly making such inquiries, members guard against the dangers of exposing and hence emphasizing the unresolvable differences among them.

The tension-reducing quality of joking was useful for handling the potentially explosive issue of an insider—the author—suddenly turning into a reporter/researcher. Two major modalities of reaction emerged in response to my revelations of intent. The first, as can by now be guessed, involved the discussion in gossip of both the project and myself. The subject became ultimately a part of the public knowledge that was passed on to all new members as they became part of the group. The second response entailed joking. Inquiries to me about the purpose and substance of my interests were quite often expressed in joking form. "You checking up on us to see if we daven every word?" "How come you don't set up a secret tape recorder inside the bimah?" To such joking inquiries, and others even more penetrating, I learned to respond with joking of my own, thereby avoiding a full and detailed revelation of the nuances of my concern, which might affect the action in the setting.

If something occurred which might reflect unfavorably on the collectivity and its members, individuals would joke to me, "Don't put that in your book," or "Better make that a footnote." On one occasion, when a shul event failed to draw a good showing of members, I jokingly asked, "What will I write in my notes?" "I'll tell you exactly what to write," the president answered with a laugh, and to the amusement of others listening. "Write that a lotta people came, and everybody had a good time."

Finally, a psychotheological explanation may be offered for the incessant joking and gossip that constitute shul conversation. This "light" chatter of sociability, almost compulsive in character, blocks out—literally as well as symbolically—the possibility of the speakers' having to come to terms with the deeper antinomies inherent in their modernity and Orthodoxy. To talk about such matters of the spirit would be to open a Pandora's box of anxieties and theological conflicts with which the everyday shul Jew refuses to deal. The "small talk" of joking and gossip is infinitely safer and more manageable.

Between their gossiping and joking, the members have other responsibilities and involvements. While in practice these often seem secondary, they are by tradition and structure much more manifestly part of proper shul behavior, and it is to them that we will now turn our attention.

7

Singing, Swaying, Appeals, and Arguments

> Is it possible to pray to the Lord with words alone?
>
> *Rabbi Nachman of Bratslav*

The analysis of gossip and joking at Kehillat Kodesh, set forth in chapters 5 and 6, was stimulated by a desire for a closer look at some of the conversational involvements that members engage in during the course of tefilah sheh be tzibbur. These two types of conversation have been treated in detail because they, more than any other types I observed, seem to constitute most of the talk in shul, both during prayers and at other times. The discussion of gossip and joking sometimes required that we range further than their use in the house of prayer. It is to this latter frame of reference that we now return. For, in addition to talk, other involvements and energizers of context exist.

I have described the prayer service as a shifting reality, defined by a series of context-marking involvements, and I have likened its participants to members of a jazz ensemble, each engaged in his own separate activity, but all periodically returning in unison to a central or basic collective involvement. In tefilah sheh be tzibbur such communion requires some activity in which the entire collectivity can engage as one. Perhaps the most outstanding and successfully encompassing of these activities at Kehillat Kodesh is group singing, for it engages most if not all of the members in the setting—including women and children.[1]

By tradition, the recitation of prayers is voiced; or, if no sound comes forth, the lips, at least, must move; it is therefore quite easy for the observer to know when a participant is at least manifestly engaged in prayer. The prayers are recited either in a whisper or, to borrow from the language of opera, in a kind of *Sprechgesang*, a type of half-singing and half-speaking.[2] The sound of people at prayer may give the impression of verging on either talk or song. When the prayer is least like song and most like speech, conversation is most likely to break out. However, when the prayer turns into melody and song, it attracts and activates general communal involvement. During the protracted singing of various prayers, even when no prohibition against being mafsik obtains, talking stops, other competing involvements decline, and people begin to pray.

The singing may take two forms. Either the participants all sing the same words in a canonic form, as is the case in quasi-chazanic activity, or they all sing in unison as members of a chorus. Only the latter includes everyone, women and children as well as men. To both the participant and the observer, such singing seems the prototypical experience of tefilah sheh be tzibbur. These are the moments when the members seem most inspired in prayer, when communion with others raises one to heights of religious inspiration. By singing together, congregants experience both sentiments of tefilah and awareness of one another's presence in the tzibbur. The words, along with the harmonies, serve to make one realize, not only that one is praying, but also that one is not alone in doing so.

Singing may be expected to become part of prayer under certain conditions. The less the profane world of everyday life impinges upon one's consciousness, the more possible does the devotion of prayer become. As individuals become inspired, they begin to sing. Prayers are at first whispered; next comes Sprechgesang; and finally there is a full burst of song. Moreover, the singing, which begins as a reflection of devotional sentiment, becomes in time its sustaining force. Accordingly, one may expect to hear singing both during periods of prayer that are free from the claims of the everyday profane world and during those that are prolonged. One is therefore not surprised to discover that the brief weekday prayers, occurring as they do amid the mundane demands of the work week, are primarily characterized by whispers and Sprechgesang, while the longer prayers of Sabbaths and holy days, those oases in time, are studded with song.

Choral singing, dependent as it is upon a union of voices, has not only a devotional dimension but also a communal one. Accordingly, one may expect to hear it when the participants need a way of affirming and displaying their union, usually when the assembled congregation is largest—again, chiefly on Sabbaths and holy days. Yet even then choral singing does not mark the early moments of the service, which are primarily conducted in Sprechgesang. These opening prayers are poorly attended, with the tzibbur not yet at full strength. By the end of the service, however, everyone who is coming is present, and the time is most favorable for the affirmation of collective experience which the singing implies. Hence Sabbath and holy-day prayers are always formally terminated with a flood of choral singing.

Singing also serves to identify and classify time, because various melodies have come to be associated with particular occasions. Sabbath has its own special tunes, and so do Passover, Yom Kippur, and so on. Moreover, Friday-night services have tunes different from Sabbath-morning ones. An individual who is praying by himself at home may repeat some of these tunes as if he were praying with a tzibbur, but neither the repetitions of the chazan nor the harmonies of a chorus are possible for the solitary worshiper.

All shul members know the standard tunes—the ones the congregation will join in singing and those it will not. The "good chazan" is the one who has learned not only these familiar melodies but also some new ones, which he occasionally introduces to the congregation. Moreover, he must know *nusach*, the hymnodical idiom combining Sprechgesang and aria, which concludes, connects, and leads the prayers. The virtue of the good chazan lies not only in his knowledge of the rules and etiquette of prayer but also in his ability to inspire congregational feelings of worship or, when the group is otherwise involved, to carry on alone with the nusach.

Learning nusach requires training, often informally acquired through years of attendance in shul. Nusach does not vary essentially from shul to shul, and this accounts for the feeling of familiarity which Orthodox Jews experience even when walking into a shul halfway across the world. Group songs, however, are more varied than nusach. Knowledge of these, like stamps on a passport, serve as indicators of the well-traveled Jew.

A conversation might run: "Do you know the tune for kedusha they use at Beth El?" "No, but I know the one at Kehillat Kodesh." Melodies thus come to stand for congregations, and knowledge of them helps to reveal the extent of one's familiarity with the rest of the Orthodox world. The member who has been to various shuls brings these tunes home to share with his fellow members. Like souvenirs, they recall tefilah sheh be tzibbur elsewhere. Furthermore, as they are learned by different congregations, they serve—much as folk songs do—to unite the dispersed Orthodox outposts into one community, one tzibbur, singing together, as it were, in a world of its own.[3]

While group singing allows the members to engage in collective action, it must not be allowed to envelop anyone so completely that he cannot afterward disengage himself and become otherwise involved. Accordingly, when members join in the singing, they do so with an undercurrent of detachment, so that they will not seem completely enraptured. As suggested earlier, the conventionalization of prayer restricts flights of ecstasy at the same time that it makes prayer possible on a day-to-day basis. Kavannah, that feeling of worshipful devotion and involvement, is rarely allowed ultimate exhibition. Indeed, one man, who appears enraptured during even the most simple of group songs, has become the object of open ridicule among the members, his exhibitions of devotional fervor having become something of a public joke. ("The guy is off his rocker; I mean he gets a little carried away," one member puts it. Others agree.)

The delicate balance between detachment and involvement is not always maintained. Some members, like this man, become captured by the song, while others remain so detached that their participation is limited to listening. Most people, however, learn to orchestrate their actions in conformity with the majority and thereby maintain the normative level of involvement.

Some occasions *are* set aside to allow for the full expression of kavannah. Such enthrallment is allowed and indeed expected during the ten "Days of Awe," from Rosh Hashona (the New Year) through Yom Kippur (the Day of Judgment); on certain fast days; and on special personal occasions, like mourning, praying for a sick kinsman, and so on. These opportunities allow an individual to step out of conventional character and, even in apparent contradiction to his normal behavior during the rest of the year's prayer, become immersed in kavannah. The same men whose amida, for example, is shortest in duration the rest of year may on Yom Kippur stand engrossed in prayer longer than anyone else. For all participants the prayers are longer, the singing more frequent, the time spent in shul protracted. Such occasions allow for a kind of religious regeneration, during which worshipers once again may experience and express the personal spirituality which prayer encourages. The atmosphere proclaims itself as different through its special rituals, reorganization of time, and modification of liturgy, and this allows for the projection of different self-presentations—presentations which need not be consistent with what has gone on the rest of the year.

Other activities also involve the members as one. Among these is the institutionalized gossip of Velvel's announcements. No matter how much talking and other involvement has occurred prior to the announcements, everything stops when these words begin. Like the group song, the public announcement, heralded by anticipatory joking and shushing, claims collective involvement. Instead of singing or praying together, the members become one as an attentive, active audience.

One must be careful not to automatically equate collective silence with undivided collective involvement, for a host of competing nonverbal engagements remain possible and may occur unnoticed, even in an atmosphere of silence. While an individual remains silent, his focus of attention may actually be mentally "away";[4] outwardly he appears to be participating in the collective activity, while he has in fact inwardly emigrated from the action. Such auto-involvements may include reading, daydreaming, playing with the fringes on one's talis, and many other like activities.[5] When most people present respond as one to the same event, one may generally assume the involvement to be collective. Since thoughts remain unobservable, however, one can never be completely certain of the depth of such involvement.

Two more kinds of collective involvement should be mentioned. In each the degree of involvement is more typical of organic than mechanical solidarity.[6] That is, everyone responds in his own fashion to the event, so that, rather than uniformity of response, as in group singing, one observes distinctly individual types of participation. Nevertheless, everyone present becomes involved in the event. In substance the two events which occasion these involvements appear quite different. One is the collection of charity, the other is resolution of open arguments.

Let us consider charity first. At various times during the year, Velvel, in his presidential role, takes his place at the pulpit and makes an appeal for funds. Such appeals are announced well beforehand, so that no insider is surprised by them. The appeal may be for money for the shul, for an outside charity, or for a special need, such as an emergency collection for a family in dire circumstances. Any appeals held in this manner imply a minimum donation of five dollars. These are not the minimum gifts given out during weekday services. Moreover, since appeals are most frequently held on Sabbath or holy-day mornings (the times of largest congregational turnout), when one is halachically prohibited from handling money, funds are always collected in the form of pledges. Pledged donations are expected to be greater than direct cash handouts.[7]

Massive attention is paid to such appeals. The members are interested not only in the total amount pledged and collected but also in who gave what. Everyone is expected to respond in accordance with his economic and institutional position. That is, different people are associated with different expectations. Originally, appeals were conducted in such a way that pledges were publicly announced by the president. However, this procedure failed to yield large collections, since the largest pledges, which always came first (having been solicited long before the actual appeal), discouraged the ten-dollar donors. The board, therefore, with the overwhelming approval of the congregation, unanimously decided to make future appeals silent. This change encouraged the smaller as well as the bigger donations. It is still possible, however, to find out the size of pledges. Now the information is simply passed via gossip. Indeed, that gossip assures that the "big giver" will not be lost behind a cover of anonymity.

Only the men are given pledge cards. Since writing is prohibited on Sabbaths and holy days, they fold down a tab corresponding to the amount of their donation. Nevertheless, many pledges are cleared in advance with wives, and this perhaps helps to explain why appeals are announced so far in advance. Men who fail to make this preparation are often seen signaling their wives or stepping out for a quick consultation on action to be taken. A pledge is, after all, a reflection not only of the individual's but of the family's position, both financially and vis-à-vis the group. The stronger one's tie to the group, the greater the proportion of one's wealth one is expected to give.[8] Indeed, being an officer or an otherwise heavily involved participant is often an expensive proposition, as the newly involved participant observer soon learns.

Members carefully watch as the gabbai collects the pledge cards. A large stack in his hand is a good sign. Soon after the appeal, perhaps the next day, the amount of the collection becomes hot news. A good collection is greeted enthusiastically. Like a good turnout at the minyan, a large collection is a sign of communal strength. If everyone has given his true maximum (an amount which is determined in gossip), a general sense of communal responsibility—a fundamental collective concern—has been adequately reaffirmed.

Money alone, however, cannot prove commitment to the collectivity. Individuals who have ceased to be active participants in the group may continue to give money to the shul. Yet such donations, no matter how generous, fail to elicit the same pride and confidence from the group as the money gathered from active members. These latter collections are evidence of a communal vitality which has a sociopsychological importance far outweighing any pride in the amount of money collected.

Because appeals may also serve as affirmations of group existence, great care is employed to make sure that the members are not exploited financially and appealed to unnecessarily. This precaution is one of the president's most important concerns. Several times I have seen him postpone or cancel an appeal that came too closely on the heels of another, more important, one. At one time when an appeal was forced on the shul by outside organizations, Velvel failed to encourage donations beforehand, as is his normal practice. Although members responded, they did so with much grumbling and complaint.

Just as appeals involve all those present at the proceedings, with some observing (i.e., children, strangers, and women) and some acting (i.e., native men and the male guests), so also do occasional public arguments. The eruption of a quarrel between two or more members brings about rapid attentiveness, awesome in its totality. Suddenly, all eyes are on the combatants, and other involvement halts; even the chazan may stop his activity. Under this social spotlight, some people move to end the fight, cajoling, ordering, and convincing the disputants to stop, while the rest of the congregation maintains its silent attention in an unspoken pressure which demands armistice. No fight is allowed to quietly smolder on the periphery of the setting. Rather, every altercation is quickly thrust to center stage, where the pressures of staged performance are enlisted to help stop it.[9] Indeed, one might even suggest that such an outburst is the quarrelers' implicit call for mediation and intercession by the collectivity. Such help is always forthcoming, for reasons that should by now be apparent.

One final point should be made with regard to these two types of collective involvement. Unlike group singing, which serves to mark the context as one of tefilah, these two involvements energize and mark a context of assembly, of collective action only indirectly related to prayer. Because these events take place within the frame of time set aside for prayer, however, they become inextricably associated, in the minds of both the actors and the observer, with the shul as house of prayer and so appear to be legitimate and anticipated involvements in that context.

One more aspect of shul as house of prayer deserves reference: *shokeling.* "Shokeling" is the Yiddish word referring to the swaying and shaking that is a common accompaniment to tefilah.

A certain mystery attaches to the origins of this practice. Some people suggest that it is called for in the psalmist's phrase, "Bless the Lord, O my soul; and my whole being bless His Holy name" (Psalms 103:1). Others suggest that it is simply a natural bodily accompaniment to devotional prayer. Whatever its sources, however, it stands now as a cultural attribute with sociological meaning.

According to common stereotypes, all Orthodox Jews shokel when they pray. Upon observation, one finds that, although such stereotypical expectations have some groundings in fact, they do not really adequately describe the practice. The observer at Kehillat Kodesh soon finds a wide variety of shokeling, associated with different classes of shul participants.

The first differentiation that one notices is that women for the most part shokel much more slowly and less vigorously than men. Their shokeling is limited to a slow swaying, either forward and back or in a small swivel, and is for the most part restricted to the amida. Some men shokel in this same way, but others go far beyond this range of movement. The more traditionally Orthodox, the occasional visitor from a yeshiva, shokels with great intensity during all parts of the service. He is swaying while he stands, undulating his upper torso while he sits. On the other hand, those who would characterize themselves as modern Orthodox sway much more intermittently and with restraint. Where the yeshiva student, for example, never seems to stop shokeling, even when he stands in conversation with another, the modern Jew is the man who shokels only during moments of most intense tefilah.

The shokeling of the young male child is perhaps the most interesting to watch. Being educated in schools run by traditional Orthodox teachers, the young boy shokels with the vigor and speed of the traditionally Orthodox. It is not surprising to see, next to a slowly swaying father, a rapidly rocking son. In jest, one parent once referred to his son's shokeling as "one of the hazards of a yeshiva education." However, as the boy matures and locates himself on the spectrum of Orthodox life, his shokeling seems to slow down. For the boy who does not leave home for a life in a yeshiva, the shokeling soon approximates that of his father. The boy who does leave home for the yeshiva, however, may establish for himself a pendulation much more vigorous than his father's. Such shokeling may serve as a public signal that a person has accepted many of the norms of behavior of traditional Orthodoxy. By itself, of course, it will not suffice as evidence, since vigorous shokeling is so easily used for deception. Together with other confirming signals (e.g., clothes, involvements in study, etc.), such rapid shokeling identifies the more frum.

Finally, because shokeling vigorously has become culturally identified with piety, one finds increased shokeling during moments when shul members seek to emphasize their piety—on the high holy days, for example. Or, within the service, group singing, qua tefilah, tends to bring forth more lively shokeling, as do the amida and the kedusha. Indeed, for the informed observer, such bodily movement may serve as a signal that an involvement shift to prayer is about to occur (although one must always be wary of the habitual shokeler or the pretender, of whom there is a sufficient number).

Shokeling during tefilah sheh be tzibbur brings to a close our discussion of the shul as a house of prayer. The next step in deciphering the setting requires looking at it as a house of study and assembly. We already know something about the nature of involvements which mark these contexts, since they have made their appearance in the serial involvements occurring in the house of prayer. Now, however, instead of being set against a basic involvement in prayer, these involvements will act as bases themselves. In the house of study, "learning" will be the involvement returned to time and again; while the house of assembly will be characterized not only by gatherings for specific purposes but by bursts of pure sociability.

In the following discussions only the baseline involvement will be detailed, not because it is the only involvement characteristic of the occasion, but because the series of involvements that are possible have already been for the most part handled in the discussion of the house of prayer. Finally, the focus will remain, as before, on the males. Renée Fox has suggested that at Kehillat Kodesh the men are like priests: they are the only ones allowed to make full use of the setting, but they are acting on behalf of the entire community.[10] A look at the houses of study and assembly in no way contradicts this proposition.

8

The House of Study

Let your house be a meeting place
for scholars.

Yosé ben Yoezer of Zeredah

"Jewish worship embraces the study of Torah."[1] "Torah" stands as
the dominant symbol of the corpus of law, lore, and rabbinic
commentary which tradition considers divinely inspired and revealed. It includes, first, the Pentateuch (the five books of Moses,
which constitute the entire Torah scroll), the writings of the
prophets (including the books of Joshua, Judges, Samuel, Kings,
Isaiah, Jeremiah, Ezekiel, and the twelve minor prophets), and the
scriptures (including the Psalms, Proverbs, Job, the Song of
Solomon, Ruth, Lamentations, Ecclesiastes, Esther, Daniel, Ezra,
Nehemiah, and Chronicles). The three together are referred to
acrostically as Tanach, after their Hebrew names: *torah, navi-im,*

and *kesuvin*. Second, and in terms of actual study perhaps more important, the Torah includes the Mishna and the Talmud, codified oral law, together with its rabbinic analysis and commentary. Third, contemporary rabbinic scholia and responsa may under certain circumstances qualify as Torah. Finally, mystical as well as exegetical texts have over time slowly been incorporated into the general definition of Torah. The study of any of these four areas may fulfill the ritual and religious obligation to study Torah.

Informally, Torah has come to symbolize and stand for the very fiber of Jewishness. To "follow the Torah" is to abide by the principles and emphases of the Jewish people and its doctrines. For the religious Jew, that alone describes the purpose and substance of life.

From almost the moment of his awakening, the observant Jew testifies to the central role which Torah plays in his life. In the liturgy which begins his morning prayers, the first blessing recited after those pertaining to the fulfillment of bodily needs is one which affirms the gift of the Torah. Moreover, as pointed out earlier, the liturgy itself is interspersed with numerous and lengthy excerpts from the Torah, which become repeated in much the same way as prayers. Moreover, the halacha states that one engaged in the study of Torah is exempt from the simultaneous obligation to fulfill other commandments. Legend even has it that one may not die while engaged in Torah study. Finally, reading from the Torah scroll and from the prophets and scriptures makes up a part of the service at regular intervals.

The preeminence of Torah study in the life of the dutiful Jew is emphasized in other ways as well. For example, as stated early in this study, no Orthodox Jewish community is complete without access to some day school where children may be educated in the ways of Torah. By the age of five the male youngster is expected to have a rudimentary knowledge of the Hebrew alphabet and to have learned (i.e., to recite and understand) a few prayers. By the age of seven he should have begun the study of the Pentateuch; and before bar mitzva, at age thirteen, the child is expected to be well along in the study of Talmud and Mishna. Throughout life these early study habits are supposed to be reinforced. What holds true for the child should remain so for his father.

For the modern Orthodox Jews of Kehillat Kodesh, many of whom are products of substantial formal Jewish education, the study of Torah remains an important principle of religious doctrine. In practice, however, relatively few attend the regular weekly formal study groups which the shul and other Orthodox institutions sponsor. Instead, members exercise their concern for Torah study in other ways—through private individual study, in conversation, through frequent halachic inquiries, and in other ways that will presently be discussed. More precisely, while shul members spend more time in Torah study than their less observant brethren, such time is not necessarily spent in formal study groups.

This neglect is not taken lightly by the members themselves, since it seems to stand as blatant evidence of an unconscionable disparity between principles of belief and realities of practice: by sponsoring and organizing formal study groups, the congregation displays its adherence to doctrine; by low attendance levels, members exhibit their deviance from that doctrine. Accordingly, the group continually calls for new classes, which disintegrate when relatively few persons attend; this leads in turn to a call for more new classes, ad infinitum. Yet always some classes exist.

For the most part it is Orthodox men who engage in Torah study. Just as women are exempt from the ritual responsibilities of prayer, so too they are exempt from Torah study. According to Jewish tradition, the woman is exempt from this obligation because her other duties leave her little time for scholarly pursuits. The *modern* Orthodox woman, like her contemporary sisters, finds that she in fact does have both time and the inclination for other than housewifely duties. Accordingly, Kehillat Kodesh women have organized several study groups of their own (groups which in longevity and size far exceed those organized by the men). These groups, however, unlike the men's, do not meet in the shul but rather, on a rotational basis, in various members' homes.

Only during lecture classes devoted to some special topic, which both sexes may attend, do women engage in Torah study in shul. Interestingly, at such times the women sit separately in the back, just as they do during prayer. They are participants—but only by invitation, not by right. In study as well as in prayer, the shul is clearly a man's world, in which the women can share only so long as the men let them.

Formal Torah study for Kehillat Kodesh members may take any of four forms: (1) small weekly study groups, (2) regular lectures on a set text, which take place between mincha and ma'ariv on Sabbath afternoons, (3) lectures on special topics, and (4) individual study. Let us look more closely at each of these types in order to decipher the primary activity of the shul as house of study.

Weekly Study Groups

The small study groups, all of which meet in the shul, have a fairly consistent format. Each has a teacher-leader who controls the proceedings. He is the one who makes the final decision on what will be studied, how long the class will last, and what issues will be emphasized. All questions are addressed to him; and although various participants may offer their own responses, the teacher's answer has the ring of final authority. Like a chazan, the teacher gives cues as to when to move on in the text, when to end digressions, and when to reiterate or amplify any point.

The props for such classes are of two types: those formally required by the dominant activity of Torah study and those informally attached to it through the other involvements associated with the class. The text is the primary formal requirement. Others besides the teacher will usually have copies of it. Indeed, regular members of such classes are often persons who have large scholarly libraries at home, and each therefore has a copy of the work under study. In fact, the class, in addition to being an opportunity for using these books, often acts as a setting where one's bibliothecal wealth may be displayed—with all the attendant advantages of any display of wealth. Members may frequently spend the warming-up period before the beginning of the class in perusing and comparing one another's books. One man finds that another has a rare and impressive volume with a great many esoteric commentaries. Another has a new edition, set in a new style of type. Still another has a cheap edition, while the last has one which was his grandfather's and which survived the Nazi holocaust. For each book there is a story; and, as the books are compared, the stories are exchanged.

Some members may not have copies of a particular text, and to them the shul offers its library. As with individual libraries, the ownership of books is an indication of the importance of study in the life of the library's owner. The ownership of books takes on added significance for the shul library. Just as the minyan indicates the strength of the religious community, so the size and variety of a library *may* express the communal commitment to study. Accordingly, members may commemorate significant occasions in their personal lives by donating books to the shul's library. The condition of the library is also important. Books that appear unused, or too old or too damaged for use, fail to express an active commitment to Torah study. The Kehillat Kodesh library is small.

Complaints on this score sometimes arise, and their frequency seems to be in direct proportion to the strength of the minyan. It is as if the first worry is to project an image of a strong house of prayer. Once that image has been satisfactorily expressed, concern about the house of study can and does emerge.

Another prop, in addition to the text, is the shulchan or table. Most of the small study groups are held upstairs, in the kiddush room. The six or seven men who attend sit around a long table, their books spread out before them. By its contact with the sacred texts the table acquires a degree of sanctity (the texts themselves must be approached with circumspection, kissed if dropped, and generally be kept from profane contact).

While certain profane objects, like pipes or ashtrays—the informal props of the activity—may be placed on the table, others, like coats and hats, which are irrelevant to the action, are removed. One has only to place the wrong objects on the table to see them quickly and quietly disappear. The sanctity of the table, however, remains understated, not, for example, as formally institutionalized and surrounded with religious ritual, as is the holy ark.

Other props, particular to the Kehillat Kodesh setting, change from time to time. At one class they may consist of extra chairs for coats and hats; at another, a supply of cigarettes, matches, and ashtrays; and, at yet another, refreshments from the nearby kitchen. These props, the arranging of which often occupies much of the warming-up period, have less to do with the formal activity of Torah study and more to do with the informal interactional needs of the particular participants at this focused gathering.[2]

Consider, for example, the distribution of cigarettes. For a long time this chore accounted for at least the first ten minutes of each class. In a ritualized manner, one or two members would pull out one or even two packs of cigarettes and place them on the table. While these men offered smokes to everyone present, beginning with Rabbi Reblem, the teacher from the Sprawl City Yeshiva, who had volunteered to lead this Talmud study group, others began a search for ashtrays and matches. When all the materials had been gathered, the smokers would light up, remark on the advantages and disadvantages of smoking, joke, share community news, and finally talk about Torah.

Almost imperceptibly, while such materials are being gathered, conversations which often last well into the first cigarette move from being concerned with pure sociability to discussions about Torah. As if warming up for the subject at hand, one member might mention a rabbinic commentary he had studied during the week, while another might bring up a question that had long been puzzling him. Still another might use this time for making a halachic inquiry about ritual practice, receiving an answer which could stimulate a long and complicated discussion among the members. When, for example, one man once asked the rabbi what should be done with beer before the Passover holy day, the question and its answer raised issues which were debated for almost the entire classtime. Topics raised during the warming-up period often resurface later in the class in the form of digressions. As such they continue to be part of the substance of the class.

Perhaps a useful way of considering such classes is in terms of Pike's conceptions of *spectacle, game,* and *miscellaneous overlapping personal hierarchies of activity.*[3] Using the example of a football game and its surrounding simultaneous and intermittent activity, Pike delineates various foci of concern. The "spectacle" includes all activities and involvements which, while related to and dependent upon the existence of the official game, are not, strictly speaking, a part of it. These include (but are by no means limited to) the pre- and postgame activities, as well as events at halftime. The spectacle is more inclusive than the "game" and occurs around it. The game remains what Pike calls "the predominant focus unit"[4] (in the present study called the "basic involvement"); still, it is by no means the only thing going on in the setting. In addition to both the spectacle and the game are other miscellaneous personal hierarchies of activity which, although ego-oriented, may temporarily merge or overlap with the spectacle. Pike mentions the cheering students in the stands, for whom participation in the spectacle is but one activity in a long series of individual involvements which he calls their "personal hierarchies of activity."

One might similarly describe the study group (to say nothing of the prayer service). The formal involvement in textual study may be seen as analogous to the "game." This is the predominant-focus unit, or basic involvement, which serves as both the stimulus for the gathering and the common activity upon which those present most regularly refocus their individual attention. The conversations, passing of cigarettes, asking of questions unrelated to the text, digressions, and exchange of gossip and jokes may, from the point of view of an observer, all be considered as part of the "spectacle." As with football, such peripheral activities may and often do take up more time and attention than the actual game and occur simultaneously or intermittently with it. Indeed, for some, if not all, persons the spectacle is more absorbing than the game.

Each man has come to the class for reasons of his own. For some, study of this kind belongs to their conception of Jewish religious observance. For others, the class offers a chance to get away from wife and family. One man admitted that by coming to the class he had found another way to get in the smoking that his wife would not let him do at home. For still others, such gatherings offer an opportunity to exchange gossip or to engage in sociability. These exemplify the "miscellaneous overlapping personal activities" in which the class is but one item in one's repertoire of active involvements. Moreover, because in the class—unlike the football game—observers are also full-fledged participants, the personal activities of one participant (e.g., his joking) become, from the point of view of the others present, *part* of the spectacle.

The group begins its formal work at the teacher's signal, commonly accomplished by his opening the text, silently perusing it, and then recapitulating the material covered during the last class. His leadership is maintained throughout the class. Whenever the group digresses from the subject at hand, it is he who brings them back to the text, most simply and frequently by reading aloud from it during a lull in the digression. Like a chazan, the teacher acts to cue the basic involvement.

As in prayer, those present try to indicate that they are knowledgeable, involved, and attuned to the activity. Such displays serve not only to advertise one's intellectual abilities but also to signal the teacher that he has made his point and can move on to the next issue. Just as quasi-chazanic activity serves many of these display and cuing functions in prayer, so reiteration and restatement do in class. For example, consider the following description:

> Reblem is explaining a fairly difficult section of the text.
> In silence we all follow along as he unravels the argument and explains the phrases of the Talmud. Some members are nodding, as if to indicate that they have assimilated and understood each point. Occasionally one or two will smile, signifying a fascination with the logic and a total comprehension of it. In the silences between various parts of the *sugia* [textual episode], the students remain silent, allowing Reblem to structure his remarks. Now, as the sugia nears its end, various participants begin to restate and reiterate Reblem's arguments.
> "So then, the *gemara* [Talmud] is saying that a man has

to be responsible for his *sheliach* [representative]?" Riff asks.
"That's right," Reblem replies. One by one the various members
repeat in their own words the points that Reblem has elucidated.

Not everyone reiterates, especially one or two of the members
who seldom seem able to follow the line of the text. Reiterations
over, Reblem begins again to read from the text.

Members may indicate their comprehension in other ways as well.
Beyond restatement and reiteration, they may respond to the
material by outlining its implications. Here the student can display
his ability not only to follow the line of the text but to penetrate its
logic and underlying theory. Such comments win for the student a
greater prestige than simple reiteration. The student who can go
beyond the text shows that he is on the way to mastery of the
material. Such statements must be made with care and are subject
to ratification by the teacher. Without his agreement and confirmation, the effect of a remark may be quite the opposite of what its
author intended. The student who draws a faulty conclusion and
spins out wrong implications indicates not only that he has
misunderstood the point of the text but also that he is perhaps less
capable and comprehending than those who have remained silent.
Accordingly, only students who have scored some successes in
their reiterative remarks will follow these up with statements of
conjecture.

The description cited from my notes makes reference to other
means of demonstrating comprehension. Many of these are nonverbal and gestural. Nods, smiles, and facial expressions may all
serve notice to the other students, as well as to the teacher, that one
has followed and understood the text. Of course, such gestures,
which attempt to manage an impression of comprehension, must at
some point be ratified and confirmed by reiteration; otherwise,
doubt will arise as to the genuineness of one's comprehension.

Yet study is more than reiteration. "Learning," as talmudic study
is called, consists also of the asking and answering of questions. In
part this format springs from the approach of the text itself. Made
up of rabbinic questions, answers, debates, and comments, the
Talmud sets up an atmosphere of questioning. Not only does the
text ask and answer questions; the teachers and students do, too.
As if using the text as a dramatic script, class participants anticipate
questions and answers, debate them, and thus bring the page before
them to life. While one speaker argues one position, another offers
its opposite. When the text moves off on tangents, so do the
students. The artful teacher elicits such reactions from his students,

or, failing to receive responses from them, plays out the drama himself by asking questions in a rhetorical manner: "But how can a person be responsible for a sheliach if he does not know what the sheliach is planning to do?" asks one member. "That's just what the gemara is really asking," the teacher replies, indicating that the student has kept up precisely with the Talmud. And so it goes, each point in the text being clarified in a gradual unfolding of questions and answers, each sugia increasingly embroiling the class members in the drama of its development.

In such a framework of questions and answers, a student's question can serve him in much the same way as a reiteration. The uncomprehending student asks digressive or misplaced questions. A proper question either anticipates the text, thus acting not only as a sign of intellectual apprehension but as a cue for the teacher to continue in the textual development, or it goes beyond the text, stimulating scholarly discussion. Questions of the latter type are the province of the more advanced students. Such questions stimulate answers and comments not only from the teacher but from the other students, who may use the discussion as an opportunity to exhibit their Jewish scholarship. Here, however, as elsewhere, the teacher retains the right to the last word; without his ratification, even a comment which may sound very learned will remain at the level of conjecture.

Questions which go beyond the text allow one to display not only one's Jewish scholarship but also one's secular knowledge. For example, during one discussion of the dietary laws of kashrut, the question of the organic composition of green olives was raised. Are such olives, because they contain lactic acid, *milchic* (dairy) or *pareve* (neutral, and thus permissible)? One member exploited the issue by indicating his special expertise in chemistry; offering a long dissertation on the composition of olives and the nature of lactic acid, he concluded, "The lactic acid in them is so broken down that it's not like milk any more." Even such comments, however, are subject to some ratifying remark by the teacher. In this case, the teacher concluded, "If that's the case, then *takeh* [indeed], we could learn up that olives are *mutor* [permissible] here."

The odd English in this last remark raises another issue inherent in the practice of learning at Kehillat Kodesh, namely, that the class context transforms language. Not only does English become intermingled with Hebrew, Yiddish, and the language of the Talmud, Aramaic; its syntax is also altered. For want of a better word, such English may be called "Yiddishized English" or, for denotative purposes, "Yinglish." The domination of Yinglish is awesome in scope. Indeed, one class member, a professor of English at a nearby university, whose command of English syntax is undoubtedly adequate, will, when engaged in Torah study, come out with a phrase like, "How *medakdek* [careful] do you have to be in learning out this *posuk* [verse]?"

This transformation of language is in part explained by the fact that the study of Torah and its transmission have for many years been in the hands of teachers whose English (Polish, German, etc.) has been less than fluent—men whose spoken language is in fact a mixture of Yiddish, Hebrew, and Aramaic, with Yiddish predominating. Thus, most students' early experiences in learning have always been in this mixed language, the use of which may in time have become habitual.

Such an explanation, however, seems to beg the sociological question. It may explain the origins of the usage but not its continuation, which seems instead to have deeper social-psychological roots. Any thoughts on the nature of such roots must, however, remain at the level of conjecture. One might speculate that because study and scholarship were and have remained essentially esoteric activities, engaged in by a limited and specialized group of virtuosi (in *spite* of being universally encouraged by religious precept), their transmission and practice have evolved a language of their own, known only by the initiated. Such a special language, like a secret code, would act to distinguish insiders from interlopers. Indeed, Yinglish has this quality. The newcomer to learning very quickly identifies himself through his accent, syntax, and inability to jumble language in the way that insiders do. Only the person who has studied the Talmud in a yeshiva or with people who have studied it there knows how to use the lingo properly. For example, the occasional Conservative Jew who makes his way into a Kehillat Kodesh class immediately exhibits his Jewish identity through his meticulous pronunciation of Hebrew and his use of unjumbled English.

To adequately decode the use of language and syntax in shul classes (and, one might add, in classes at other Orthodox institutions), one would have to begin with a precise analysis of the speech patterns of such classes. Such work requires a full and exact treatment and collection of all Yinglish terms utilized. Analysis of this sort is beyond the scope of this study and outside the ken of this writer and remains as an area for further study by social linguists. Some tentative remarks are, however, in order.

The Talmud in its text makes use of shorthand terms for various of its conceptualizations. Such terms act as representations of complex Judaic legal arguments. When translated literally, they make little or no sense, since they are usually composed of key words of the argument. Although these words could be translated into English abstractions, to do so would destroy their codical and referent qualities. Moreover, such efforts are intellectually gratuitous, since they often obliterate important nuances of meaning in the interests of coining some pithy neologism. Accordingly, such terms remain untranslated. For example, in the sentence *"Hasholayach es ha kayn* is the principle working here," the first words refer to a legal principle which mandates one to chase away a mother bird from a nest before taking away her eggs. The words themselves make little sense if literally translated. However, they act as simple referents to the complex argument of which they are the opening words. In much the same way as a pope's encyclical may be referred to by its opening words, so certain legal and talmudic principles become epigrammatized. Familiarity with many of these terms is another indication of scholarship and the mark of one who is an insider to the class, if not to the study of Talmud in general. This particular use of non-English is thus explained both by the conventions of talmudic terminology and by the strategic displays of status which occur in the social context of Talmud study.

Other non-English terms defy such relatively simple explanation. In many cases the non-English term is one that might be considered to be emotionally or socially charged: *moichel* is used instead of "forgiven"; *chiyuv ahava* appears instead of "the obligation to love"; *pilegesh* in the place of "concubine." Why such terms are spoken in non-English is not immediately clear. One is tempted to make vaguely psychoanalytic statements pertaining to the associated guilt, fear, and shame upon which ritual behavior, including study, is presumed to be predicated, but such comments are not warranted by the ethnographic data; that is, no corroborative evidence of such feelings was displayed.

Moreover, not all non-English terms are so blatantly affective. The use of *hachonos* rather than "preparations" or *zochur* instead of "male" defies psychological explanation. Many of these are idiomatic and stylized expressions which have become a part of Torah study. To "be *makdim"* instead of "to preface," to "give a *payrush"* instead of "offering an explanation," is to speak in Yiddishisms transplanted from a Judeo-European world in which they were marks of cultural eloquence. In their accentuation and in the context of Yinglish these expressions have, however, lost their original veneer of eloquence. Like a noble lost on a linguistic skid row, such phrases are memories of a language that once was. To the speaker these are often formulaic phrases of whose historic linguistic roots he is unaware.

The question of Yinglish syntax is perhaps the most intriguing of all and the hardest to answer. The speculation above, regarding the segregationary and distinguishing qualities of such language, does not unravel the puzzle of its specific rules of usage, nor does it account for the fact that those who use Yinglish vocabulary and syntax are commonly unaware of what they are doing to language. Switching from one language to another within the same sentence, the speakers seem oblivious of their shifts.[5] In their minds, they are speaking only one language, consistently throughout the class. Only when he is stopped in mid-sentence and asked to account for his phrasing and language will the speaker realize the composite character of his speech. Laughing sheepishly, one member responded to an inquiry of this kind by saying, "Well, you know, gemara is a special language."

In part, some language-shifting is mandated by the exegetical quality of Torah study, for much of the classwork consists in translating text and commentaries into the contemporary, and hence more comprehensible, language of the student. While one might properly expect this approach to promote the use of contemporary syntax and a predominance of English, one finds instead that the translations blend Yinglish with English. One possible explanation might view this mix as symbolic of the mix between the parochial and the secular so characteristic of modern Orthodox Jewishness. While the more frum continue to study in Hebrew, Aramaic, and Yiddish and the less frum study primarily if not completely in English, these shul Jews, living at once in the modern English-speaking world and the traditional Jewish world, study in Yinglish, that linguistic blend which reflects their character and situation.

One final point should be made in regard to this multilinguistic behavior, namely, that those who engage in it in class are often quite capable of speaking perfect English; some are even native-born Americans. Outside the frame of the class such individuals are seldom heard speaking extensively in Yinglish. In fact, its only other regular use occurs during informal conversations held in shul, possibly for many of the same reasons it occurs in class. The modern Orthodox shul, one might suggest, is in its social dimension generally a crossroads between the contemporary world and the traditional Jewish one. Often the teacher, as group leader, sets the argot for the event. His phrases, set out early in the proceedings, are repeated in students' questions and reiterations, making him seem like a director of a drama, who, by setting out the phrases and words to be used in class provides the fundamentals of the script.

The series of involvements defining the situation of these small, formal study groups is affected by the small number of participants in them. With at most seven people in any given class, the group can ill afford the luxury of allowing *individual* participants to shift their involvement from the primary activity (i.e., basic involvement) so as to create a definitional anarchy. Consequently, the small study groups are characterized by what Goffman calls "tightness." That is, they are situations in which "each person present may be obliged to show constant orientation to the gathering as a whole and constant devotion to the spirit of the occasion" in order to maintain the relatively fragile *group* definition of the situation.[6] The few participants present retain expectations of mutual involvement in the subject at hand, because deviations from such involvement threaten disruption of the paramount reality. Consequently, when persons shift involvement away from the primary task of learning the text, they do so with great circumspection and detachment, so that they will be able to return quickly and easily to the primary involvement. They do so both out of fidelity to the situation and in order to avoid the negative repercussions of defiant deviance. Thus, for example, personal conversations are whispered and brief.

Yet, in spite of the pressures of tightness, involvements other than those of study occur here, just as in other shul situations. In this frame of action, however, contextual shifts, when they do occur, involve the entire collectivity. That is, shifts suggested by engagement in involvements other than the primary one either include everyone present or else dissipate themselves shortly after being initiated. The entire class stops its primary involvement in textual study and does something else. Such collective shifts may be called *digressions*. Although digressions in class are primarily verbal in nature (i.e., digressive discussions), they may at times be digressions of action—gathering props, servicing the setting, smoking, and so on.

The first point to be made in connection with digressive discussions is that such talks do not irreparably disrupt the primary involvement in study. Indeed, the teacher, like the chazan, is often the one who calls the participants back to the primary involvement. For the informed, "learning," the activity of Torah study, ineluctably includes such digressions. Moreover, classes that are replete with digressions turn out to be the ones that participants describe as "one of the best classes we've had in a long time."

The topics raised during digressive discussions often act as hints to the character of the assembled collectivity. When the members of the group perceive the gathering as essentially a social occasion, they indicate this by broad-ranging digressions which at times have no clear connection to the text. When those present sense the learning dimension of the class, digressions tend to be scholarly in nature. Moreover, groups composed of young professionals, the most modern, tend to digress into their areas of secular interest, while the more traditional older members digress to less contemporary (though not necessarily less esoteric) topics. Just as warming-up periods reflect participants, situational definitions, and plans of action, so digressions indicate the kind of involvement desired. Together, digression, warming up, and, of course, the primary activity help the observer to decipher the direction and character of the action.

As suggested, not all classes digress in the same way. Digressions in the small Talmud groups meeting at Happiton are quite different from those in the Kehillat Kodesh class led by Rabbi Reblem. Each reflects its respective membership. The former contains more novices to Torah study, while the latter consists of former yeshiva students. Not surprisingly, digressions in the former group are not patently related to Torah, while, in the latter, group deviations from text study often include the asking of halachic questions, the sharing of Torah scholarship, and discussion of various ritual observances, as well as occasional jokes and news. Where the Happiton class is study sandwiched between jokes and anecdotes, the Reblem class is study interspersed with other scholarly involvements.

Having already described the Talmud-class proceedings as a drama which mirrors the text and brings it to life in the actions and involvements of the students, one should note that the digressions are also a part of that drama. The Talmud, in itself digressive, weaving its text with the most tenuous of connecting threads, creates an atmosphere of digression. While the wanderings of the students do not necessarily parallel those of the text in content, they do so in large measure in structure. Both text and students go off on tangents.

No treatment of digressive discussion would be complete without a presentation of some clarifying examples. Accordingly, I offer, below, eleven episodes that occurred during one ninety-minute class. Although these examples are not completely representative of the full scope and variety of digressions, they display their general character. Some seem to be stimulated by subjects raised in the text, while others simply spring spontaneously out of the silence that occurs between readings in the text and the elaborations made on them. Some of the spontaneous digressions turn out to be continuations of broken-off conversations begun during the warming-up period.

1. The rabbi, having just made reference to Jewish practice during "rabbinic times," is bombarded with several questions about such practices. Although he could easily delay answering by saying that such a discussion would be digressive, he does not do so. The conversation quickly moves far afield as the entire group begins to talk about Jewish practice then and now.

2. At a particular mention of an anecdote about a rabbi in the text, the teacher leaves the text and tells a joke about the rabbinic role. Self-deprecatory in nature, this digression is brief, the other class members offering one-word or one-line rejoinders before allowing the teacher to return to the text.

3. Prior to this class one of the members has raised a question about preparations for the upcoming Passover holy day. Now, during a lull in the class, another member bounces back with further inquiry about Passover procedures. Instead of answering this question directly, the rabbi and the others launch into a recitation of the list of places in Sprawl City where special Passover-preparation seminars will be held in the coming weeks.

4. Directly stimulated by the text, which outlines an important halachic principle, one member suggests that this principle is similar to one outlined in a recent state supreme-court decision. As he sets forth the details of the case, but before its legal principles can be deciphered, the other members begin to ask all sorts of questions about the particulars—almost as if they were gathering gossip information. In the end, the case seems to have very little if anything in common with the principle stated in the Talmud text under study.

5. A talmudic tale is recounted by the rabbi in response to a point made in the text. This digressive talk does not, strictly speaking, completely abandon involvement in the text; it might qualify as an effort to elaborate it. The tale may, however, be

considered digressive because many of its details and much of
its substance seem completely off the original subject.

6. A mention of the law of yartzeit prompts a long series
of questions and tales of personal experience related to this
observance.

7. The mention of the law of atonement brings about a rather
lengthy discussion of Christian versus Jewish modes of atonement. The underlying theme of these comparisons delineates
the emotional superiority of Jewish atonement.

8. The text has just mentioned the Exodus from Egypt. Now
members try to construct a detailed map of the forty-year
journey through the wilderness. The map is first described in
terms of the countries inhabiting the land in Mosaic times, then
in terms of the contemporary map. The subject stimulates much
debate and disagreement, which the rabbi's opinion seems to
end.

9. Soon after the digressive discussion described above, a
member stops the discussion of the text with, "I know this is
off the subject, but I was just thinking. . . ." He proceeds to
detail what to him appears an inconsistency in the description
of the Exodus: the fact that one source describes all the Jews
as having maintained the rites of circumcision throughout their
forty-year journey, while another source asserts that Joshua saw
the entire nation circumcised just prior to its entry into Canaan.
"How can both sources be correct?" the member asks. This
question, discussed with a sense of urgency, stimulates a great
deal of discussion, with various members guessing and hypothe-
sizing replies. The rabbi, puzzled as well, stops the class to fetch
another book, which might provide an answer. All watch him
and wait, occasionally reiterating their own hypotheses. Finally,
the rabbi provides an answer which seems to reconcile the two
sources, and the group, satisfied, returns with him to the text.

10. The subject of Passover is raised again during a silent
moment. Now all sorts of questions break out about procedures.
Some of these are answered and discussed. Finally, a decision
is reached to devote the next few classes to Passover study.

11. After this last digression, with the class nearly over,
the rabbi returns to the text only to be struck, almost at once,
with another digressive discussion. This one is another continuation of material discussed during the warming-up period. The
subject now concerns the various types of tefillin, or phylacteries, worn by various persuasions of Jews. After this digression, the teacher closes his book, a signal that the class is over.

During the class, it is often the case that digressions become more
numerous and protracted as time passes; thus, by the end of the

class, digressions have often taken up more time than the references to the text. The observer gets the impression that classes have two endings: the first occurring when the group signals, by its constant digressions, that it can no longer be held by the text for any extended period of time, the second occurring afterward, when the teacher, reciting one more point from the text, either closes his book or formally indicates closure. Always, it is the teacher who either explicitly, or, as here, indirectly, signals and ratifies the conclusion of the formal period of study.

Two more important points, each related to the other, must be made with reference to the small formal study group. The first concerns the fact that it is the teacher who chooses the material to be studied. Implied in this is the fact that, no matter what text is chosen and what subject of study, people will attend. Some members may be deterred from talmudic study because of a lack of expertise and ability, but this is not necessarily the case. Indeed, Talmud classes are often attended by members who could never study such material on their own. They do so because the regular study of Torah is a ritual activity. What one studies is less important than that one continue to study *something*. Only with great admissions of guilt do members admit that they have missed a particular chance to study. Like prayer, Torah study, in some form, is expected of all men. As with prayer, different people involve themselves in the activity in different ways. Yet somehow, either in small study groups or in other formats, people "learn."

The second and related point concerns the fact that men study Torah in shuls. Just as their prayer is often in shul, so their study is there. The women need not come to shul to pray, so, analogously, their study, which also is not legally mandated, takes place in private homes, away from the public shul. The house of study, like the house of prayer, remains a male territory, where others may sojourn but never nest.

Sabbath-Afternoon Lectures

The small attendance at the small formal study groups suggests that, if shul members engage in Torah study, they must do so for the most part in other formats. One of these is the brief lecture on the Torah (again usually the Talmud) given during the break between mincha and ma'ariv on Sabbath afternoons. Before anything can be said about this class, the special nature of this time must be made clear.

Although the Sabbath begins at sunset on Friday afternoon, it does not end until nightfall on Saturday night. Practically, this means that ma'ariv, the first prayer of the week after Sabbath, cannot begin one moment too early, while mincha, the last prayer of Sabbath, cannot begin too late, lest it end after Sabbath. Institutionally, this halachic issue has been handled by scheduling mincha in the late afternoon; this makes for a break of forty-five minutes, lasting through the twilight hours of dusk, between the end of mincha and the beginning of the ma'ariv service. This gap (which does not occur during the week for more than a few minutes, unless members are deep in conversation) is filled with Torah study.[7]

The substance and nature of this study is somewhat different from the formal type. First, it always takes place in the sanctuary, with the teacher, Rabbi Housmann, standing at the bimah, facing what to an outsider seems very much like an audience. Unlike the participants in the small study groups, these people have not manifestly come to shul to study. Rather, they have come for tefilah sheh be tzibbur, with all of its associated activities—only one of which may be study. Many are thus a captive audience, and many often refuse to define the situation as being a class. Some, rebelling against their captivity, repair to the foyers or the yard for conversation. Others may simply go to the back of the sanctuary or upstairs, to engage in private study, poring over some volume of the Talmud, and completely ignore the class.

Those who do attend do not remain constantly involved in the text and thus define the situation as "loose"—a situation "in which the regulation barely constrain[s] the participants to display their respect for the gathering."[8] A condition of looseness allows participants to engage in a series of individual involvements, including some which do not absolutely conform to the basic activity. Hence, members may talk among themselves, read, stand (to catch up on prayers they have missed), or otherwise openly deviate from involvement in the class. In short, during Housmann's class one observes many of the same sorts of involvements that occur during the loose periods in tefilah sheh be tzibbur. There one returns to the basic involvement by returning to prayer; here, however, one returns to listening to Housmann. The same man who seems engrossed in conversation with his neighbor will in a moment turn his attention to Housmann and may even raise a question or reiterate a point made. Collective digressions occur, more frequently when the number of people attending this class is small. When the group reaches fifteen or more, the situation becomes loose enough to allow for individual involvement shifts. When these occur, the situation seems at one moment defined as a sociable assembly, at another as an extension of mincha prayers, and at a third as indisputably a class in the Talmud.

Another distinction obtains between the small formal study groups and these short lecture periods. Here only a minority of the participants hold copies of the text that is being studied. This further facilitates situational looseness. Forced into the role of passive auditors who cannot on their own delve into the meaning of the text, students are implicitly encouraged in their involvement-shifting.

Although the class is regular and is always taught by Housmann, those attending it vary from week to week. A man who, for example, one week finds people with whom to go out for conversation will, the next week, find himself alone, with little else to do but remain inside for the class. Accordingly, the class lacks a sense of continuity, and this also tends to foster looseness.

In spite of the loose nature of the class situation, Housmann retains many of the prerogatives of the teacher role. It is he who calls the beginning and end of the class, accomplishing the former by standing up and opening the text and the latter by closing it. Often the participants insistently signal him to end. A rising tide of involvements other than attentive study shows him that he cannot long maintain the class as a legitimate baseline definition of the situation. Terminal squirms, an increasing volume of talk, and joking amens also serve to express the students' impatience. Finally, an influx of members returning from the foyers may force Housmann to close his text. Nevertheless, without his signal, the class is still on, regardless of others' lack of participation. Like the chazan, the teacher declares when the event has reached its formal conclusion. Like the chazan, however, he must be sensitive to cues from the group if he is to continue as its leader.

For many members, this Sabbath class is a chance to fulfill the ritual obligation to study. However, widespread dissatisfaction with its character ("This is really just a chance for Housmann to make speeches," one member admitted) has given the class a reputation that makes it difficult for a member to point to his attendance at it as an adequate fulfillment of his obligation.

Lectures on Special Topics

There is a third type of class, which, although infrequent, enables members to express, exhibit, and feel as if they have met the obligation of Torah study: the lecture on a special topic. Essentially such occasions are programmatic events dealing with a specific and circumscribed subject. Commonly held for only one session, they may occasionally be part of a regular but relatively infrequent lecture series. Although such seminars may occur at any time during the year, they are most common during the period immediately preceding holy days. Indeed, on two occasions of the year such special classes have become a part of Ashkenazic Jewish tradition.[9] Before Yom Kippur, on Shabbos Shuva, the Sabbath of Repentful Return, and prior to Passover, on Shabbos Hagadol, the Great Sabbath, Torah discourses have become an institutionalized ritual of shul life. Such class lectures are attended by all segments of the community—even by the women and children.

The substance of the seminars preceding holy days tends to be fairly similar from year to year. These classes must be distinguished from the sermons which also occur during these periods, but usually during a prayer service, for the classes are special occasions set aside distinctly for study and not for homily. Seminars before Passover inevitably deal with dietary-law observance. Before Yom Kippur, lessons focus on Atonement. Before Succos, the Holy Day of Booths, classes pertain to the laws of building and using the booth.

A point about the symbolic character of these annual classes can be made, particularly with reference to the Succos class. According to Jewish tradition, Succos commemorates the journey of the Jewish people following their Exodus from Egypt. During that time the people dwelt in booths (*succos*), small huts with three or more walls and a roof made of branches or reeds, through which the sky was visible. In order to relive this experience, Jews are to "dwell" (i.e., eat, study and—in some cases—sleep) in succos during the seven days of the holy-day period.

For the urban Jew, Succos presents logistical, but not insurmountable, difficulties, since he finds few spots outdoors where he can build a booth. Accordingly, the synagogue often provides a community succah (booth) for all its members to use. While Kehillat Kodesh offers such a facility—which members help construct and decorate each year, just before the start of the holy day—many members, living in private homes which have back yards, build their own succos and invite those lacking one to join them for meals in the succah. Consequently, the shul succah remains relatively unused—a good sign from the point of view of the members, since it indicates a self-sufficient community which sees to it that the obligations of the holy day are fulfilled. To "prove" that the shul succah is empty, not out of neglect of tradition but because of the members' scrupulous care in fulfilling by themselves the demands of the holy day, the community sponsors and attends the special-topic classes on the laws of Succos, a matter of interest only for the actively observant—i.e., Orthodox Jews. Attendance at such classes has thus the latent function of indicating a general communal frumkeit in the face of an empty shul succah. Hence, *building* a shul succah indicates to the outside, non-Orthodox world—for example, passersby on the street who may see the structure—the communal concern for observing the laws of the holy day. Leaving it *empty*, along with the ritualized attendance at the anticipatory classes, symbolizes, to the insider, the same sort of concern.

Let us examine in greater detail one of these special-topic classes, one dealing with the laws and observances of Passover, in order to get a clearer understanding of their nature, structure, and function. The seminars preceding Passover are the most common and perhaps the best-attended events of their kind. More than any other holy day, Passover, during which all *chometz* (leavened foodstuffs) must be systematically removed from one's possession, requires anticipatory adjustment and preparation. For the Orthodox Jewish woman, whose dominion over the workings of the home is in some spheres nearly absolute, this period is therefore filled with comprehensive cleaning and preparation. While this is not the place to summarize the many and complex laws of Passover, we may generally say that for those who strictly observe halacha the tasks are gargantuan.

As might well be expected, those preparing for the holy day must have a practical and fairly thorough familiarity with the laws of Passover. In many cases such knowledge is accumulated through years of experience. One often hears explanations of procedures phrased in terms of, "My father or my mother did things this way." The laws are, however, so complex, and the coefficients of modern life so unsettled, that new questions, requiring authoritative legal responsa, may sometimes arise.

For such questions, as well as for review of traditional preparatory practices, Passover seminars have become institutionalized. Upon closer analysis, however, one finds that in spite of the manifest educational justification for seminar attendance—"to learn the laws of Pesach [Passover]"—few of the annual questions are new, and most of the time is spent in the reiteration of laws already known and complied with. The purpose of the class must thus go beyond instruction. Indeed, the class becomes, as will be apparent, no less a symbolic and ritual event than the class held before Succos.

The announcement of a special Passover seminar to be taught by Rabbi Shofetman, a teacher from the very large yeshiva in Bayberg, 250 miles south of Sprawl City, came two weeks before Passover. If people had been waiting for such a class before making their Passover preparations, they would have been caught with too little time. The cleanings and anticipatory arrangements had to begin at least four weeks earlier in order to be satisfactorily completed by the beginning of the holy day, which, by the time the class met, would be less than a week away. If anything, the seminar would, from the practical point of view, serve at best as a checklist event and at worst as a notification that, when it was too late to change, everything had been done wrong—a possibility which few if any people expected.

The occasion of Shofetman's seminar was announced by Velvel on the two preceding Sabbaths, while notification for the rest of Sprawl City Orthodoxy went out by newsletters and word of mouth. In addition, Sprawl City Yeshiva students were urged to attend, since Shofetman was renowned for his expertise in the matters of practical halacha. Although women were invited as well, they were told that there would be separate seating for them (in deference to the more frum—including the speaker). They could, therefore, expect to take a back seat in the proceedings—symbolically as well as in fact. Thus, although the affair was to be held in the shul sanctuary, it would not, strictly speaking, be a completely Kehillat Kodesh event.

The talk was scheduled for 8:00 P.M., with a ma'ariv service posted for 7:45 P.M. Latecomers who had missed the prayers organized a second minyan at the conclusion of the class. The alignment of these two events is neither unusual nor serendipitous. Traditionally and halachically the relationship between prayer and study is a close one, so that a house of study may also be considered a proper place for communal prayer. Moreover, halacha requires that all public study sessions where at least ten males have gathered be followed by some recitation of prayer. Finally, as mentioned earlier, much prayer consists of repeating the same texts that in other contexts one studies.

Before the beginning of the lecture, people, as always, warmed up, talking about Torah more than is usually the case before tefilah sheh be tzibbur. More than the usual number of members perused volumes of the Talmud and other scholarly books. Women whose conversations I could overhear also seemed to talk a great deal about the halachic questions that they had about Passover preparations (many of which had been resolved long before Shofetman's arrival). The few local yeshiva students set themselves up with paper and pencil, ready to take notes. Two students had even brought a tape recorder, which they installed in front.

As always, gossip was exchanged. With so many outsiders present, most of the information passed was of the news variety. Who was sick, who was out of town and not to be expected— this made up the substance of such conversation. News is of course by definition open to anyone present, but only shul members, among those present, seemed at all interested in the details about Kehillat Kodesh, particularly in the matter of who would and would not be coming tonight.

Any insider could easily catalogue and identify the various participants. In front sat the men, divided into the following groups. Yeshiva students sat together near the front, on the left side of the sanctuary, while shul members sat at the back, on the right, close to the mechitza. The large middle section was occupied by a miscellany of outsiders, most of whom were members of the Aguda, an Orthodox association which had partially sponsored the lecture. The women, fewer in number, sat behind the mechitza in groups much like the men's. Most of them were members' wives (single women are seldom responsible for preparing a home for Passover and hence have no manifest reason to attend a lecture of this kind).

The various participants further identified themselves and their association by their clothing. Yeshiva students, in traditional dark suit and backward-tilted hat, where the easiest to spot. Other nonmembers, most of whom, as Aguda members, were more traditionally Orthodox than shul members, also wore hats, but without the yeshiva tilt. Shul members wore yarmulkes, the skullcaps which the more frum usually reserve for wear in the home. Women wore headcoverings; since they were barred from view and careful observation, I noticed no other features of their dress.

Of all the distinctions among the participants in the setting, the most interesting, sociologically, seemed to be in the nature and content of the questions each group asked. The format of the class consisted of a short lecture by Shofetman followed by a longer period of questioning.

Shofetman spoke mainly about two common legal problems of

the season. The first concerned the halachic procedures involved in holding onto chometz whose value is sufficiently high that to remove it from one's premises and ownership constitutes a substantial financial loss and hardship. Traditionally, halachic virtuosi have found loopholes in the law to mitigate and in some cases avoid such hardships. One such loophole, the selling of chometz to a Gentile for the entire eight days of Passover, only to repurchase it after the holy day, has become an institutionalized procedure. To use it invariably requires the help of a rabbi, who acts as an agent for the sale and repurchase. Although every Orthodox and observant Jew knows the general aspects of this procedure, it is complex enough so that explanation of it can always make for part of a seminar. As could be expected, Shofetman described this procedure in detail. He colored his words with humor, as if realizing that the facts themselves were not as important as their repetition. Almost as in telling a folktale, one could repeat the laws either directly and without embellishment or with new nuances and flair. By choosing the latter, Shofetman set the tone for a successful and popular presentation. He described the hypothetical befuddlement of the Gentile who had to be "pulled out of a bar by a rabbi and confused with all this business about buying and then selling chometz." The participants enthusiastically chuckled, obviously enjoying the humor, which made the recitation of what was well known appear new and fresh.

In addition to the laws of selling and buying chometz, Shofetman described procedures for using dishes on Passover—dishes which might be cleansed of their "chometzdik" qualities and thus become acceptable. In all his comments, Shofetman made clear that he was maikail, a fact which would be reemphasized as the evening progressed. He did not, for example, require women to move heavy refrigerators in order to check for chometz which might have fallen behind. Such chometz was "buried," he said, and did not require any further attention. The members with whom I sat nodded and whispered approvingly at many of these lenient decisions.

With the end of the formal remarks, questions began to be called out by the participants. Shofetman fielded all these without hesitation, the only exception occurring on the occasion of the first question called out by one of the invisible ladies. Exhibiting what appeared to be some reticence at answering the lady in public (women are, after all, not to be included actively in yeshiva study—but this was no yeshiva), Shofetman at first seemed to ignore the question. When a Kehillat Kodesh member called out to the woman, "A little louder, he couldn't hear you," Shofetman answered, obviously realizing that he was expected to respond to the women as well as the men. From then on questions and answers continued unhesitatingly and unabated for almost two hours.

As stated earlier, the various participants in the class defined and identified themselves through the content of their questions. Women's questions were all practical ones, relating to tasks of housework and the cleaning of kitchens in preparation for the Passover. Women made inquiries such as "Will you discuss the use of ovens on Passover?"; "May baking pans be lined with waxed paper and be baked in?"; "Is yeast chometz?"; and "Do cabinets have to be lined with paper before Passover?" To each of these questions Shofetman had a succinct and ready reply. From the practical standpoint most of these questions must be seen as superfluous, since the women had for the most part already acted on these matters. After all, these were not women who were observing and preparing Passover for the first time in their lives. Instead the women seemed to be asking the questions almost ritually, as part of what Eliade might call "the ceaseless repetition of gestures"—in this case, verbal ones.[10]

The men, especially the modern Orthodox ones of Kehillat Kodesh, also asked practical questions, but of a larger scope. Just as the women were physically preparing the home for Passover, the men seemed to be preparing themselves to act as specialized virtuosi in halacha, consultants who could provide solutions for the questions most likely to arise. These men asked such questions as "What is the case with chometz brought into a man's place of business?," "What is the reason for not eating gebrochts [dunking unleavened foodstuff into liquid] on Passover?," "How long after Passover before you can buy chometz from a Jewish shopkeeper?," "Can more than one kind of wine be used for the four required cups at the Passover seder?," and "Why is the law so strict on the use of ovens?" These questions and others like them seemed aimed at amassing a store of knowledge which could be dispensed when necessary throughout the holy-day period. Here again, as was true for the women, many if not all of the inquirers had observed Passover before and knew or had once heard answers to these questions, so again the asking may be seen as more important than the receiving of answers; for it is the asking—and the preliminary thought which it implies—which exhibits one's preparations for Passover, as well as one's ongoing involvement in Torah study.

Such involvement in learning, perhaps more than the actual substance of what is learned, is what counts. Indeed, according to tradition, if one has finished studying the entire Torah, one begins again. What is studied is never quite as important as the act of studying.

The Sprawl City Yeshiva students and some of the adults, as immersed in study as any student in a yeshiva, asked questions of a different order. Theirs were intricate and esoteric legal inquiries aimed at acquiring and displaying the special knowledge of a halachic virtuoso. Such questions are to be expected of yeshiva students. Trained as they are for ultimate ordination, Torah study is more than just a ritual act; it is part of their active daily life. Accordingly, the seminar and its questions are a part of their course of study. Put simply, for yeshiva students (and to some extent for their adult counterparts), Torah questions are shoptalk. Examples of their questions include: "Is there a *chiyuv* [obligation] to eat two *kezaisim* [a unit of measure] even if there are too many people present for all of them to have enough?," "How long before someone has to swallow the matzah in his mouth?," "Should you rush to end the *seder* [Passover meal] before *chatzos* [midnight]?," and "How do you appoint someone else to appoint a rabbi to sell your chometz?" To each such inquiry Shofetman would reply with a smile, adding once, "I'm used to these *yeshivadik* [yeshiva-like] questions." While many people laughed at some of these questions, no one challenged their legitimacy; nor did the rabbi try to ignore or inadequately answer them. For the students, as for the others, the act of asking and the content of one's question were at least as important as the substance of the information received. Through the act of questioning, that archetypical vehicle of Jewish scholarship, they became actively involved in the learning; through the content of the question, they acted to identify themselves.

If one searches for one remark which hints at the instrumental and symbolic qualities of the session as being even more important to the participants than the actual substance of it, none could be more suggestive than one made by Shofetman at the conclusion of the evening as he walked out among the women in their foyer. Many people were following him with specific questions that they had not had an opportunity to ask. In an almost offhand manner, Shofetman at one point said, "Look, no one really listens to *rabonim* [rabbis] anyhow. You all come to classes, but you'll do what you want anyway." He smiled, as did those who heard him. Learning Torah around holy-day time has an importance all of its own, independent of any questions of its substance.

Perhaps one final point should be emphasized. Although many of the questions asked during the seminar seemed to be technical or even obscurely legalistic, such questions are the very tissue of Jewish religious study and learning. While some classes allow for homily and theological sermonizing, especially around the time of various holy days, for the Orthodox Jew, true Torah learning consists of intellectual navigations in halacha. No high-flown theology or homiletic expostulation exists without the halachic nexus. What to do when one man's bull gores someone in a third man's meadow, how to become another's agent, how to prepare dishes for Passover use—these inquiries are the stuff of Torah learning, from which prodigious and monumental theological implications may emerge. But the latter can never stand without a firm basis in halacha.

Individual Study

There is a fourth type of study at Kehillat Kodesh: individual Torah study. Although persons may engage in such study in shul, it is not confined to shul, and no special time is institutionally set aside for it. Rather, each man must find his own way of integrating such study into his everyday life. For the modern Orthodox Jews of Kehillat Kodesh, daily Torah study is difficult and sometimes impossible. Many, however, try to set aside some time during the week which they devote to Torah study. Sabbath afternoons and Friday evenings are the most common times reserved. Reviewing the biblical reading for the week, exploring a difficult talmudic argument, and reviewing the laws of Sabbath or holy days are examples of the subject matter common to individual study.

In the shul, the primary locus of my observations, persons engage in individual Torah study most commonly within the context of, or immediately before and after, tefilah sheh be tzibbur, as described in chapter 4. Instead of picking up a prayer book upon entering the shul, some members grab a scholarly book to peruse as they recite the words of the prayers, which they have already committed to memory. Many of them chant words from the scholarly text with the same Sprechgesang used for prayer.[11] Moreover, such persons often spend much if not all of their warming-up period immersed in study, indicating by this that the time for praying is not to be completely separated from the time for studying.

Such involvement is not always devoted purely to study. Other ends may be served as well. For example, immersion in Torah study during the warming-up period serves latently to avoid sociability. The person involved in Torah study is shielded by it from other kinds of involvement. This quality is particularly useful for the stranger who knows no one else in the setting. By immersing himself in Torah study, he avoids the uncomfortable and vulnerable position of appearing open to invasion and conversational intrusion. Furthermore, he also displays his status as a knowledgeable Jew. Finally, he exhibits his familiarity with the shul setting, with what is legitimate or "occasioned activity" in it.[12] He knows that study is appropriate in shul, especially during the warming-up period before prayers. Just as the stranger who engages in quasichazanic activity exhibits his familiarity with the "activities that are intrinsically part of the occasion,"[13] so too does the stranger who involves himself in individual study (or at least appears to be so involved).

While no one in the shul setting negatively sanctions individual Torah study, efforts to disrupt such auto-involvement are pronounced and frequent.[14] The person who uses individual Torah study to remove himself from involvement in a setting which is essentially group-oriented and dominated is deplored. Thus, a man engaged in such study may often be approached by others with inquiries about the subject of his study. This draws him back into the group, and what was individual study turns into group study. Indeed, he may himself realize the group's claims upon him and volunteer scholarly insights even before being asked for them. To fail to do so is to risk the disfavor of the group and isolation in one form or another.

Turning the individual study into a group effort is not the only way of disrupting such auto-involvement. Sometimes the student may be approached by others who seek to completely reorient his involvement and interest. The joker, the gossiper, the friend may all act to force the student to close his book and chat. Many are the members who begin warming up with study but end up in conversation, their book lying closed on a nearby seat.

Contemporization

One more point should be made in connection with Torah study in its specific setting among the modern Orthodox Jews of Kehillat Kodesh, and that is that the material studied is constantly undergoing a process that might be termed "contemporization." By contemporization I mean the explanation, exemplification, and elaboration of Torah material in present-day terms. Even the most archaic-seeming and obscure references are supplied with contemporary parallels. Sensitive to accusations of intellectual obsolescence, the modern Orthodox Jewish Torah student enthusiastically delineates such analogues and examples. The Torah seems for him enhanced with added significance and power when its seemingly parochial concerns can be discovered to be not completely removed from present reality and to speak to contemporary concerns. Such contemporization is, therefore, frequently observable in Kehillat Kodesh classes. On one occasion, for example, during a class studying the Haggadah, the rabbinic text used as a guide for the traditional Passover seder, one of the participants pointed out with great enthusiasm:

> "The Haggadah is really a great textbook in education. Look how it goes: first, background; then reinforcement and motivation, stimulation, stories and legends—midrash—and finally praise of God."

The others present were quite impressed with this insight, reiterating its major points and at times elaborating them. With this statement, something they already believed was once again confirmed—that Torah belongs in the contemporary world. For persons who invest a great deal of emotional and physical energy in maintaining simultaneously allegiance to both a modern and a traditionally Jewish set of guiding principles, finding such parallels is of no small importance.

Recall the comment quoted earlier in this chapter in which one class participant compared a point made in the Talmud with a recent state supreme-court decision. That reference aroused a great deal of interest and discussion, even causing digression from the original text. Making the parallel stick is often a crucial part of modern Orthodox Jewish study. In short, while the study of Torah has intrinsic religious and ritual value, the advantages in finding that it applies to the contemporary world and can be presented and understood in those terms are not to be overlooked.

There is the other side, or complement, of contemporization as well. Not only can one in the course of Torah study find parallels and applications to the modern world, but one is also never so fully engrossed in contemporary life that one is not on occasion reminded of the wisdom of the Torah. The Orthodox Jew, accordingly, often appears as the narrator of maxims, the citer of texts. His mind is forever in search of and finding text analogues for the vagaries of contemporary life. An oversight at work reminds one of a talmudic quotation on how to avoid forgetfulness; a mistake in procedure can be described as one would describe the procedures of making food kosher, and so on. These references to the Torah are frequent reminders of one's adherence to Jewishness in the midst of a modern-world involvement.

Even during what appear to be the most mundane of conversations, speakers may suddenly shift to "talking Torah." The man who is at one moment gossiping, joking, or otherwise engaged may in the next find himself deeply immersed in a discussion of Torah. Thus, when one member was chatting with another about problems he was having in securing the support of his coworkers, the other responded, "Yeah, it's just like with Moshe Rabeinu [Moses, Our Teacher]; no matter how hard he worked, he couldn't count on help from the others." That comment stimulated an extended conversation about Moses, his relations with the Israelites, and other related issues of Torah. For shul members, such serendipitous conversations are often the most vigorous forms of Torah study.

Finally, questions about halachic performance inevitably arise in the course of daily religious and ritual observance. These questions, along with their responsa, may also serve as stimuli and occasions for Torah study. In order to properly formulate a question, a member may have to delve into the Torah. To comprehend an answer, he may have to do the same. Indeed, one rabbi, in constant search of ways to enlist his congregation in study, refuses to answer any halachic questions without obtaining a promise that the questioner will join him in the scholarly search for an answer. In this way he ensures that the desire to maintain halacha in the contemporary world is coupled with active Torah learning.

That Torah learning is not to be separated from other religious and ritual obligations is recognized by shul members. While relatively few of these moderns are immersed and involved in regular formal Torah study groups, almost all agree on the need to continue shul sponsorship of such opportunities for learning. As one member plainly put it, "An Orthodox shul ought to have regular *shiurim* [Torah classes]." Learning is a ritual responsibility which a synagogue ought to make practicable.

Like all ritual acts, Torah study can transform those who perform it. At no time more than the eve of the Passover holy day is this fact more clearly exemplified. At this time all first-born Jewish males are required to fast. However, if these males attend a Torah class where some volume of study is completed, they are freed from the obligation to fast. Torah study has changed their state of being.

Indeed, all young Orthodox Jews learn very early in life that the way to become a good Jew is to study Torah. The study of Torah is a way to atone for sin, to achieve sainthood, to change one's position in the cosmos. Yet, just as modernity makes the minyan suffer from poor attendance, so does it affect study groups. Just as everyone—including those who seldom attend—wants the minyan to continue to stand, as a monument to both the religiosity and the existence of the group, so do they want the formal study groups to flourish. Torah study affirms the existence of a shul; regular Torah study affirms the Orthodoxy of that shul and its members.

As should by now be clear, the congregation in its informal life exudes an involvement in Torah. The conversations, the inquiries, the one-session classes make up the lifeblood and tissue of everyday shul life. Every Torah-dominated conversation can thus be seen as an act which defines a situation as one of Torah study and transforms the location into a house of study. When shul men assemble and talk Torah, their place of gathering becomes not only a house of assembly but also a house of study. In this way, perhaps more than any other, the congregation in its house seeks to fulfill the talmudic dictum: "Make the study of Torah a regular habit."

9

The House of Assembly

Do not remove yourself from the
assembly.

Hillel

Life is with people.

*Mark Zborowski and
Elizabeth Herzog*

By now the reader should realize that activities which define the
shul as house of assembly are inherent in its use both as house of
prayer and house of study. That is, while members may be
manifestly involved in actions characteristic of prayer or study,
they are at the same time latently engaged in the bonding behavior
characteristic of the house of assembly. Put differently, one might
say that there exists little public behavior in the shul that does not
in some way also define the situation as one of assembly. When
people attend the shul for purposes of communal prayer, or when
they come to study Torah together, they come to share sociable
union as well, as expressed in their exchange of gossip, jokes, and

ideas. In sum, while the shul may at times cease to be a house of prayer or a house of study, it hardly ever stops being a house of assembly—at least insofar as a setting is defined by the action considered legitimate in it. Indeed, there are those who would suggest that a shul is really nothing more than a house of assembly: that while people claim to come to shul for prayer or study, they have really come only to be with one another, to bond together and ratify their communion.[1]

Because assembly is so much a part of everything else occurring in the setting, relatively little that is new in the way of description needs to be added here. What remains to be done, therefore, is to cull some of the major aspects of assembly from earlier depictions of the setting, to describe other circumstances during which it occurs, and to analyze the phenomenon by drawing out its underlying sociological and social-psychological implications.

We may begin by outlining assemblies other than the formal gatherings for prayer and study, already delineated.[2] Such meetings may occur either in shul or elsewhere, but they are sponsored by and open to the entire congregation. Included here are assemblies which have some manifest purpose beyond pure sociability, such as dinners promoting the sale of Israel bonds, banquets benefiting the day-school treasury, *malava malkas* (after-Sabbath feasts) to bolster the shul's precarious finances, and the like. Although the stated purpose of such assemblies is ostensibly pecuniary, the affairs are also planned so that people may, as one member put it, "enjoy themselves at the same time that money is raised."

Planning such gatherings is no simple task, since often, in the attempt to make them financially successful, invitations are extended not only to shul members but also to the more traditional Orthodox element in the Sprawl City area. Often what the Kehillat Kodesh moderns might approve, and prefer, as an organizing theme for the event stands in opposition to what the more frum would find appropriate. Accordingly, assemblies come to be organized around the lowest common religious denominator—that which religiously offends the fewest but which also excites the least enthusiasm.

One member tried to explain the problem analytically. Using his experience as a leader of a now dormant group of Orthodox Jewish collegiates, he illustrated the inevitable pressures of compromise:

> I used to try to figure out something new for these get-
> togethers—but let me tell you, it was hell finding something

that everyone could come to, and after a while I gave up.

Mixed dancing was out—not because the people who actually came were against it, but because if we scheduled mixed dancing some people would be *automatically* ruled out.

(You mean it was like ruling out potential members?)

Well, not exactly. We knew these people wouldn't come, but we couldn't make it like it was impossible for them to come if they wanted to.

Then a lecture in gemara or something might have drawn some, but it would have turned off most of the active inter-collegiates.

So in the end you choose something neutral, like bowling or something—which nobody is really crazy about but which doesn't insult anybody either. I mean you don't want to tear apart the group or anything.

It's just the same way in the shul; they always end up having the same kinds of affairs. It's usually a *malava malka*, a banquet or dinner or something like that. You have food, some story-telling, games, slides, something like that. You know, the stuff nobody minds but is a little bit dull. I mean it's nice and all—but it's not exactly an exciting evening, you know what I mean?

In spite of the bland nature of the planned activities, people continue to attend in relatively large numbers. Such events draw about as many people as the lectures on special topics but not as many as a Sabbath morning service. I asked my informant why people came to such gatherings in spite of the obviously uninspiring entertainment. He explained without hesitation.

Look, people come out of a sense of obligation to the shul. In a way it's like when they come to the [weekday] minyan or a *shiur* [class]. I mean, you can't let the shul set up all these affairs and things and nobody comes.

In other words, in addition to immediate financial needs and those of entertainment, assemblies are stimulated and sustained by another, deeper social need. As one participant explained, "This is a chance to show support for the organization." Although the donation of money to the shul is strategically important and an indication of one's concern for and allegiance to the collectivity, the simple fact of attendance at its gatherings has as much, if not more, symbolic importance. A member's presence, often more than his presents, is vital to the continued life of the group. In small and fragile groups like Kehillat Kodesh, the absence of the former makes the latter superfluous. Indeed, the total in the shul treasury is not as frequently discussed as the total number of members attending a particular event.³ The size of assemblies, the identities of those who attend and those who are absent, and the number of outsiders present are commonly of paramount importance and are much discussed. Whether the gathering is a minyan, class, or social event, it is, as Velvel says, "always important that we should have a lot of our people there."

Besides money-raising, there are other manifest reasons for organizing such meetings. There are administrative meetings held for the purpose of governing and managing the institution, and there are assemblies organized for the celebration of certain non-sacred holidays, including the anniversary of the founding of the State of Israel, the commemoration of the holocaust in Europe, and the observance of the retaking of the city of Jerusalem in the Six-Day War. Attendance at such affairs is also considered important and may act as a show of communal and collective strength if the group is a large one.

In addition to such shul-sponsored assemblies are those summoned by individual members. Indeed, as mentioned in chapter 3, no *simcha*, or joyous occasion, enjoyed by a member can pass by without his sharing the event with the other members in some sort of assembly, always based on the theme of eating and drinking together. A large attendance at such affairs is also evidence of the strength of the group. Here, however, participants come not only out of a sense of obligation to the collectivity but also to express relationship with the host. Even at the most inopportune times, members will go out of their way to join in another member's simcha. For example, an afternoon circumcision in the middle of the week can still draw a sizable attendance if the bearer of the simcha is a full-fledged member of the shul.

Members assemble for sad occasions. The turnout for funerals is impressive. One member whose father was to be buried on the eve of Yom Kippur, one of the busiest days of the year, when individual energies and concerns commonly turn inward, found that almost the entire congregation had turned out to honor both his bereavement and the memory of the deceased.

One would, however, be mistaken to suppose that the only reasons for assembly are those having to do with obligation to and affirmation of the collectivity or its members. Another explanation, not necessarily denying but rather enlarging the earlier hypothesis, is possible. To understand this further explanation, one must comprehend some of the major characteristics of action in the house of assembly.

Whenever shul members gather, regardless of their manifest purpose, they always accompany that activity with a great deal of conversation. In fact, one might say that, in addition to the phenomenal world emergent from that manifest action, there is a second cosmos, created in the conversations. The parameters of the latter are not necessarily identical with those of the former. In it the dead may come to life, the living may be as if dead, the absent may be made present, the impossible can be conceived as possible, innuendo appears as fact, the unexpected becomes normative, and so on. Such talk, the kind that occurs, for example, in gossip and joking, transforms the situation from one defined only by the manifest activity to something more. Moreover, because of the nature and substance of the talk and the interaction that it requires, the conversationalists transform themselves as they transform the situation. The house of prayer or study becomes simultaneously a place of sociation, a house of assembly, and the actors become associates as well as coworshipers and fellow students. Protracted conversation, like that engaged in in the shul, bonds people, ultimately modifying the setting so that it remains always to some extent—sometimes more and sometimes less—a house of assembly.

All the manifest public uses of the shul—for worship, study, meeting—latently foster interaction among the participants. Communal prayer requires union and interaction, both of a formal kind, as demanded by ritual liturgy, and informal kinds, which have become institutionalized by the group. Study can be described in much the same way, and so can many of the public meetings. In addition to the basic involvements of such contexts, participants come together not simply to pray, study, or formally meet but also to joke, gossip, share concerns, compare experiences, give one another advice, and, what is perhaps most important, simply to be with one another, tasting the benefits of union and sociability. As one member explained, "Sometimes I come to shul just because I want to see and be with my friends."

The transformation of the "mere aggregation of isolated individuals into specific forms of being with and for one another"[4] occurs by other means than conversation. As already indicated, prayer, especially through singing, may serve to stir such sociability. Study may do so as well. Moreover, the members of Kehillat Kodesh are people who on certain holy days and on other joyous occasions may dance together, linked arm in arm in a large circle. Such dancing discourages the formation of an indifferent or dispassionate "lonely crowd"[5] and literally propels participants toward and into emotional unity with one another. The collective breaking of bread at the kiddush or other meals also acts to stimulate and sustain sociability. Collective atonement before God, in which all members may see themselves at least once a year as equal before Heaven, also serves to bond shul members. Finally, stigmatization by outsiders often results in a sense of relationship with "sympathetic others."[6]

In response to these various stimuli to cohesion, members have embraced the collectivity, turning it into something akin to a large extended family which uses the shul as the locus of its assembly. No item of personal life is categorically excluded from being shared within the group. As is the case with all extended families, the strength of the relationship varies with various segments of the group, but some measure of collective feeling obtains for all. As one of the members reported:

> In the shul context, I socialize with everybody—especially the
> men, because the women are ... [voice drops off]. I mean,
> they're all a nice bunch of people. I would say that I could
> be friends with most of the people. With some I might be a little
> closer than with others—but maybe that's just because I haven't
> tried. [Mentions some of these by name.]
> Most of the friends I have are from shul—I mean real close
> friends, not just acquaintances. I think that's because we live
> in the same community; we have similar things in common.
> I suppose I could be friends with someone who's not Ortho-
> dox. It really has nothing to do with it, as far as being friends.
> But when you're talking about doing things together, then you
> wind up, well, you end up with Orthodox people a lot. I mean
> the restrictions and all. So maybe in theory your friends don't
> have to be kosher, for example, but then, when you want to
> go out, they find out that you can't go where they go; and
> they don't want to go where you can go. You just stick out.
> But anyway, the shul is the place where it's kind of like
> a family. It's where you most feel at home with the people in
> general. I mean, you always end up getting together with them
> for one thing or another. They know you and care about you,
> and it's mutual.

The measure of concern expressed by members for one another is perhaps most eloquently reflected in the fact that they are willing to assemble even at great expense to their individual life-pursuits. One is not surprised to be called suddenly—from bed, from the dinner table—even, at times, from work—to come to shul for a minyan, a class, a meeting, or some other assembly. When such a summons comes—and it may come not only from the group but also from a particular member, as, for example, when a chiyuv calls for help at a minyan in the fulfillment of religious and ritual responsibilities— we have seen that attendance is all but assured. On the most inclement of nights, in the most dangerous of neighborhoods, the one who calls can count on his fellow members to come out when asked. Even if a man has already prayed, he will not refuse to come and help fill out the necessary quorum. Furthermore, members often spend extra time in shul in order to enable a late-comer to recite prayers for which a minyan is necessary, often at personal expense, as one member discovered after regularly missing his train for work several mornings because he stayed to "keep the minyan."

In assembly, as in study and prayer, the men rule the shul. While all-male assemblies may take place in the shul, all-female ones hardly ever do. When women assemble in shul, they do so only with male escort or introduction. An all-female class which met in the shul was opened with a lecture by a male. Women's auxiliary meetings, like their classes, take place at various members' homes and never in shul. Male governmental meetings always take place in the shul. In short, while the shul is a sociability spot, it is so primarily for the men and only incidentally for the women.

The regularity of assembly among the people of Kehillat Kodesh is no small matter, especially when one recalls that it takes place in an essentially urban environment, where, more often than not,

> contacts . . . may indeed be face to face, but they are neverthe-
> less impersonal, superficial, transitory, and segmental, [and
> where] [t]he reserve, the indifference, and the blasé outlook
> which urbanites manifest in their relationships may . . . be
> regarded as devices for immunizing themselves against the
> personal claims and expectations of others.[7]

For shul members neither of these dimensions of urban life is dominant. Here is a group whose contacts are lasting and whose personal expectations and claims are part of the fabric of everyday life. Here is a setting, the shul, where urban dwellers can be found who are not scarred by disaffection and loneliness.

One member tried to explain the importance of the shul in the lives of its congregants:

> You've got to see it as an atmosphere of *achrayus* [respon-
> sibility]; because the children should see that, to be frum, you
> need other people, that you need other frum Jews to be a member
> of Kllal Yisroel [the collectivity of Israel]. That's what this shul
> is all about; it's a community.

Assembly is not only an affirmation of group life, nor is it only an opportunity to affect and experience the benefits of sociability; for it is a part of one's religious responsibility, part of being frum. To be frum is to assemble with other frum Jews, to share community with them.

I have chosen the pseudonym "Kehillat Kodesh" for this congregation; that choice can now be explained. Literally the words mean "holy community." However, the implication is not that the community is composed of the holy, but rather that here is a collectivity for whom community is holy, for whom regular assembly in a house of assembly, for whom union with other like Jews, is "what this shul is all about."

10 *Final Words*

> As long as your words are in your
> mouth, you are their lord; once you
> utter them, you are their slave.
>
> *Ibn Gabirol*

Although the social facts presented in the foregoing chapters ought to speak for themselves, the temptation to voice certain lingering ideas stimulated by these facts is a strong one. Many such comments have already been scattered through this monograph and need not be elaborately repeated here. Nevertheless, certain points are worth some final reflections.

Throughout this book, I have tried to create a portrait of the life of a synagogue. Portraits, however, are paradoxical in that at the same time that they reveal, they also conceal. By offering its particular perspective, that of interactional analysis—the microscopic and microcosmic examination of human sociation—this portrait in a sense rules out other perspectives and perhaps tempts critical observers to wonder what has been missed or not fully detailed. These critics might ask: How would matters look from another viewpoint? Could the frame of the portrait not have been expanded to include more centrally those matters which at present remain either at the periphery or outside the picture completely? Why is there not more depth in the portrait, so that what is now in the background could be brought forward to allow for more careful scrutiny? Why are some things outlined in bold strokes, while others remain blurred or subtle?

More specifically, one might ask, for example: How would the synagogue appear if it were considered historically, structurally, theologically, or from some other analytic perspective? Why is it, in a book which describes many of the practices, rituals, and behaviors in an Orthodox synagogue, one learns little if anything about what leads people to be Orthodox Jews and to constrain themselves by its strict demands? Why, in a book about those who are modern Orthodox Jews, is there little or no explanation for why these people adopt ways of living so fraught with ambivalence instead of becoming *either* modern *or* Orthodox? Why is so little said about the evolution of certain Orthodox Jewish practices or their religious meaning? Why are certain informal dimensions of synagogue behavior emphasized while formal characteristics are only briefly treated? To these and questions like them, I can in part reply that—as I indicated in the preface—the perspective of inter-actional analysis illuminates only those matters concerned with the imperatives of relations and behavior in public and fails to shed light directly on these other questions, which it nevertheless raises.

This being the case, I readily admit the limitations of my perspective. To suggest that what I have presented in this book presents a full view of the synagogue is as wrong as to suggest that the microscope reveals all that there is to see in the human organism. Still, the view from the microscope does reveal the human organism in a way which no other perspective allows; so, too, interactional analysis presents the synagogue in a way which no other perspective allows. To fully comprehend the synagogue and its inhabitants, one needs a series of perspectives. I have tried in this book to offer a piece of the portrait which was, until now, missing.

One may well ask a different kind of question: is the view presented here, even with its specific limitations, an accurate one? Is it consistent with what is already known about modern Ortho-dox Jews and their synagogues? I believe that it is; but to prove that would require another book, a concordance of sorts. I cannot hope to provide that here.

Finally, portraits, no matter how detailed, necessarily give the impression of stasis. Their creator commits his vision to paper, canvas, or stone, and there it remains, forever unchanged. In describing Kehillat Kodesh, I have tried to present the underlying structure and sense of the setting. Even if I have succeeded, the description may seem to be of a social organism in such perfect balance that one cannot imagine it throbbing with life. But the shul is a dynamic rather than a static reality, a fluid and shifting structure made up of a series of interlocking involvements and activities. In their actions, members are always energizing one another. Whether they do so in the quasi-chazanic activity of prayer, the questions and answers of Talmud study, the dispensing of kibbudim, or the exchange of gossip and jokes, members sustain a vital system of ebb-and-flow which turns the shul into a living and changing community.

While efforts are made toward achieving interactional equilibrium, each action stimulates reaction, which in turn brings on counterreaction, and so on. The action never really ends, even though an account of it must.

Perhaps the essence of this interactional dynamic is the sense of obligation which shul members feel toward one another. Initiating and fulfilling obligations occur unendingly in almost every aspect of group life, both formal and informal. The examples are numerous, but a few are worth recollecting.

Kibbud, that major medium of exchange, may be understood in terms of obligation. More than honoring people, it ties them together by the prestation of privilege. Repayment, of course, does not end the dynamic of obligation. As Goffman has succinctly put it, "Prestation ... leads to counter-prestation"[1]—to which one might add: "leads to counter-counter-prestation." In a never-ending cycle of obligation, a member who responds to a kibbud with the proper repayment is presented with another kibbud, and so on forever.

Near the end of my stay at Kehillat Kodesh, when I had already received a substantial number of kibbudim in close succession, I was told by Velvel, "We got to pay you back [for all you've done in the past] and get in a few kibbudim for you before you leave town." Since the obligatory and compensatory qualities of such honors are not unfelt by members, one might even speculate that one way in which the congregation retains its hold over departing members is by saddling them with obligations which flow from the many and high-status kibbudim which such emigrants usually receive. An unresolved obligation between two parties may act to maintain some bond between them. The visits of some former members seems best explained by the desire to repay communal obligation with the honor of one's presence. The visits reaffirm the existence of the group and the individual's continuing relationship to it.

Gossip also reflects the interactional dynamic of obligation, and the persistent preoccupation with it at Kehillat Kodesh may be understood as simply another means by which the members build up obligations among one another. No piece of gossip is ever given freely; rather, each implies the notion of credit and the obligation of some sort of repayment. Moreover, the complex lines of gossip exchange may in this light be seen as a network of obligations through which the entire membership is bonded.

Mutual obligations are also part of congregational religious life and observance. The fulfillment of religious responsibilities, a matter of general concern, often requires the aid of other members. Such assistance is viewed as an important personal as well as religious obligation. Hence, no man called to make a minyan for a friend can or will refuse to do so. Such nonmaterial prestations establish ties between the donors and recipients. Furthermore, the frequent and regular interaction among members which Orthodox ritual observance—to say nothing of friendship—fosters assures the production of such obligations. Whether one helps another to acquire kosher food, to get to the mikva, or to make a minyan, each act of assistance fixes a universally recognized obligation to give help in return.

In the case of Torah study, obligation and repayment are often the very reason that study groups persist as long as they do. Members frequently come to the group merely to enable someone else to fulfill the religious responsibility of Torah study. One member, reluctantly on his way to a class, once explained, "I don't really feel like going, but I don't want to stop anybody else from studying—and they're counting on me to come."

Assemblies, parties, and meetings are all subject to these feelings of obligation. People inevitably describe their attendance in such terms as "We owe it to the shul to go," or "We owe it to Velvel to come, since he put so much work into this affair." Indeed, one affair which I had wanted to skip I found myself finally attending. I had been told: "You really have to go"; "After all the information we gave you, you'd better come to this banquet"; "Your book is not coming for free, you know." In an environment where information is a medium of exchange with obligations for repayment, the researcher finds that participation is not gratuitous but rather, ultimately, obligatory.

The sources of obligation are myriad, appearing in many other dimensions of congregational life. Whether one looks at charity donation, joking, dinner invitations, or elsewhere, one finds that the people inexorably establish mutual obligations. Like members of a family, the congregants cannot help tying themselves together in numerous ways simply because they continue to share so much of their lives with one another. They are coreligionists, friends, neighbors, kin, and, ultimately, bound to the same cultural destiny.

Beyond acting as a source of bonding among the congregants, obligations serve as mechanisms of social control. If one couples the religious and ritual obligations prescribed by halacha with the particular communal and institutional obligations of Kehillat Kodesh, one discovers a system of behavior which in many ways restrains individuality. The food that the members eat, the times that they assemble, their intellectual life, their careers, and, indeed, even their conversations are subject to the controls of obligation. Some are the responsibilities of reciprocity, while others are reflections of a commitment to Orthodoxy and modernity. Such social control does not differ qualitatively from that found in all societies which exercise "a coercive influence on individual consciousness,"[2] but that is, after all, one of the points of this study—to find that *one* society sheds light upon *all* society.

An analysis of the described behavior of these Jews divulges an underlying motif of control in almost every act. Whether one looks at the microdynamics of interaction in the house of prayer, where, among other things, the members act to control and conventionalize the progress and character of the service; whether one studies the practice of gossip to discover its social-control dimensions; or whether one looks at the macrodynamics of career choices and housing location, one finds a collectivity within which every kind of individual behavior is always subject to control.

The scope of that control is so great that even the religiously deviant may be redefined as normal. Consider, for example, the conventionalization of prayer in the face of halachic doctrine, which prescribes, instead, intense devotion. Yet not only prayer, but most of what characterizes modernity, may be seen as halachic deviation which has *de facto* been made normative. Secular careers, kinds of entertainment, styles of life and dress, and topics of conversation all characterize the members of Kehillat Kodesh as modern but can also characterize them as less than completely Orthodox.

These deviations toward modernity serve further to bind the members together. As modern Orthodox Jews, the members stand between two sources of stigmatization: the contemporary world, which considers their Orthodoxy a stigma, and the traditional Orthodox community which looks upon their modernity with disapproval. As such, modern Orthodox Jews have only themselves.

Being so few in number, they cannot afford such isolation, and so they often, in order to widen their social ties, seek to disguise either their modernity or their Orthodoxy. Although it is not always apparent in the cloistered environment of the shul, these Jews are forever trying to engage in "passing" behavior. To their more traditional Orthodox brethren, they must appear strictly Orthodox. Accordingly, the shul is constructed and organized around the strictest of halachic demands. Few members, for example, are concerned about the height of the mechitza (the partition between the men and the women), but it was made "high enough so that anyone from the [Sprawl City] Yeshiva could daven here."

To their contemporary colleagues, modern Orthodox Jews must, on the other hand, seem to be completely engaged with the present and with downplaying their Orthodoxy and the anachronism it connotes. Secular-world colleagues discover, long after first impressions have been established, that these people are also Orthodox Jews.

These two foci of identity—modernity and Orthodox Judaism—are the poles between which the everyday life of the shul member hovers. In a sense, one might describe that existence as one characterized by shifting involvements. At one moment a member finds himself at prayer, immersed in a context of Judaism; the next moment he is at work in the contemporary American world. At lunch, when he takes out his kosher food and retreats to a place where he can wash his hands before partaking of bread and cover his head to make the blessings, he reverts to the world of Orthodox Judaism. Again after lunch, or perhaps in the midst of it, he is thrust back into the secular world, and so on. At any moment, the modern Orthodox Jew must be prepared to shift his involvement from the Orthodox Jewish to the modern secular world and vice versa. Such rapid, and often sudden, shifting is an integral part of his life. Indeed, the shifting involvements in shul might in a sense be regarded as microcosmic reflections of this underlying dynamic of modern Orthodoxy.

Even gossip can be related to this issue, for it is a way of catching up on what one has missed while away from the scene. Shul Jews gossip so much when they are together because they are so often apart.

In the final analysis, the ultimate identity for shul members is the Jewish one. By definition, those who have remained tied to the shul have asserted their abiding commitment to Jewish life and observance. The dropout rate is negligible. Few members abandon Orthodoxy even when they leave the shul (or so, at least, the gossip would seem to suggest). While only time will reveal the long-term strength of the Orthodox commitment, at the time of my research almost all of the children, at least, openly maintain the Orthodoxy of their parents. Modernity only gradually erodes Orthodoxy. Whether these dual foci of identity can continue to coexist without destroying each other remains to be seen.

Epilogue

Geertz, in his notes on Bali, writes: "The culture of a people is an ensemble of texts, themselves ensembles, which the anthropologist strains to read over the shoulders of those to whom they properly belong."[3] In the cultural context of modern Orthodox Judaism, the shul is one of the most important of such texts. At its center is the Word. Accordingly, those who would comprehend the shul must also recognize the role which words play in it. For the shul Jew, to speak is to worship, study, socialize, sanction, lead, guide, exalt, degrade, indicate involvement, and define context. To be able to speak easily and freely is to be in and of the shul. To be able to recite the founding story is to be implicated in it. To quarrel is to talk violently. To talk when talk is prohibited is to sin. To be silent during gossip and joking is to transgress the claims of interaction and deny the rules of prestation. By words the mundane is sacralized and the sacred made conventional. In short, through words, more than any other behavior, the people of Kehillat Kodesh reveal themselves. With words I have tried to describe them.

Notes

Chapter 1. Background, Beginnings, and Definitions

1. R. K. Merton, *Social Theory and Social Structure*, rev. ed. (New York: Free Press, 1968), p. 447.

2. E. C. Hughes, *The Sociological Eye: Selected Papers* (Chicago: Aldine, 1971), p. 334.

3. Merton, *Social Theory and Social Structure*, p. 447.

4. Ronald Frankenberg, *Village on the Border* (London: Cohen & West, 1957), p. 65.

5. P. E. Slater, *Microcosm: Structural, Psychological and Religious Evolution in Groups* (New York: Wiley, 1966), p. 1.

6. Ibid., pp. 46, 56.

7. Ibid., p. 56.

8. Merton, *Social Theory and Social Structure*, pp. 185–246.

9. Ferdinand Toennies, *Community and Society*, trans. C. P. Loomis (New York: Harper, 1957), pp. 239–40.

10. Ibid., p. 239.

11. S. Fichter, *A Southern Parish* (Chicago: University of Chicago Press, 1951), p. 260.

12. R. K. Merton and Elinor Barber, "Sociological Ambivalence," in *Sociological Theory, Values, and Sociocultural Change: Essays in Honor of Pitirim A. Sorokin*, ed. E. A. Tiryakian (New York: Free Press, 1963), pp. 92, 95.

13. For a full discussion of reference-group theory see Merton, *Social Theory and Social Structure*, esp. pp. 286–88.

14. This is often the case when members of Kehillat Kodesh try to explain the difference between themselves and other Orthodox Jews, specifically Chassidim, to outsiders who see all Orthodox Jews as identical and cannot account for the fact that Kehillat Kodesh people do not all wear beards, satin coats, etc.

15. Jews in general and Orthodox Jews in particular tend to be highly endogamous. One of the more interesting ways in which Orthodox Jews of all types express links to other Orthodox Jewish congregations is through kinship lines. The more Orthodox, the more isolated from others, the more endogamous they are. Thus members of one Orthodox shul are very often related to members of another. Interestingly, while modern Orthodox Jews have such kin, too, these kin are frequently members of Orthodox shuls outside the immediate geographic area. The cosmopolitanism of modern Orthodox Jews does not do away with their endogamy, for many of the things that they value in a spouse are concerned with Orthodox Jewishness; but it does raise the possibility that the Orthodox kin will be located far away. Thus, while much of Sprawl City Orthodoxy is kin-linked, Kehillat Kodesh and Happiton, the two modern Orthodox shuls (I do not know about Drumlin) have members whose Orthodox kin are not in Sprawl City but rather in other Orthodox communities—in New York, Boston, Baltimore, etc. Hence, when members of Kehillat Kodesh express linkage to modern Orthodox shuls elsewhere, they often base such assertions on the fact that they have relatives in these other shuls.

Chapter 2.   The Setting

1. Rudolf Otto, *The Idea of the Holy*, trans. J. W. Harvey (New York: Oxford University Press, 1958), p. 52.

2. Georg Simmel, "On Sociability," in *Theories of Society*, ed. T. Parsons, E. Shils, K. Naegele, and J. Pitts (New York: Free Press, 1961), p. 458.

3. Erving Goffman, *Relations in Public: Micro Studies of the Public Order* (New York: Basic Books, 1971), p. 32.

4. Max Weber, *Theory of Social and Economic Organization*, trans. T. Parsons (New York: Free Press, 1947), p. 139.

5. Under the contemporary pressures by women for a greater parity with men, even the Orthodox synagogue has been affected. As modern Orthodox communities plan their new buildings, the mechitza is more and more frequently placed along the vertical axis; this brings the women as far forward as the men. One large modern Orthodox synagogue, located on the upper west side of Manhattan and serving a particularly cosmopolitan congregation, has gone so far as to make its sanctuary circular, thereby circumventing the issue of who is in front and who is in back. Whether the new placement of the mechitza reflects or presages a change in the Orthodox woman's role in the synagogue is, however, a question which cannot be considered here.

6. Erving Goffman, *The Presentation of Self in Everyday Life* (New York: Doubleday, 1959), p. 91, footnote.

7. *The Zohar*, trans. H. Sperling and M. Simon (London: Soncino Press, 1949), Gen. 167b.

8. At Kehillat Kodesh, the women never get close enough to the Torah scroll to make even indirect contact with it (except on Simchas Torah, that most frenetic of holy days)—even further evidence of their exclusion from much of shul activity, specifically, in this instance, in the house of prayer.

9. Otto, *Idea of the Holy*, p. 31.

10. Erving Goffman, *Behavior in Public Places: Notes on the Social Organization of Gatherings* (New York: Free Press, 1963), p. 84.

11. An item is invested with sanctity in various ways; if, for example, the name of God appears on it or in it, its sanctity is assumed. Nevertheless, though the Torah scroll, the tefillin, and the books mentioned in the text all bear the name of God, the degrees of holiness associated with them are different.

12. Simmel, "On Sociability," p. 158.

13. Ibid., p. 161.

14. Goffman defines a "primary framework" as the original organization of an event or thing, its fundamental character, which, however, is not its only or final perceptual incarnation. For a fuller treatment of this concept, see Erving Goffman, *Frame Analysis* (Cambridge, Mass.: Harvard University Press, 1974), esp. pp. 21–39.

15. Goffman, *Relations in Public*, p. 38.

16. The mandatory religious uniform is not identical for men and women, even among the most modern of Orthodox Jews. Indeed, the halacha, strictly observed, prohibits men from wearing women's clothing, and vice versa. The people of Kehillat Kodesh observe this halacha.

17. J. Schwartz, "Men's Clothing and the Negro," *Phylon* 24 (1960): 224.

18. Thorstein Veblen, *The Theory of the Leisure Class* (New York: New American Library, Mentor Books, 1954), p. 119.

19. Solomon Poll, *The Hasidic Community of Williamsburg: A Study in the Sociology of Religion* (New York: Shocken, 1969), p. 223.

20. The requirement for males to wear a talis during the performance of certain religious rituals has its source in the complexities of Jewish law. Nevertheless, the sociological observer cannot help but note that it is

implied in this requirement that often only the married man is completely equipped for religious ritual duty. The traditional Jewish endorsement of marriage thus reveals itself even in the symbolic expressiveness of ritual garb.

21. Mark Zborowski and Elizabeth Herzog, *Life Is with People: The Jewish Little-Town of Eastern Europe* (New York: International Universities Press, 1952), pp. 41–42.

22. These infants are kept at home under the care of either their mother or some other woman. Thus the manifest halachic and social prohibition of their appearance in shul latently serves as a mechanism for discouraging women's shul attendance.

23. Philippe Ariès, *Centuries of Childhood* (New York: Knopf, 1962), pp. 30–50.

24. Interestingly, one Chassidic sect which specializes in turning unobservant Jews toward a life of ritual observance uses as its instrument of recall the procedure of putting on tefillin. Implicit in this practice is the belief that clothes make the man or, more specifically, that ritual garb makes a ritually observant man. These Chassidim are trying to create in others the same excitement that they can recall from their own first experiences as adult Jews. The problem of bringing unobservant women back to religion is evidently not so simple.

Chapter 3.   The House of Prayer: The Cast of Characters

1. P. L. Berger, *The Sacred Canopy: Elements of a Sociological Theory of Religion* (New York: Doubleday, 1967), p. 3.

2. Ibid., pp. 8, 11.

3. This activity is a specific instance of what Goffman, in a significantly more abstract way, has described as "keying"—the transformation of "a given activity, one already meaningful in terms of some primary framework ... into something patterned on this activity but seen by the participants to be something quite else" (Erving Goffman, *Frame Analysis* [Cambridge, Mass.: Harvard University Press, 1974], pp. 43–44). The subject will be further considered below, in chapter 4.

4. A. E. Milgram, *Jewish Worship* (Philadelphia: Jewish Publication Society, 1971), p. 9.

5. Henri Hubert and Marcel Mauss, *Sacrifice: Its Nature and Functions*, trans. W. D. Halls (London: Cohen & West, 1964), p. 13; italics added.

6. Milgram, *Jewish Worship*, p. 11.

7. Emile Durkheim, *The Elementary Forms of the Religious Life*, trans. J. W. Swain (New York: Free Press, 1954), p. 473.

8. Milgram, *Jewish Worship*, p. 26.

9. Erving Goffman, *Encounters: Two Studies in the Sociology of Interaction* (Indianapolis: Bobbs-Merrill, 1961), p. 93.

10. Consider, for example, the following item from page 32 of the New York *Times* of 21 April 1975:

GROSSINGER, N.Y., April 20—The head of the Conservative rabbinical movement predicted today that women would be serving in his denomination's pulpits "in the foreseeable future."

Two years ago, the committee on Jewish law and standards, composed of leaders of various bodies of Conservative Judaism, endorsed the policy authorizing individual congregations to accept women as part of the minyan. . . .

Women in Reform Judaism now participate equally with men in rituals of religious worship. Reform Judaism has ordained one woman as a rabbi, and a second is expected to be ordained in June.

Orthodox Judaism, in accordance with Jewish religious law, separates women from men in religious worship, and women may not be . . . counted in a quorum of ten.

11. Marcel Mauss, *The Gift*, trans. Ian Cunnison (New York: Norton, 1967), p. xi.

12. Ibid., pp. 3, 21.

13. Ibid., p. 21.

14. Durkheim, *Elementary Forms of Religious Life*, p. 466.

15. Ibid., pp. 474–79.

16. This description holds true only in an Ashkenazic Jewish service, i.e., one derived from the Jewish traditions of Europe. The Sephardic, or Oriental, Jewish service requires, on the contrary, that the chazan rather than the congregation recite the entire stanza, with the congregation repeating only the first and last lines. This liturgical difference stems in part from educational variations between these two Jewish communities. The former used the chazan to cue and guide their prayers, while the latter used him as a surrogate. Indeed, among Sephardic Jews, the chazan became *chacham* (wise man) as well, being one of the few who knew all the texts of prayers. Thus, in many modern Sephardic congregations, the roles of spiritual leader and chazan have become intertwined in one person.

17. On the subject of "performances" and impressions both "given" and "given off," see Erving Goffman, *The Presentation of Self in Everyday Life* (New York: Doubleday, 1959), pp. 1 ff.

18. Durkheim, *Elementary Forms of Religious Life*, p. 483.

19. I say "weekday," for Sabbaths and holy days never lack a minyan.

20. Durkheim, *Elementary Forms of Religious Life*, pp. 485, 488.

21. W. I. Thomas, *The Unadjusted Girl* (New York: Harper & Row, 1969), p. 68.

22. In my role of participant observer, I had to attend every minyan. I thus achieved the status of a "regular" and suddenly found myself with more power than I had bargained for and a concomitant difficulty in remaining unobtrusive. An advantage accrued to this, however. In being a regular, I often received information that might not otherwise have been obtainable—particularly from the chiyuvim I met at the daily minyan.

23. W. Schmalenbach, "The Sociological Category of Communion," in

Theories of Society, ed. T. Parsons, E. Shils, K. Naegele, and J. Pitts (New York: Free Press, 1961), p. 331.

24. Mark Zborowski and Elizabeth Herzog, *Life Is with People: The Jewish Little-Town of Eastern Europe* (New York: International Universities Press, 1952), p. 74.

25. The reader must recall that the focus here is on the rabbi's role in light of the discussion of the shul as house of prayer. The rabbinic needs of the congregation in the house of study are different. Study requires a regular rabbinic teacher. A class is always a "season" for rabbis. Here the Sprawl City Yeshiva also supplies such rabbi/teachers. The regularity of the class role, however, seems qualitatively different from the relatively sporadic use of outside full-fledged rabbis in the house of prayer.

26. Georg Simmel, *The Sociology of Georg Simmel*, trans. K. Wolff (New York: Free Press, 1950), p. 402.

27. Excluded from such honor, at least in the house of prayer, are female guests, children, and those who, although halachically adult, are not socially adult—for example, teenagers. These persons may, however, be treated with all the prerogatives of guests in other contexts, specifically, in the house of assembly, as, for example, at a kiddush, where the stranger gets the best drink, the first serving, etc.

28. Schmalenbach, "The Sociological Category of Communion," p. 335.

29. Goffman, *The Presentation of Self*, p. 25.

30. An extended discussion of these Jewish mendicants considered in the context of theories of reciprocity and stigma may be found in S. C. Heilman, "The Gift of Alms: Face-to-Face Almsgiving among Orthodox Jews," in *Urban Life and Culture* 3, no. 4 (January 1975): 371–95.

31. Schmalenbach, "The Sociological Category of Communion," pp. 341, 340.

32. Mauss, *The Gift*, p. 31.

33. Ibid., p. 10.

34. A. Gouldner, "The Norm of Reciprocity: A Preliminary Statement," *American Sociological Review* 25 (April 1960): 172.

35. Erving Goffman, *Relations in Public: Micro Studies of the Public Order* (New York: Basic Books, 1971), p. 38.

36. Eric Wolf, "Kinship, Friendship, and Patron-Client Relations in Complex Societies," *The Social Anthropology of Complex Societies*, A.S.A. Monograph no. 4, ed. M. Banton (London: Tavistock, 1966), pp. 16–17.

Chapter 4. Shifting Involvements

1. Henri Hubert and Marcel Mauss, *Sacrifice: Its Nature and Functions*, trans. W. D. Halls (London:Cohen & West, 1964), p. 13.

2. A point made in various places in the liturgy, for example in the Sabbath prayers.

3. Erving Goffman, *Relations in Public: Micro Studies of the Public Order* (New York: Basic Books, 1971), p. xiii.

4. Mary Douglas, *Natural Symbols: Explorations in Cosmology* (New York: Pantheon, 1970), p. 16.

5. W. I. Thomas, *The Unadjusted Girl* (New York: Harper & Row, 1969), p. 42.

6. Erving Goffman, *Behavior in Public Places: Notes on the Social Organization of Gatherings* (New York: Free Press, 1963), pp. 43–44.

7. For a full discussion of Goffman's concept of "supportive interchange," see Goffman, *Relations in Public*, pp. 62 ff.

8. Goffman, *Behavior in Public Places*, p. 69.

9. See ibid., p. 38.

10. Mary Douglas, "Deciphering a Meal," *Daedalus: Journal of the American Academy of Arts and Sciences*, Winter 1972, p. 66.

11. Goffman defines a "remedial interchange" as a corrective action, verbal or nonverbal, by which one may account, apologize, or otherwise compensate for some normative violation (*Relations in Public*, pp. 95–187).

12. S. Y. Agnon describes such a childhood moment of his own:

The heavens were pure and the earth silent, and all the streets were clean, and a new spirit wafted through the cavity of the universe. And I, a small child of about four, dressed in the clothing of the holy day, was being taken by a kinsman to be near my father and grandfather in the house of prayer. And the house of prayer was filled with those wrapped in prayer cloaks, the silver-ornamented collars about their heads, their clothing white, their hands holding prayerbooks. And the lines of candles, melting onto the long sand-covered tables, filled me with their light, and the fragrance of their burning wax. An old man stood at the bimah, his prayer cloak reached down below his heart, sweet and pleasant sounds coming out from beneath it. And I stood near the window of the house of prayer, trembling and awed by these sweet voices, silver-ornamented collars, eerie light, and sweet smell of candles. And it seemed to me that all the earth upon which I had walked in my life, and streets I had passed, and indeed the entire universe were but a vestibule of this house. I did not yet know or comprehend the notion of penitence, nor did I recognize the face of holiness. Yet, there is no doubt in my mind that at that very moment I experienced the sanctity of the Place and the sanctity of the day and the sanctity of the men who stood in that house. [S. Y. Agnon, *Yomim Noraim* (Jerusalem: Schocken, 1946), p. 3; trans. S. C. Heilman.]

13. Those who seldom frequent the synagogue sometimes have difficulty in understanding this point. For them, prayer seems much easier to sustain precisely because it is an unusual experience, not repeated three times a day, seven days a week. The regular shul participant, however, must try to reach the rare spiritual peak in spite of the contempt-breeding familiarity of the setting and its inhabitants. Thus, paradoxically, the Jew who seldom comes to shul may be able to pray with more kavannah than the Jew who, because

of his intense commitment to his faith, comes to shul every day. To the former, the latter appear as hypocrites; and to the latter, the former seem charlatans.

14. Indeed, Agnon continues his description:

And thus I stood and watched the house and the men who stood in this house, not able to distinguish between one man and another, for all were united with the house and with one another, seeming to me like a single strand. . . . Slowly, one by one, the murmurs of prayer stopped, and finally one solitary voice remained—until it, too, stopped. And my soul shuddered and I broke into tears. . . .

Now I shall tell you what made me cry. The moment that the prayer stopped, the strand was broken. A few men uncovered their heads, dropping their prayer cloaks; a few began to chat with one another. Those whose faces had been so moved in prayer became transformed and changed their countenance into the profane look of the every day and changed the atmosphere of the house and of the day. [*Yomim Noraim*, pp. 3–4; trans. Heilman.]

15. Georg Simmel, *The Sociology of Georg Simmel*, trans. K. Wolff (New York: Free Press, 1950), pp. 5, 52.

16. Ibid., p. 53.

17. In saying "members," I specifically exclude outsiders, for whom such talking is not always permissible. This is particularly the case for those who are not only outsiders at Kehillat Kodesh but at Orthodox shuls in general. In his biography, David Daiches quotes one of the members of his Orthodox shul in Scotland on the matter of such outsiders talking in shul during the prayers:

I remember Motty Rifkind, a shambling, grizzled man, the elder and the more uncouth of two extremely pious brothers. He sat next to me once in shul one Passover morning, and was indignant with some young men, infrequent visitors to the synagogue, who were chattering loudly throughout the chazan's repetition of the *Amidah*. . . . As old Motty himself used the synagogue as if it were his club, sleeping, snoring, talking, arguing, or praying as the spirit moved him, I was a little surprised at this stern view of the talkers, and indicated as much. In reply he told me a story.

"Two me'," he said, "vent into a poob and ordered a glass of beer. Dey hadna been in dat poob more dan vonce or tvice before. Vell, dey sip deir beer un' dey sit talking un' *shmoosing*. Dey sit un' talk un' talk. At lest de barman leans over de counter und he says to dem: 'Drink op yer beer. Get oot frae here. Ye coom into ma poob vonce a year un' ye tink ye can set here un' shmoos for hours as do' ye owned de place. Ma regular customers can sit un' talk over deir beer as long as dey like. But no' you. Oot!'

"*Nu* dat's hoo is mit a shul. I come here every week und *Hakodush Boruch Hu* [The Holy One Blessed Be He] kens me vell, un' he don't mind if I take it easy. But dess bleggages, dat come vonce or tvice a year—no! Dey daven or dey shot op." [David Daiches, *Two Worlds*:

An Edinburgh Jewish Childhood (New York: Harcourt, Brace, 1956), pp. 154–55.]

Sociability is for members of the group only, or at times for their guests.

18. Sherri Cavan, *Hippies of the Haight* (mimeographed; unpaged).

19. There is a mandatory liturgy which everyone—including late-comers—must recite. Most Kehillat Kodesh males strictly comply with this religious requirement.

20. Cited in D. Fitzgerald, "The Language of Ritual Events: An Analysis of the Structure of Anti-Structure," Conference on the Ethnography of Speaking, University of Texas, April 1972, p. 15 (unpublished).

21. Erving Goffman, *Frame Analysis* (Cambridge, Mass.: Harvard University Press, 1974), pp. 40–82.

22. S. Freud, *Civilization and Its Discontents*, trans. J. Riviere (London: Hogarth Press and Institute for Psychoanalysis, 1961 [based on 1930 translation]), p. 81.

Chapter 5.   Gossip

1. *Random House Dictionary* (unabridged) (New York: Random House, 1968), p. 611.

2. Robert Paine, "What Is Gossip About? An Alternative Hypothesis," *Man: Journal of the Royal Anthropological Institute* 2, no. 2 (June 1967): 283.

3. For an interesting discussion of scandal (category 3), see Rowland Evans and Robert Novak, "What's Whiter than White, Brighter than Bright, Lemon-Scented and Squeaky Clean?" *Esquire* 83 (June 1974): 69–71, 176.

4. W. I. Thomas, *The Unadjusted Girl* (New York: Harper & Row, 1969), p. 42.

5. Max Gluckman, "Gossip and Scandal," *Current Anthropology* 4, no. 3 (June 1963): 312, 308, 314, 315.

6. R. B. Stirling, "Some Psychological Mechanisms Operative in Gossip," *Social Forces* 34 (March 1956): 264.

7. Albert Blumenthal, "The Nature of Gossip," *Sociology and Social Research* 22 (1932): 32.

8. Paine, "What Is Gossip About?," p. 282.

9. Erving Goffman, *The Presentation of Self in Everyday Life* (New York: Doubleday, 1959), p. 3.

10. Stirling, "Some Psychological Mechanisms," p. 262.

11. John Szwed, "Gossip, Drinking, and Social Control: Consensus and Communication in a Newfoundland Parish," *Ethnology* 3, no. 4 (October 1966): 435.

12. James West, *Plainville, U.S.A.* (New York: Columbia University Press, 1945), p. 162.

13. Stirling, "Some Psychological Mechanisms," p. 266.

14. Erving Goffman, *Relations in Public: Micro Studies of the Public Order* (New York: Basic Books, 1971), p. 38.

15. B. A. Cox, "What Is Hopi Gossip About? Information Management and Hopi Factions," *Man: Journal of the Royal Anthropological Institute* 5, no. 1 (March 1970): 88; H. Garfinkel, *Studies in Ethnomethodology* (Englewood Cliffs, N.J.: Prentice-Hall, 1967). See also Stirling, "Some Psychological Mechanisms," p. 265.

16. Gluckman, "Gossip and Scandal," p. 309.

17. Stirling, "Some Psychological Mechanisms," p. 265.

18. Ibid.

19. Gluckman, "Gossip and Scandal," p. 308; Elizabeth Colson, *The Makah Indians* (Manchester, Eng.: Manchester University Press, 1953).

20. Ronald Frankenberg, *Village on the Border* (London: Cohen & West, 1957), p. 20.

21. Thomas, *The Unadjusted Girl*, p. 44.

22. Stirling, "Some Psychological Mechanisms," p. 263.

23. Max Gluckman, "Psychological, Sociological, and Anthropological Explanation of Witchcraft and Gossip: A Clarification," *Man: Journal of the Royal Anthropological Institute* 3, no. 1 (March 1968): 30.

24. Emile Durkheim, *The Elementary Forms of the Religious Life*, trans. J. W. Swain (New York: Free Press, 1954), pp. 474–75.

25. Barbara Kirshenblatt-Gimblett, "Types of Narrative Events in Ashkenazic Jewish Culture," Conference on the Ethnography of Speaking, University of Texas, April 1972, p. 27 (unpublished).

26. J. K. Cambell, *Honour, Family, and Patronage* (New York: Oxford University Press, 1964), p. 314; Gluckman, "Gossip and Scandal," p. 308.

27. Gluckman, "Gossip and Scandal," p. 313.

28. Ibid., p. 309.

29. Ibid.

30. Goffman, *Relations in Public*, p. 69; West, *Plainville, U.S.A.*, p. 102.

31. Marcel Mauss, *The Gift*, trans. Ian Cunnison (New York: Norton, 1967), p. 35.

32. Ibid., Introduction by E. E. Evans-Pritchard, p. vi.

33. Ibid., p. 11.

34. A. Vidich and Joseph Bensman, *Small Town in Mass Society* (Princeton: Princeton University Press, 1958), p. 36.

35. Mauss, *The Gift*, p. 11.

36. T. Shibutani, *Improvised News* (Indianapolis: Bobbs-Merrill, 1966), p. 14; italics added.

37. Thorstein Veblen, *The Theory of the Leisure Class* (New York: New American Library, Mentor Books, 1953), pp. 41–80.

38. Mauss, *The Gift*, p. 37.

39. Ibid., p. 21.

40. Ibid., p. 10.

41. Ibid.

42. Peter L. Berger and Thomas Luckmann, *The Social Construction of Reality* (New York: Doubleday, 1967), pp. 150–51.

43. Gluckman, "Gossip and Scandal," pp. 314, 313.

44. G. T. Marx, "Thoughts on a Neglected Category of Social Movement Participant: The Agent Provocateur and the Informant," *American Journal of Sociology* 30 (1974): 417.

45. S. Kierkegaard, *The Present Age*, trans. A. Dru (New York: Harper Torchbooks, 1962), p. 72.

46. Shibutani, *Improvised News*, p. 25.

47. J. N. Rosenau, *Public Opinion and Foreign Policy* (New York: Random House, 1961), p. 40.

48. Gluckman, "Gossip and Scandal," p. 309.

49. Kirshenblatt-Gimblett, "Types of Narrative Events in Ashkenazic Jewish Culture," pp. 5–6.

50. Ibid., p. 7.

51. Erving Goffman, *Strategic Interaction* (Philadelphia: University of Pennsylvania Press, 1972), p. 10.

52. Vidich and Bensman, *Small Town in Mass Society*, p. 42.

53. G. Simmel, *The Sociology of Georg Simmel*, trans. Kurt Wolff (New York: Free Press, 1950). Recall that Simmel included dyads within the meaning of "society."

54. Ibid., p. 230.

55. Vidich and Bensman, *Small Town in Mass Society*, p. 303.

56. Simmel, *Sociology*, pp. 333–34.

57. It is important to reiterate here the fact that even secret gossip must appear to be communicated in a casual manner rather than be the central theme or blatant purpose of the communication. If the nonchalance of the communication is neglected, the donor may appear to be a malicious gossipmonger even to his closest confidants.

58. With regard to the connection between gossip and time, Kierkegaard interestingly observes, "If we could suppose for a moment that there was a law which did not forbid people talking, but simply ordered that everything which was spoken about should be treated as though it happened fifty years ago, the gossips would be done for, they would be in despair" (S. Kierkegaard, *The Present Age*, trans. A. Dru, pp. 71–72). If gossip cannot freely manipulate time and make even the past seem fresh and new, its entire purpose, pleasure, and existence become threatened; and, one might add, so do its users.

59. Goffman, *Relations in Public*, p. 361.

60. Gluckman, "Gossip and Scandal," p. 314.

61. E. Wolf, "Kinship, Friendship and Patron-Client Relations in Complex Societies," *The Social Anthropology of Complex Societies*, A.S.A. Monograph no. 4, ed. H. Banton (London: Tavistock, 1966), p. 10.

62. Berger and Luckmann, *The Social Construction of Reality*, p. 183.

Chapter 6. Joking

1. See Erving Goffman, *Relations in Public: Micro Studies of the Public Order* (New York: Basic Books, 1971), p. 67.

2. Harvey Sacks, "An Analysis of a Dirty Joke," Conference on the Ethnography of Speaking, University of Texas, April 1972, p. 28 (unpublished).

3. Barbara Kirshenblatt-Gimblett, "Types of Narrative Events in Ashkenazic Jewish Culture," ibid., p. 26.

4. Cf. A. R. Radcliffe-Brown, *Structure and Function in Primitive Society* (New York: Free Press, 1952), p. 91.

5. D. Ben-Amos and J. Enobakhare, "Igbogie: Funny Insults in Benin," Conference on the Ethnography of Speaking, University of Texas, April 1972, p. 2.

6. Cf. Horace Kallen, quoted in W. F. Fry, Jr., *Sweet Madness: A Study of Humor* (San Francisco: Pacific Books, 1968), p. 106.

7. Beyond the simple social implications of shaming, its potential for divisiveness and tension, is the halachic sanction against it. The Talmud points out—and it is a dictum frequently quoted by congregants—that to embarrass another is tantamount to killing him. Literally, "He who pales [whitens] the face of his neighbor has done as if to kill him." Embarrassment is thus not only socially dangerous but halachically reprehensible.

8. Ben-Amos and Enobakhare, "Igbogie," p. 4.

9. Radcliffe-Brown, *Structure and Function in Primitive Society*, p. 90.

10. Consider, for example, the following report on page 31 of the New York *Times* of 8 June 1975:

FALLSBURG, N.Y., June 5—The head of the major Orthodox rabbinic body has called for the immediate establishment of a commission of rabbinic and lay leaders to diminish what he called the factionalism within the Orthodox movement. He warned that these divisions posed a "grave threat" to the development of Orthodox Judaism on the American scene.

11. Of course, the person who jokes excessively becomes the unesteemed *laitz*, the clown whose joking is desperate rather than artfully strategic.

12. Philip Rieff (*Fellow Teachers* [New York: Harper & Row, 1973], p. 77 n.) explains, "An ex-Jew is someone who, having stopped going to the synagogue, declines to go to church." For further discussion of this term, see ibid., pp. 77 ff.

13. That some relationship with a Gentile is necessary at times for the Jew's observance of halacha illustrates, albeit indirectly, that even the most parochial Orthodox Jew must maintain linkage—mix sympathy with antipathy, in Toennies' terms—with the manifestly alien non-Jewish world.

14. See F. Toennies, *Community and Society*, trans. C. P. Loomis (New York: Harper, 1957), p. 33.

Chapter 7.   Singing, Swaying, Appeals, and Arguments

1. The range of legitimate involvements for children is very different from that allowed to adults. This is explained in part by the fact that each of these groups defines the situation differently. Thus, the children may become involved in play, while their fathers are involved in conversation. Indeed, one of the marks of a youngster's maturity occurs when he stays in shul during the prayers and, instead of playing, begins to talk.

Yet, even the child joins in singing and some of the other collective experiences to be discussed below. He is, after all, to some extent a part of the collectivity, the tzibbur.

2. The term was invented by Arnold Schönberg to describe the style he used in *Pierrot Lunaire*. See W. Apel and R. T. Daniel, *Harvard Brief Dictionary of Music* (Cambridge, Mass.: Harvard University Press, 1958), p. 282.

3. On occasion, tunes from Reform or Conservative congregations may be learned and introduced. These may be perfectly acceptable in and of themselves, but, once their source is learned, the person who has introduced them becomes stigmatized as one who has prayed in a non-Orthodox synagogue. Moreover, his knowledge of the tune suggests that he has been in such places on Sabbaths or holy days, an action which is anathema to shul members.

4. See Gregory Bateson and Margaret Mead, *Balinese Character* (New York: New York Academy of Sciences, 1942), pp. 68–69.

5. For a full discussion of auto-involvement, see Erving Goffman, *Behavior in Public Places: Notes on the Social Organization of Gatherings* (New York: Free Press, 1963), pp. 64–69.

6. On the difference between mechanical and organic solidarity, see Emile Durkheim, *The Division of Labor in Society*, trans. G. Simpson (New York: Free Press, 1949), pp. 61–69.

7. This relationship between manner of giving and size of gift holds true only for money given in shul. Donations made to meschulachim or schnorrers who visit one at home may be as big or bigger than pledges, even though they are directly and immediately paid.

8. In fact, only strangers escape the obligation of giving. Guests do not, and the size of their gifts often reflects on their hosts. The Orthodox Jewish guest, knowing this from his own experience as a host, will often ask, "How much do you think they expect me to give?" His host will of course always tactfully answer, "Whatever you want; I guess about. . . ."

9. For a full discussion of these performance pressures, see Erving

Goffman, *The Presentation of Self in Everyday Life* (New York: Double-day, 1959).

10. Personal communication.

Chapter 8.   The House of Study

1. A. E. Milgram, *Jewish Worship* (Philadelphia: Jewish Publication Society, 1971), p. 15.

2. For the term "focused gathering," see Erving Goffman, *Behavior in Public Places: Notes on the Social Organization of Gatherings* (New York: Free Press, 1963), p. 24.

3. K. Pike, *Language in Relation to a Unified Theory of the Structure of Human Behavior* (Glendale, Cal.: Summer Institute of Linguistics, 1955), pp. 44–48.

4. Ibid., p. 48.

5. Indeed, because I too had assimilated and acquired skill in such language-switching, it was one of the last observations that I was to make in my study of the setting and the behavior in it. The discovery was quite serendipitous and came only as I began to look at various quotations I had gathered in my notes of the classes.

6. Goffman, *Behavior in Public Places*, p. 199.

7. In many congregations this period is filled with *seudah shelishis*, the third ritual meal of the Sabbath, during which eating is complemented with Torah study and sociability. The financial burden of providing such refreshments is too great for the small Kehillat Kodesh congregation to bear. Accordingly, perhaps to compensate for this ritual nonobservance, the group has substituted the ritual activity of study.

8. Goffman, *Behavior in Public Places*, p. 198.

9. The ritual nature of these classes is captured in the following joke told by one of my informants, a rabbi:

A rabbi who had been giving the same biannual lecture for seventeen years finally decided that he had had enough. Accordingly, one Shabbos Shuva he asked his congregants:

"I've been making the same points year after year for seventeen years; do you all understand it now?"

Not wanting to appear dumb, all responded: "Yes."

"If so, then I need not make them any more," the rabbi replied with a smile.

Recognizing that the rabbi was trying to get out of his job and deprive them of an opportunity for study, the members decided that if he should ask the same question on Shabbos Hagadol, they would answer "No," so that he would have to continue the classes. Accordingly, when the rabbi asked the same question six months later, everyone answered "No."

"If in seventeen years you didn't understand these points, then there is no sense in my continuing to teach you," the rabbi replied, again with a sly smile.

The congregation planned their strategy anew, deciding that, the next time, half the members would answer "Yes," while the others would answer "No," in order to foil the rabbi and maintain the ritual of Torah study. Accordingly, after six months, when again on Shabbos Shuva the rabbi asked his expected question, the members gave him their mixed reply.

"Good. Those who understood, please explain the matters to those who did not," the rabbi remarked, laughing heartily.

Beyond the one-upmanship here, the story displays the efforts to keep the class going. In spite of the fact that they were learning nothing new, the members of the congregation were committed to the ritualized continuation of the class. This is the case at Kehillat Kodesh also.

10. Mircea Eliade, *Cosmos and History* (New York: Harcourt, Brace, 1965), p. 5.

11. Traditional Torah study, especially as it is practiced in yeshivas, requires a kind of Sprechgesang throughout. Indeed, the untrained ear often cannot be sure, on hearing men at study, whether they are praying or studying. The trained one recognizes subtle tonal differences, to say nothing of specific words. This similarity between the two involvements is but one more hint at the religious and ritual qualities of study—it even sounds like praying.

12. See Goffman, *Behavior in Public Places*, p. 36.

13. Ibid., p. 35.

14. For a fuller discussion of the concept of auto-involvement, see ibid., pp. 64–65.

Chapter 9. The House of Assembly

1. In fact, the traditional Hebrew term most commonly used to denote a synagogue is *Bais Ha-Kenesses*, which, literally translated, means "House of Assembly."

2. While it is not true of Kehillat Kodesh, many synagogues, especially those with larger and more varied facilities, may present themselves primarily as community centers, in which assemblies for study and prayer are but two among many occasions for gathering. Such synagogues may offer their members the opportunity to assemble for athletic recreation in a gym or pool, bingo in a social hall, arts and crafts in utility rooms, and so on. While such facilities emphasize the synagogue as a house of assembly, they do not necessarily define either the house of prayer or the house of study.

3. While the general treasury is not commonly discussed, appeals (as noted in chapter 7), insofar as they are seen as symbolic as well as pecuniary events, do of course stimulate much concerned discussion. At such times financial presents come to represent social presence.

4. Georg Simmel, *The Sociology of Georg Simmel*, trans. K. Wolff (New York: Free Press, 1950), p. 41.

5. David Riesman, Reuel Denney, and Nathan Glazer are responsible

for this marvelously revealing phrase (*The Lonely Crowd: A Study of the Changing American Character* [New Haven: Yale University Press, 1950]).

6. See Erving Goffman, *Stigma* (Englewood Cliffs, N.J.: Prentice-Hall, 1963), p. 20.

7. Louis Wirth, "Urbanism as a Way of Life," *American Journal of Sociology* 44 (July 1938): 12.

Chapter 10. Final Words

1. Erving Goffman, *Relations in Public: Micro Studies of the Public Order* (New York: Basic Books, 1971), p. 63.

2. Emile Durkheim, *The Rules of Sociological Method* (Chicago: University of Chicago Press, 1938), p. liii.

3. Clifford Geertz, "Deep Play: Notes on the Balinese Cockfight," *Daedalus: Journal of the American Academy of Arts and Sciences*, Winter 1972, p. 29.

Glossary

Although I have throughout the book been careful to define, at least at their initial appearance, every Hebrew or Yiddish term used, I am including a glossary of *frequently used* words for easy reference. While some words are either Hebrew or Yiddish, others, depending upon intonation and pronunciation, may be either. Some words are Aramaic, the language of the Talmud, used by the Jewish people during their Babylonian exile and ultimately incorporated into the liturgy and culture. I have identified words along these lines as well as translated them.

All pronunciation is as suggested by spelling, the only exception being in the "ch" sound, which is guttural, as in the name *Bach*.

aliya (Hebrew) Literally, "going up"; commonly refers to one's going up to the *bimah* (see below) during the *Torah* reading. For the event to qualify as an *aliya*, one must be ceremonially called to the bimah.

amida (Hebrew) Literally, "standing"; commonly refers to the silent prayer (composed of a series of benedictions, usually nineteen) which, recited without interruption, with feet touching at the instep, makes up the structural core of each prayer service.

aron (Hebrew) Closet or ark; commonly refers to the *aron ha kodesh*, holy ark, in which the Torah scrolls are stored.

bimah (Hebrew) Pulpit on which the *Torah* scroll is placed while being read. Commonly located in the center of the men's section of the synagogue, it is frequently several feet above ground level—hence the term *aliya* (see above), "going *up*" to the *Torah*. Also called "shulehan" (see below).

chazan (Hebrew) Cantor.

chiyuv (Hebrew) Responsibility or obligation; (Yiddish) commonly refers to one who must say the memorial *kaddish* prayer (see below).

chol (Hebrew) Profane; also at times refers to weekdays, the profane days of the week—those other than Sabbath or holy days.

chometz (Hebrew) Leavened bread, forbidden during Passover. It includes not only actual bread but all other edibles which are the result of leavening, such as beer.

chumash, pl. **chumashim** (Hebrew) The Pentateuch (the first *five* books of the Old Testament).

daven (Yiddish) Pray.

frum (Yiddish) Adhering strictly to the doctrines and practices of Orthodox Judaism.

frumkeit (Yiddish) The state of being *frum*.

gabbai (Hebrew/Yiddish) The man responsible for the dispensation of ritual tasks and generally in charge of the conduct of prayer services. Historically, he was first the congregational treasurer.

gemara (Aramaic/Yiddish) The *Talmud* (see below).

goyim (Hebrew/Yiddish) Literally, "nations"; commonly refers to Gentiles.

haftora (Hebrew) The portion of scripture, selected from the writings of the prophets, read after the *Torah* scroll (see below) readings on Sabbath and holy-day mornings and occasionally following afternoon Torah readings. These selections usually contain something related either to the Torah reading or to the occasion of the holy day.

Hakodush Boruch Hu (Hebrew) "The Holy One, Blessed Be He, God."

halacha (Hebrew) The corpus of Jewish law; literally, "the way."

kaddish (Hebrew) The Aramaic prayer of praise recited by a male relative in response to the death of a kinsman. It is recited during the morning, afternoon, and evening prayers during the first eleven months following bereavement and then afterward on the anniversary of the death. One can recite it only in the presence of ten or more males, all of whom must respond in formulaic language. The root of the word is the same as for the word *kadosh*, meaning "holy."

kashrut (Hebrew) The maintenance of Jewish dietary laws, the state of being kosher.

kavannah (Hebrew) Devotion, concentration, intensity, and determined intention. It is the subjective attitude which should properly accompany all conscious action, including, most especially, religious action.

kedusha (Hebrew) Literally, "sanctity"; commonly refers to a prayer recited during the repetition of the *amida* (see above), during which no interruptions are permitted and during which one must stand erect, feet touching at the instep.

kibbud, pl. kibbudim (Hebrew) The public honor associated with the ceremonial performance of a ritual act.

kiddush (Hebrew) Literally, "sanctification"; commonly refers to the public meal shared by the congregation following Sabbath or holy-day morning services or to celebrate some joyous occasion. A kiddush is usually a buffet meal.

ma'ariv (Hebrew) The evening prayer.

machmir (Hebrew) One who is strict in his interpretation of the laws of Jewish life and observance.

mafsik (Hebrew) One who disturbs or interrupts involvement in an ongoing activity, usually prayer. One may be *mafsik* in words or in movement or indeed in action.

maikail (Hebrew) One who is lenient or liberal in his interpretation of the laws of Jewish life and observance.

mechitza (Hebrew) Literally, "separation"; commonly refers to the partition separating men from women in the sanctuary.

meshulach (Hebrew/Yiddish) Literally, a "messenger," "one who is sent"; commonly refers to one who is sent by others to act as their agent in the collection of funds.

mikva (Hebrew) A ritual bath; commonly used by women seven days after the end of their menstrual cycle but also by men before Sabbaths and holy days and for the purification of newly acquired dishes. The water in the *mikva* must to some degree be organic—i.e., minus chemical additives.

mincha (Hebrew) The afternoon prayer.

minyan (Hebrew)   Literally, "number"; commonly refers to the quorum of ten or more men necessary for the convening of communal prayer. It must consist of males over the age of thirteen. While others may participate in the service, only adult Jewish males are counted in the minyan.

mitzva (Hebrew/Yiddish)   A commandment; "doing a *mitzva*" denotes the fulfillment of a commandment, but it has gradually come to connote the doing of good deeds generally.

musaf (Hebrew)   The additional prayer said at the conclusion of the morning prayers on Sabbaths and holy days.

nusach (Hebrew)   The hymnodical idiom—a combination of Sprechgesang and aria, which concludes, connects, and leads the prayers.

pesukay d'zimrah (Aramaic)   The name for the stanzas of prayer, hymn, and scripture which precede the main portion of the morning prayers.

pushke (Yiddish)   The charity box.

schnorrer (Yiddish)   The Jewish mendicant, temporarily fallen upon hard times.

seforim (Hebrew)   Literally, "books"; commonly refers to religious or scholarly books written in Hebrew, Aramaic, and occasionally Yiddish and pertaining to Jewish matters.

shabbos (Hebrew)   Sabbath.

shacharis (Hebrew)   The morning prayer.

sheliach tzibbur (Hebrew)   Literally, "communal messenger"; commonly refers to the cantor.

shmoosing (Yiddish)   Chatting.

shokeling (Yiddish)   Swaying (in prayer).

shul (Yiddish)   The synagogue, the congregation, the synagogue building.

shulchan (Hebrew)   Literally, "table"; commonly refers to the *bimah* (see above), on which the Torah scroll is read.

siddur (Hebrew)   Prayer book.

sugia (Aramaic)   An episode in the *Talmud* (see below), marked off from what precedes and follows it by contextual and thematic boundaries.

talis (Hebrew)   A four-cornered cloak with *tzitzis* (ritually knotted fringes), on each of the corners. The garment is commonly worn only by married men but may on occasion be worn by any Jewish male over the age of thirteen and must be worn by the cantor during morning and afternoon prayers. Although often made of silk or cotton, the traditional *talis* is all wool, with a white background and black stripes.

Talmud   (Hebrew)   The codified oral law, together with its rabbinic analysis and commentary.

tefilah   (Hebrew)   Prayer; sometimes refers to the *amida* in particular (see above).

tefilah sheh be tzibbur   (Hebrew)   Literally, "prayer which is [said] in assembly"; commonly refers to communal prayer.

tefilah sheh be yochid   (Hebrew)   Literally, "prayer which is [said] alone"; commonly refers to individual prayer.

Torah   (Hebrew)   The corpus of Jewish law, lore and rabbinic commentary which is the central organizing element of Jewish religion and tradition and which is considered by believers to be divinely inspired and revealed.

Torah scroll   (Hebrew)   The parchment scroll which contains the Pentateuch and whose reading is a mandatory part of communal prayer on Sabbaths, holy days, and other specified occasions.

yarmulke   (Yiddish)   A skullcap to be worn by all Jewish males all the time.

yartzeit   (Yiddish)   Literally "a year's time"; the anniversary of one's bereavement of a parent, child, or sibling.

yeshiva   (Hebrew)   An academy of higher or advanced Jewish learning.

Bibliography

Agnon, S. Y. *Yomim Noraim*. Jerusalem: Shocken, 1946.

Apel, W., and Daniel, R. T. *Harvard Brief Dictionary of Music*. Cambridge: Harvard University Press, 1958.

Ariès, Philippe. *Centuries of Childhood*. New York: Knopf, 1962.

Barth, F. "Models of Social Organization." *Occasional Papers, Royal Anthropological Institute* 23 (London, 1966): 6.

Bateson, G., and Mead, M. *Balinese Character*. New York: New York Academy of Sciences, 1942.

Ben-Amos, D., and Enobakhare, J. "Igbogie: Funny Insults in Benin." Conference on the Ethnography of Speaking, University of Texas, April 1972. Unpublished.

Berger, P. L. *The Sacred Canopy: Elements of a Sociological Theory of Religion*. New York: Doubleday, 1967.

————, and Luckmann, T. *The Social Construction of Reality.* New York: Doubleday, 1966.

Blumenthal, A. "The Nature of Gossip." *Sociology and Social Research* 22 (1932): 31–37.

Campbell, J. *Honour, Family, and Patronage.* New York: Oxford University Press, 1964.

Cavan, Sherri. *Hippies of the Haight.* Mimeographed.

Cohen, Elliott, ed. *Commentary on the American Scene.* New York: Knopf, 1953.

Colson, Elizabeth. *The Makah Indians.* Manchester, Eng.: Manchester University Press, 1953.

Cox, B. A. "What Is Hopi Gossip About? Information Management and Hopi Factions." *Man: Journal of the Royal Anthropological Institute* 5, no. 1 (March 1970): 88–98.

Daiches, David. *Two Worlds: An Edinburgh Jewish Childhood.* New York: Harcourt, Brace, 1956.

Douglas, Mary. *Natural Symbols: Explorations in Cosmology.* New York: Pantheon, 1970.

————. "Deciphering a Meal." *Daedalus: Journal of the American Academy of Arts and Sciences,* Winter, 1972, pp. 61–81.

Durkheim, Emile. *The Elementary Forms of the Religious Life.* Trans. J. W. Swain. New York: Free Press, 1954.

————. *The Division of Labor in Society.* Trans. G. Simpson. New York: Free Press, 1949.

————. *The Rules of Sociological Method.* Chicago: University of Chicago Press, 1968.

Eliade, Mircea. *Cosmos and History.* New York: Harcourt, Brace, 1965.

————. *The Sacred and the Profane: The Nature of Religion.* New York: Harcourt, Brace, 1968.

Evans, R., and Novak, R. "What's Whiter than White, Brighter than Bright, Lemon-Scented and Squeaky Clean?" *Esquire,* June 1974, pp. 69–71, 176.

Evans-Pritchard, E. E. *Witchcraft, Oracles and Magic among the Azande.* New York: Oxford University Press, 1937.

Fichter, S. *A Southern Parish.* Chicago: University of Chicago Press, 1951.

Fitzgerald, D. "The Language of Ritual Events: An Analysis of the Structure of Anti-Structure." Conference on the Ethnography of Speaking, University of Texas, April 1972. Unpublished.

Frankenberg, Ronald. *Village on the Border.* London: Cohen & West, 1957.

Freud, S. *Civilization and Its Discontents.* Trans. J. Riviere. London: The Hogarth Press & The Institute of Psychoanalysis, 1961. Based on 1930 translation.

Fry, W. F., Jr. *Sweet Madness: A Study of Humor.* San Francisco: Pacific Books, 1968.

Garfinkel, H. *Studies in Ethnomethodology*. Englewood Cliffs, N.J.: Prentice-Hall, 1967.

Geertz, Clifford, "Deep Play: Notes on the Balinese Cockfight." *Daedalus: Journal of the American Academy of Arts and Sciences*, Winter, 1972, pp. 1–37.

Gluckman, Max. "Gossip and Scandal." *Current Anthropology* 4, no. 3 (June 1963): 308–15.

———. "Psychological, Sociological, and Anthropological Explanation of Witchcraft and Gossip: A Clarification." *Man: Journal of the Royal Anthropological Institute* 3, no. 1 (March 1968): 20–34.

Goffman, Erving. *The Presentation of Self in Everyday Life*. New York: Doubleday, 1959.

———. *Encounters: Two Studies in the Sociology of Interaction*. Indianapolis: Bobbs-Merrill, 1961.

———. *Asylums*. New York: Doubleday, 1961.

———. *Behavior in Public Places: Notes on the Social Organization of Gatherings*. New York: Free Press, 1963.

———. *Stigma*. Englewood Cliffs, N.J.: Prentice-Hall, 1963.

———. *Relations in Public: Micro Studies of the Public Order*. New York: Basic Books, 1971.

———. *Strategic Interaction*. Philadelphia: University of Pennsylvania Press, 1972.

———. *Frame Analysis*. Cambridge: Harvard University Press, 1974.

Goody, Jack. "Religion and Ritual: The Definitional Problem." *British Journal of Sociology* 12 (June 1961): 142–64.

Gouldner, A. "The Norm of Reciprocity: A Preliminary Statement." *American Sociological Review* 25 (April 1960): 164–77.

Handlin, Oscar. *The Uprooted: The Epic Story of the Great Migrations*. Boston: Little, Brown, 1951.

Heilman, S. C. "The Gift of Alms: Face-to-Face Almsgiving among Orthodox Jews." *Urban Life and Culture* 3 (January 1975): 371–95.

Hertz, Robert. *Death and the Right Hand*. London: Cohen & West, 1960.

Hubert, Henri, and Mauss, Marcel. *Sacrifice: Its Nature and Functions*. Trans. W. D. Halls. London: Cohen & West, 1964.

Hughes, E. C. *The Sociological Eye: Selected Papers*. Chicago: Aldine, 1971.

Kierkegaard, S. *The Present Age*. Translated by A. Dru. New York: Harper Torchbooks, 1962.

Kirshenblatt-Gimblett, Barbara. "Types of Narrative Events in Ashkenazic Jewish Culture." Conference on the Ethnography of Speaking, University of Texas, April 1972. Unpublished.

Leach, E. *Political Systems of Highland Burma*. Boston: Beacon Press, 1965.

Marx, G. T. "Thoughts on a Neglected Category of Social Movement Participant: The Agent Provocateur and the Informant." *American Journal of Sociology* 80 (September 1974): 402–42.

Mauss, Marcel. *The Gift.* Trans. Ian Cunnison. New York: Norton, 1967.

Mayer, A. C. "The Significance of Quasi-Groups in the Study of Complex Societies." *The Social Anthropology of Complex Societies,* A.S.A. Monograph no. 4. Edited by M. Banton. London: Tavistock, 1966.

Merton, R. K. *Social Theory and Social Structure.* Rev. ed. New York: Free Press, 1968.

———, and Barber, Elinor. "Sociological Ambivalence." In *Sociological Theory, Values, and Sociocultural Change: Essays in Honor of Pitirim A. Sorokin,* edited by E. A. Tiryakian. New York: Free Press, 1963.

Milgram, A. E. *Jewish Worship.* Philadelphia: Jewish Publication Society, 1971.

Mitchell, J. C. *The Yao Village.* Manchester, Eng.: Manchester University Press, 1956.

Otto, Rudolf. *The Idea of the Holy.* Trans. J. W. Harvey. New York: Oxford University Press, 1958.

Paine, Robert. "What Is Gossip About? An Alternative Hypothesis." *Man: Journal of the Royal Anthropological Institute* 2, no. 2 (June 1967): 278–83.

———. "Lappish Decisions, Partnerships, Information Management and Sanctions—A Nomadic Pastoral Adaption." *Ethnology* 9 (1970): 52–67.

Parsons, T. *The Social System.* New York: Free Press, 1951.

Pike, K. L. *Language in Relation to a Unified Theory of the Structure of Human Behavior.* Glendale, Cal.: Summer Institute of Linguistics, 1955.

Poll, Solomon. *The Hasidic Community of Williamsburg: A Study in the Sociology of Religion.* New York: Schocken, 1969.

Radcliffe-Brown, A. R. *Structure and Function in Primitive Society.* New York: Free Press, 1952.

Radin, Paul. *Primitive Man as Philosopher.* New York: Dover, 1927.

Riesman, David; Denney, Reuel; and Glazer, Nathan. *The Lonely Crowd: A Study of the Changing American Character.* New Haven: Yale University Press, 1950.

Rieff, Phillip. *Fellow Teachers.* New York: Harper, 1973.

Rosenau, J. N. *Public Opinion and Foreign Policy.* New York: Random House, 1961.

Rosten, L. *Treasury of Jewish Quotations.* New York: McGraw-Hill, 1972.

Roth, J. A. *Timetables: Structuring the Passage of Time in*

Hospital Treatment and Other Careers. Indianapolis: Bobbs-Merrill, 1963.

Sacks, Harvey. "An Analysis of a Dirty Joke." Conference on Ethnography of Speaking, University of Texas, April 1972. Unpublished.

Schmalenbach, W. "The Sociological Category of Communion." In *Theories of Society,* edited by T. Parsons, E. Shils, K. Naegele, and J. Pitts. New York: Free Press, 1961.

Schwartz, J. "Men's Clothing and the Negro," *Phylon* 24 (1960): 222–25.

Seeley, J., Sim, R., and Loosley, E. W. *Crestwood Heights.* New York: Basic Books, 1956.

Shibutani, T. *Improvised News.* Indianapolis: Bobbs-Merrill, 1966.

Simmel, Georg. *The Sociology of Georg Simmel.* Trans. K. Wolff. New York: Free Press, 1950.

———. "On Sociability." In *Theories of Society,* edited by T. Parsons, E. Shils, K. Naegele, and J. Pitts. New York: Free Press, 1961.

Singelmann, Peter. "Exchange as Symbolic Interaction: Convergences between Two Theoretical Perspectives." *American Sociological Review* 37, no. 4 (1972): 414–24.

Slater, P. E. *Microcosm: Structural, Psychological and Religious Evolution in Groups.* New York: Wiley, 1966.

Stirling, R. B. "Some Psychological Mechanisms Operative in Gossip." *Social Forces* 34 (March 1956): 262–67.

Szwed, John. "Gossip, Drinking, and Social Control: Consensus and Communication in a Newfoundland Parish." *Ethnology* 5, no. 4 (October 1966): 434–41.

Thomas, W. I. *The Unadjusted Girl.* New York: Harper & Row, 1969.

Toennies, Ferdinand. *Community and Society.* Trans. C. P. Loomis. New York: Harper, 1957.

Van Gennep, A. *The Rites of Passage.* Trans. M. B. Vizedom and G. L. Caffee. Chicago: University of Chicago Press, 1960.

Veblen, Thorstein. *The Theory of the Leisure Class.* New York: Mentor, 1954.

Vidich, A., and Bensman, J. *Small Town in Mass Society.* Princeton, N.J.: Princeton University Press, 1958.

Weber, Max. *Theory of Social and Economic Organization.* Trans. T. Parsons. New York: Free Press, 1947.

West, James. *Plainville, U.S.A.* New York: Columbia University Press, 1945.

Wirth, Louis. "Urbanism as a Way of Life." *American Journal of Sociology* 64 (July 1938): 12–22.

———. *The Ghetto.* Chicago: University of Chicago Press, 1968.

Wolf, Eric. "Kinship, Friendship, and Patron-Client Relations in Complex Societies." A.S.A. Monograph no. 4. Edited by M. Banton. London: Tavistock, 1966.

Zborowski, Mark, and Herzog, Elizabeth. *Life Is with People: The Jewish Little-Town of Eastern Europe.* New York: International Universities Press, 1952.

The Zohar. Translated by H. Sperling and M. Simon. London: Soncino Press, 1949.

Index

Ambivalence: about almsgiving, 117; religious, 107–8; sociological, 20

Amen, use of term, 199

Arguments. *See* Kehillat Kodesh, and conflict

Assembly: and bonding behavior, 253; as a collective representation, 255–56; conversation and, 257; dinners and, 254; religious considerations surrounding, 254

Auto-involvement, 215, 248, 281n5. *See also* Involvement shield(s), individual Torah study as

Authority. *See* Kehillat Kodesh; Orthodox Jews, and authority; Rabbinic authority

Basic involvement: cuing of, 227; definition of, 132, 133; formal definition of the situation and, 133; in house of prayer, 132, 212, 219; in house of study, 219 (*see also* Torah study, as "learning"); "looseness" and, 238–39; as "predominant focus unit," 226; "tightness" and, 233

Beggars: charity box (pushke) and, 29, 114–15; guests versus, 113;